Communicating
with Strangers

Gerri Parker

nov 1987

How HEOK LIM

Communicating with Strangers

An Approach to Intercultural Communication

William B. Gudykunst
State University of New York at Albany

Young Yun Kim
Governors State University

ADDISON-WESLEY PUBLISHING COMPANY
Reading, Massachusetts • Menlo Park, California
London • Amsterdam • Don Milis, Ontario • Sydney

This book is in the Addison-Wesley Series in Speech Communication.

Library of Congress Cataloging in Publication Data

Gudykunst, William B.
  Communicating with strangers.

  Bibliography: p.
    1. Intercultural communication.   I. Kim, Young Yun.
II. Title.
HM258.G84   1984   303.4'82   83-15458
ISBN 0-201-11374-0

ABCDEFGHIJ-AL-89876543

Preface

Anyone who communicates with people from other cultures, either for pleasure or as part of his or her job, should find this book useful. For example, Foreign Service officers, Peace Corps volunteers, businesspersons in multinational corporations, social workers, teachers in integrated schools, staff members of hospitals in urban settings, and police officers dealing with ethnic communities should find this book helpful in the performance of their work.

We concentrate on theoretical issues more than do many of the existing analyses of intercultural communication. In order to understand the process of intercultural communication and to improve intercultural effectiveness, it is crucial to have the relevant conceptual tools. Following Kurt Lewin, we believe that a good theoretical perspective is also highly practical; it provides a framework by which many specific phenomena in real-life situations—for example, our encounters with people from other cultures—can be described and explained more accurately.

The enormous complexity and scope of the process of intercultural communication necessitates the use of perspectives and concepts from diverse academic disciplines, including social psychology, sociology, cultural anthropology, and sociolinguistics, and, of course, communication. We owe an intellectual debt to Georg Simmel, sociologist, and Edward T. Hall, anthropologist, whose work significantly influences our approach to intercultural communication.

To organize the various elements of the process of intercultural communication, we present a model of intercultural communication in Part One. Our model is based on the premise that communication between people from different cultures is essentially the same as communication between people from different subcultures. In fact, we go even further to assume that all interactions between people share essentially the same underlying communication process, which we outline in Part One.

We conceptualize the common underlying process of communication with people who are unknown and unfamiliar as communication with strangers. In this view, intercultural communication is a special case only in the sense that the unknown and unfamiliar qualities of strangers are primarily culturally based. This fact, in turn, permeates all other sources of interpersonal differences, including sociocultural, psychocultural, and environmental influences, on which we elaborate in Part Two.

Our communication with strangers presents the challenge of having to understand their cultural backgrounds and their communication patterns. As we acquire knowledge of how strangers express themselves and interpret the world, we also recognize the fundamental universalities of communication that are shared by people in all cultures. In Part Three we look at some of the recognized variations and universalities of human communication.

The development of interpersonal relationships with strangers requires that we have some understanding of their culture and patterns of communication and that they have some understanding of ours. Being able to communicate effectively plays a vital role in determining the nature and the quality of the relationships we establish with strangers. As our relationships with strangers become more meaningful, we begin to deal with the strangers, who in the meantime, go through a process of cultural adaptation into our environment. Through cumulative experiences of communicating with strangers, we, as well as the strangers, may enter the process of becoming intercultural—a gradual change of psychic growth beyond our respective cultural parameters. Through intercultural communication, we are therefore able to broaden our perspective on life, people, and ourselves and to expand our behavioral capacity to adapt in our changing world. In Part Four we discuss these and other related topics.

We would like to take this opportunity to express our gratitude to friends and colleagues who contributed their time and expertise in reviewing various versions of the book. The "official" reviewers—Milton Bennett, Larry Sarbaugh, and Dennis Tafoya—read the entire manuscript and provided detailed critiques and suggestions. Even though we did not incorporate all of their suggestions, their comments were invaluable in helping us to clarify our thinking. Several others who reviewed various chapters and gave us useful feedback include Gordon Craigo, Huber Ellingsworth, Joan Hojek, Lois Silverman, and Stella Ting-Toomey. In addition, we want to thank the staff of Addison-Wesley, especially San Rao, who encouraged us to write the book, and Linda Fisher, our editor, who was a constant source of support throughout the completion of the manuscript.

Albany, New York   W.B.G.
October 1983   Y.Y.K.

Contents

PART ONE

CONCEPTUAL FOUNDATIONS

On April 8, 1960, the world entered a new era. On this date, the first attempt was made to "communicate" with extraterrestrial life as part of Project Ozma organized by Frank Drake of the National Radio Astronomy Observatory in Green Bank, West Virginia. Although this first attempt was "passive" in that no attempt was made to transmit signals to extraterrestrial beings, Pioneer 10—launched on March 3, 1972—included a six-by-nine-inch gold-plated aluminum plaque with a message for any extraterrestrial being coming across it. The plaque on Pioneer 10 was designed by the astronomer Carl Sagan. The left side of the plaque contained a representation of the periods of pulsars to indicate the solar system of origin, while across the bottom the planets of the solar system were drawn with an indication that Pioneer 10 originated on the third planet. The right side of the plaque contained drawings of unclothed male and female figures, the man having his right arm raised with the palm extending outward. Pictures of the plaque appeared in newspapers around the world when Pioneer 10 was launched.

What does the plaque on Pioneer 10 have to do with the study of intercultural communication? Think about it for a moment. Does the plaque have anything in common with your attempts to communicate with people from other cultures? The plaque illustrates what often happens when two people who do not share a common language try to communicate—they try to get their ideas across nonverbally. Reactions to the plaque when it appeared in newspapers around the world further illustrate what can happen when we use this method in our everyday encounters with people from other cultures. People in some cultures interpreted the man's gesture to be a universal gesture of friendliness, while people in other cultures interpreted it as one of hostility. One can only imagine how extraterrestrial beings would interpret the gesture; they might take it to mean that one arm of one of the sexes is permanently angled at the elbow while that of the other sex is not. The point is that gestures used by people in one culture often do not mean the same thing in another culture. Trying to communicate through nonverbal means may, therefore, lead to misunderstandings.

In order to minimize misunderstandings when we communicate with people from other cultures, we need to understand the process of intercultural communication. The importance of understanding this process is called to our attention by two former presidents of the United States:

> So let us not be blind to our differences, but let us direct our attention to our common interests and to the means by which those differences can be resolved. And if we cannot end now our differences, at least we can make the world safe for diversity.
>
> John F. Kennedy

> It is . . . in our interest—and the interest of other nations—that Americans have the opportunity to understand the histories, cultures and problems of others, so that we can understand their hopes, perceptions and aspirations. [These efforts] will contribute to our capacity as a people and a government to manage our foreign affairs with sensitivity, in an effective and responsible way.
>
> Jimmy Carter

These two former presidents imply that understanding people of other cultures and their patterns of communication is important not only to decrease misunderstandings but also to make the world a safer place in which to live.

Throughout the book we focus on the concepts necessary to understand people from other cultures, their patterns of communication, and our interactions with them. More specifically, our intent is to present a framework for understanding your encounters with people from other cultures and subcultures, for determining when misunderstandings occur, and for improving the effectiveness of your intercultural communication.

The purpose of Part One is to outline our perspective on communication in general and intercultural communication in particular. In Chapter 1 we specify the assumptions we make about the process of communication and define the two major terms, communication and culture, used in the book. Our approach to intercultural communication is presented in Chapter 2, where we examine the concept of the stranger and outline the model we use to organize the elements in the process of communication.

1
Introduction

*We travel together, passengers on a little spaceship,
dependent upon its vulnerable resources of air and
soil; all committed for our safety to its security and
peace; preserved from annihilation only by the
care, the work, and I will say the love we give our
fragile craft.*

Adlai Stevenson

In the past most human beings were born, lived, and died within a limited geographical area, never encountering people of other races and/or cultural backgrounds. Such an existence, however, no longer prevails in the world. Even once isolated groups of people like the Tasadays in the Philippines now frequently have contact with other cultural groups. Marshall McLuhan characterizes today's world as a "global village" because of the rapid expansion of worldwide communication networks (e.g., jet airplanes, communication satellites, and telephones). It is now possible for any person from an industrialized country to communicate with any person in another industrialized country within minutes by phone or within hours face to face. In fact, we are at a point in history when important or interesting events (presidential debates in the United States, major sporting events, royal weddings, etc.) in one country are often transmitted simultaneously to more than 100 different countries.

The expansion of worldwide communication networks, combined with increases in travel for pleasure or business and in international migration of refugees, heightens our awareness of the need for understanding other cultures and their people. The work of the Presidential Commission on Foreign Language and International Studies (1979) illustrates this increased awareness. In their final report to the president of the United States, the Commission points out:

Nothing less is at issue than the nation's security. At a time when the resur-
gent forces of nationalism and of ethnic and linguistic consciousness so
directly affect global realities, the United States requires far more reliable
capacities to communicate with its allies, analyze the behavior of potential
adversaries, and earn the trust and sympathies of the uncommitted. Yet
there is a widening gap between these needs and the American competence
to understand and deal successfully with other peoples in a world in a flux.
(pp. 1–2)

The Commission sets forth a number of recommendations in order for the
people of the United States to understand and deal successfully with other
peoples of the world, including increased foreign language instruction, more
international educational exchanges, citizen education in international affairs,
and increases in international training for business and government personnel.
Although it is not stated explicitly, central to most of the Commission's recommendations is the need for an increased awareness and understanding of communication between people from different cultures.

In a world of international interdependence, the ability to understand and
communicate effectively with people from other cultures takes on greater ur-
gency. The need for intercultural understanding, however, does not begin or end
with national boundaries. Within any nation a multitude of racial and ethnic
groups exist, and their members interact daily. Recent legislation and legal
rulings in the United States on affirmative action, school busing, and desegregation underscore the importance of nondiscriminatory contact between members
of different racial and ethnic groups. To accomplish this end, people of different
racial and ethnic groups need to understand one another's cultures and patterns
of communication.

It is recognized widely that one of the characteristics separating humans
from other animals is our development of culture. The development of human
culture is made possible through communication, and it is through communication that culture is transmitted from one generation to another. Culture and
communication are intertwined so closely that one writer, Edward T. Hall
(1959), has maintained "culture is communication" and "communication is
culture." In other words, we communicate the way we do because we are raised
in a particular culture and learn its language, rules, and norms. Because we learn
the language, rules, and norms of our culture by a very early age (between five
and ten years old), however, we generally are unaware of how culture influences
our behavior in general and our communication in particular.

When we communicate with people from other cultures, we often are confronted with languages, rules, and norms different from our own. Confronting
these differences can be a source of insight into the rules and norms of our own
culture, as well as being a source of frustration or gratification. Although the
presence of cultural differences may suggest the need for accommodation in
our communication, it cannot be taken automatically as either a "barrier" or a

"facilitator" of effective communication (Ellingsworth, 1977). Communication between people from different cultures can be as effective as communication between people from the same culture (Taylor and Simard, 1975). Stated in another way, communicating with a person from another culture may be either easier or more difficult than communicating with someone from the same culture.

One of the major factors influencing our effectiveness in communicating with people from other cultures is our ability to understand their culture. It probably is impossible to understand the communication of people from other cultures if we are highly ethnocentric. Sumner (1940) characterizes ethnocentrism as the "view of things in which one's own group is the center of everything, and all others are scaled and rated with reference to it" (p. 27). Ethnocentrism leads people to see their own culture's ways of doing things as "right" and all others as "wrong." While the tendency to make judgments according to our own cultural standards is natural, it hinders our understanding of other cultures and the patterns of communication of their people.

Becoming more culturally relativistic, on the other hand, can be conducive to understanding. Cultural relativism suggests the only way we can understand the behavior of others is in the context of their culture. Herskovits (1973) succinctly summarizes this position when he says evaluations must be "relative to the cultural background out of which they arise" (p. 14). He goes on to argue, "judgments are based on experience, and experience is interpreted by each individual in terms of his enculturation" (p. 15). In other words, no one cultural trait is "right" or "wrong"; it is merely "different" from alternative cultural traits. This is not to say we must never make value judgments of people in other cultures. Making them is often necessary. Postponing these value judgments, or recognizing their tentative nature, until adequate information is gathered, however, greatly facilitates understanding.

The purpose of this book is to provide the conceptual tools needed to understand culture, communication, how culture influences communication, and the process of communication between people from different cultures. Such knowledge is extremely important—in fact, necessary—if we are to comprehend fully the daily events of today's multicultural world. The concepts discussed should help you to better understand your communication with people from other cultures and many international situations such as the holding of United States diplomats in Iran. Understanding the material presented should help you not only to analyze your intercultural encounters in order to determine where misunderstandings occur but also to determine how these misunderstandings can be minimized in future interactions.

Before proceeding further, we must be more specific about what we mean when we use the terms communication, culture, and intercultural communication. In the next section we outline the assumptions we make about the nature of communication. Following this we examine the concept of culture and develop a working definition for intercultural communication.

CONCEPTUALIZING COMMUNICATION

Everyone communicates, and thus has a preconceived notion of what communication is and how it takes place. Our purpose here is to specify our preconceived notions about the nature of communication. It is not necessary for you to agree with our conceptualization; however, while reading the remainder of the book, you need to remember we take the ideas expressed here for granted. Because we take these ideas for granted, we present them as assumptions.

Assumption 1: Communication Is a Symbolic Activity

Communication involves the use of symbols. Symbols are things used to stand for, or represent, something else. Symbols are not limited to words; they also include nonverbal displays and other objects (e.g., the flag). The important thing to remember is symbols are symbols only because a group of people agree to consider them as such. There is no natural connection between any symbol and its referent; the relationships are arbitrary and vary from culture to culture. Bram (1955) points out:

> The relationship between symbols and the "things" which they symbolize is not a self-evident or natural one. . . . Symbols derive their specific function from group consensus or social convention and have no effect whatever (outside their rather trivial physical characteristics) on any person not acquainted with such consensus or convention. (p. 2)

It is the human ability to utilize symbols that makes possible the development of speech and language and the capacity to deal with relationships among people and objects in the absence of those people and objects.

Assumption 2: Communication Is a Process
Involving the Encoding and Decoding of Messages

Since it is impossible to transmit electrical impulses directly from our brain to that of another person, it is necessary for us to put our ideas into codes that can be transmitted, either verbally or nonverbally. *Encoding* refers to the process of putting thoughts, feelings, emotions, or attitudes, for example, in a form recognizable by others. The symbols used may be written, verbal, nonverbal, mathematical, or musical, to cite only a few. We refer to the encoded set of symbols as a message. *Decoding* is the process of perceiving and interpreting, or making sense of, incoming messages and stimuli from the environment. How we encode and decode messages is influenced by our experiential background, including not only our unique individual experiences but also our shared group and cultural ones.

Berlo (1960) points out if we conceptualize communication as a process, "we view events and relationships as dynamic, on-going, ever-changing, continuous. . . . we also mean that it does not have a beginning, an end, a fixed sequence of events. It is not static, at rest. It is moving. The ingredients within a process interact: each affects all of the others" (p. 24). Viewing communication as a process, therefore, allows for recognition of its continuity, complexity, unrepeatability, and irreversibility.

To say communication is a process is to recognize that the encoding and decoding of messages take place simultaneously. We do not simply encode a message and then wait for a response to decode. Rather, we continually are encoding and decoding information simultaneously whenever we communicate. The information we decode influences what we encode, and what we encode influences how we decode incoming stimuli.

Assumption 3: Communication Is Transactional

Communication is the "product of both environmental objects (or stimuli) and internal mental states" (Miller and Steinberg, 1975, p. 38). Not only do the environment and objects in it influence our communication, but our perceptions of the environment also influence the way we behave. Viewing communication as a transaction further implies that the people with whom we communicate have an impact on us and we have an impact on them.

If communication is a transaction, then the meanings we attach to encoded messages are a function of the messages, the people who encoded the messages, the environment (or context) in which the communication takes place, and our "conceptual filters." Conceptual filters, according to Fisher (1978), "comprise the internal states of the human organism. . . . They are not directly observable . . . but are assumed to affect the communicative event significantly" (p. 145).

Although messages can be transmitted from one person to another, meanings cannot. Since meanings are not determined solely by the message, the net result of any communication is a partial difference between the meanings held by the communicators. In other words, the meaning of the message one person encodes is never exactly the same as the meaning another person decodes. "To say that meaning in communication is never totally the same for all communicators is not to say that communication is impossible or even difficult—only that it is imperfect" (Fisher, 1978, p. 257).

Assumption 4: Communication Takes
Place at Varying Levels of Awareness

As we are socialized into our culture, we learn much of our behavior unconsciously. Learning to walk is a good illustration. No one told us to do this and that when we learned to walk. We just did it and eventually mastered it. Much of our communication behavior was learned the same way. Because we learned much of it unconsciously, we are not usually aware of our behavior when we communicate.

Several recent writers have taken the position that a large amount of social interaction occurs at very low levels of awareness (see, for example, Abelson, 1976; Berger, 1982; Langer, 1978). These writers argue, and we concur, that we behave with low levels of awareness in situations we consider "normal," or routine. When we encounter new or novel situations, however, we become aware of our behavior (our behavior is consciously enacted). One difference to be expected between our communication with people from our own culture and people from other cultures, therefore, is the level of awareness we have of our behavior. We are more aware of our behavior with people who are from other cultures than we are of our behavior with people from our own culture. This is because interaction with people from other cultures is less routine; it involves new and novel situations.

Assumption 5: Communicators Make Predictions About the Outcomes of Their Communication Behavior

Miller and Steinberg (1975) argue: "When people communicate, they make predictions about the effects, or outcomes, of their communication behaviors; that is, they choose among various communicative strategies on the basis of how the person receiving the message will respond" (p. 7). These authors go on to recognize that communication behaviors, including predictions, are not always conscious. Specifically, they argue that awareness of making predictions varies with the degree to which we are aware of alternative outcomes for the situation in which we find ourselves. The more aware we are of alternative outcomes, the more aware we are of making predictions. When our behavior is unconscious (outside of our awareness), generally we are not aware of making predictions. When our behavior is conscious, we are more aware of the predictions we make.

Assumption 6: Intention Is Not a Necessary Condition for Communication

This assumption is derived from the first of three axioms of communication proposed by Watzlawick, Beavin, and Jackson (1967): "one cannot not communicate" (p. 51, emphasis deleted). The basis for this axiom is any behavior, or the absence of any behavior, communicates something if there is someone in the environment to notice the behavior, or its absence. In making this assumption, we are not contending all behavior is communication; rather, communication occurs any time one person attributes meaning to his or her own or another person's behavior. Taking this view implies it is not necessary for a person to transmit a message intentionally in order to communicate. Many intercultural misunderstandings, in fact, are due to the unintentional behavior of a person from one culture being perceived, interpreted, and reacted to by a person from another culture. In other words, behavior that was not meant to communicate did.

Assumption 7: Every Communication Message Has a Content Dimension and a Relationship Dimension

In their second axiom of communication, Watzlawick, Beavin, and Jackson (1967) argue that every communication message can be interpreted on two levels: <u>what is said (the content level), and how it is said (the relationship level)</u>. The content level specifies the substance of the message, while the relationship level indicates how the substance is to be interpreted. The relationship dimension is "only rarely defined deliberately or with full awareness" (p. 52); it is, therefore, usually encoded and decoded unconsciously. The content level usually is encoded verbally, while the relationship level tends to be encoded nonverbally. As we will show later, cultures vary with respect to the emphasis they place on these two levels.

Assumption 8: Communicators Impose Structure on Their Interactions

The third axiom of Watzlawick, Beavin, and Jackson (1967) states: "The nature of a relationship is contingent upon the punctuation of the communicational sequences between the communicants" (p. 59, emphasis deleted). By punctuation of the sequence of events they mean the grouping of elements into a recognizable pattern, or the imposition of structure on the communication process. Without this grouping of elements, or imposition of structure, interaction would be uninterpretable. People not only impose a beginning and an ending on a sequence of events but also interpret a particular event as being a "cause" or an "effect" of their behavior. For example, a husband may say he drinks (an effect) because his wife always works late (a cause). In contrast, the wife may say she works late (an effect) because her husband drinks (a cause).

Every time we communicate we impose structure on the process. "Culturally, we share many conventions of punctuation which, while no more or less accurate than other views of the same events, serve to organize common and important interactional sequences" (Watzlawick, Beavin, and Jackson, 1967, p. 56). When communicating with people from our own culture, therefore, we usually are safe in assuming the structure we impose is roughly the same as the one they impose. When communicating with people from another culture, however, we must determine how they impose structure on the process of communication if we are to interpret and predict their behavior accurately.

The assumptions outlined above present a relatively clear picture of how we view communication. We elaborate on our conceptualization in the next chapter, but the above specification of our assumptions is sufficient to show what we mean by communication. To review, those aspects of our assumptions necessary for delimiting communication are as follows: (1) it is a symbolic activity; (2) it is a process; (3) it involves the encoding and decoding of messages; (4) it is transactional; (5) it takes place at varying levels of conscious awareness; and (6) intention is not necessary for it to take place.

CONCEPTUALIZING CULTURE

Culture is a term that means many different things to different people. More than a hundred definitions of the concept can be found in the social science literature. Some writers discuss culture in terms that suggest it is the same as society, while others define it in such a way that they can talk about male and female cultures. In order to clarify our conceptualization of culture, we will take a brief excursus into the more general study of social organization. Through an understanding of social organization we will generate a working definition for culture.

The Process of Social Organization

The study of social organization is concerned with the way in which human activity is coordinated or organized. Our view of social organization draws upon Olsen's (1978) work. According to Olsen, social life is "a process that is continually being created and recreated as individuals bring order and meaning to their collective social life" (p. 4). In other words, like communication, social life is a dynamic, ongoing process without a beginning or an end.

Social organization cannot come about unless some degree of "order" exists. Olsen (1978) differentiates three levels of ordering involved in social life: personal, social, and cultural. Personal ordering refers to the process that "gives coherence and stability to the various cognitive and affective psychological processes occurring within an individual" (p. 7). This level of ordering takes place within each of us as our "minds" bring together our feelings, attitudes, needs, etc., into a coherent whole, which we call a "personality."

For social ordering to exist, two or more individuals must interact with each other over time. Social interaction, according to Olsen, occurs whenever the behavior of one person influences another person's thoughts and/or behavior. As individuals interact over time, ongoing social relationships are formed among them. When these patterns of behavior become "stable," we can say social ordering takes place. Stated differently, social ordering "grows out of the interactions and relationships of individuals as these activities become patterned and recurrent through time" (Olsen, 1978, p. 7).

Obviously, different levels of social ordering occur. For example, when two people interact for an extended period of time and their behavior becomes patterned, one form of social ordering takes place (a friendship is formed). Similarly, when a man and a woman get married and have children and interact on a daily basis, their behavior becomes patterned and another type of social ordering occurs (a family). Furthermore, when people within some geographical area interact over time and their behavior becomes patterned, we again can say that social ordering develops (a society is "born"). If a group of people interact together over time and their behavior becomes patterned (i.e., social ordering has taken place), they develop shared agreements about how to interpret the world they inhabit. Stated differently, patterned and recurrent social interactions "give rise to shared sets of cultural ideas that symbolize, reflect and give meaning to the social order" (Olsen, 1978, p. 163).

Given the above, we can say cultural ordering involves the development of a set of shared symbolic ideas associated with patterns of social ordering. Cultural ordering is, therefore, different from social ordering, but any group that develops social ordering also displays cultural ordering. In other words, cultural ordering is associated not only with large collectivities (such as nations) but also with smaller collectivities (such as ethnic groups and families) that interact on an ongoing basis. To the extent collectivities are interrelated or overlap with each other, they share cultural ideas; therefore, most forms of cultural ordering are not entirely unique (Olsen, 1978).

A Working Definition for Culture

Since each level of social ordering (families, ethnic groups, etc.) displays cultural ordering, it can be argued that each also has a culture of its own. Taking this position, however, leads to problems in labeling the different levels of culture associated with each level of social ordering. In order to avoid the problems inherent in this approach, we reserve the term *culture* to refer to the pattern of cultural ordering associated with the societal level of social ordering. Given this position, we stipulate: *culture refers to that relatively unified set of shared symbolic ideas associated with societal patterns of cultural ordering.* Olsen (1978) elaborates:

> As people communicate the meanings of their actions to each other and work out shared interpretations of activities and definitions of situations, they develop a common culture that is shared by all the participants. Shared culture in turn influences and guides—but does not fully determine—these people's collective activities by providing them with interpretations of social life, role expectations, common definitions of situations, and social norms. (p. 107)

If the term culture is reserved for cultural ordering at the societal level, we need a term to use to refer to cultural ordering at lower levels of social ordering. The term traditionally used for this purpose is "subculture." A subculture, therefore, involves a set of shared symbolic ideas held by a collectivity within a larger society. A subculture's set of cultural ideas generally is derived from the larger (societal) culture but differs in some respect. Although the term subculture often is used to refer to racial and/or ethnic groups, there obviously are other types of subcultures. For example, we can talk about a student subculture, a medical subculture (people who work in medicine), a lower-class subculture, a middle-class subculture, or a business subculture, to name only a few. Each of these groups shares many common cultural ideas with a larger culture but has some that are unique.

Components of Culture

Three components of culture can be differentiated: postulates, ends, and means (Olsen, 1978). Postulates consist of cultural ideas accepted as "the way things are." Postulates are thus assumptions, accepted without being questioned; they are "the facts of life." The most general postulate held by people in a culture is their world view. Our world view delimits the objectives of social life and tells us our place in the universe and our relationship to nature and the supernatural.

The goals of social life, or cultural ends, constitute the second component of culture. According to Olsen, the ends of social life involve the desired objectives or outcomes sought by the people of the culture. "Social values, the most basic of these cultural ends, are shared conceptions of what is more desirable in social life" (Olsen, 1978, p. 166).

Within any culture there are prescribed and proscribed ways of reaching the acceptable ends; that is, each culture has acceptable means to reach cultural goals. The means to reach cultural goals involve shared agreements about how people are expected to behave. These shared agreements are referred to as cultural norms and rules.

These three components are found in every culture, as well as in every subculture. There is, however, a tendency for members of subcultures within a culture to share cultural postulates. Differences between subcultures tend to be manifested with respect to their cultural ends and means.

High-Context and Low-Context Cultures

One of the leading intercultural theorists, Edward T. Hall, presents a simple, but elegant, way of thinking about how cultures differ. According to Hall (1976), culture provides a "highly selective screen" between us and the outside world. Culture influences what stimuli we take in and what we ignore. It also provides a "screen" that influences how we encode messages. The way in which messages are encoded and decoded, maintains Hall, depends on the context, and cultures vary in the importance they place on the context of communication. In order to illustrate how cultures differ with respect to context, Hall (1976) draws a distinction between cultures characterized by high-context messages and those characterized by low-context messages:

> A high-context (HC) communication or message is one in which most of the information is either in the physical context or internalized in the person, while very little is in the coded, explicit, transmitted part of the message. A low-context (LC) communication is just the opposite; i.e., the mass of the message is vested in the explicit code. (p. 79)

One example of low-context communication is programming a computer. Everything must be specified in the coded message (the program) or the program will not run. Communication between twins raised together who communicate with shortened sentences and words is an example of high-context communication.

Hall applies his scheme of cultural variability to what we call societal cultures. High-context and low-context messages may both exist in any one culture, but one type tends to predominate. The culture of the United States, while not at the end of the scale, is a relatively low-context culture. Several cultures can be considered lower in context; according to Hall, these include the German, Scandinavian, and German-Swiss cultures. On the other hand, most Asian cultures are considered high-context cultures. As an illustration, think of the languages using Chinese characters. If one does not know the context in which a particular character is used, it is impossible to look the character up in a dictionary because the context influences what it means (Hall, 1976). Drawing upon Hall and Kohls (1978), we can list 12 cultures on a continuum from low-context to high-context: Swiss-German, German, Scandinavian, United States, French, English, Italian, Spanish, Greek, Arab, Chinese, and Japanese.

Hall (1976) claims context influences everything about the way we communicate. He argues high-context communication is a long-lived, cohesive force, which is slow to change and, therefore, unifies the group using it. Low-context communication, in contrast, does not unify the group using it because it changes rapidly and easily. Because of these differences, people in high-context cultures are more aware of culture's screening process than are people in low-context cultures. Hall's conceptualization of high-context and low-context communication is similar to the linguist Basil Bernstein's (1971) notion of "elaborated" and "restricted" codes. In using an elaborated code, "the speaker will select from a relatively extensive range of alternatives and therefore the probability of predicting the pattern of organizing elements is considerably reduced" (p. 77). Even though the probability of predicting the pattern is reduced, an elaborated code draws more accurate distinctions and is universalistic with respect to meaning. Elaborated codes are, therefore, similar to low-context messages. Use of restricted codes decreases the number of alternatives, and thus the "probability of predicting the pattern is greatly increased" (p. 77). Restricted codes involve the use of shortened and collapsed words and sentences. They, therefore, are particularistic with respect to their meaning and are similar to Hall's high-context messages. (We elaborate on Bernstein's perspective in Chapter 8.)

DIFFERENTIATING TERMINOLOGY

Given the preceding conceptualizations of communication and culture, we are now ready to present a working definition for intercultural communication. Putting the two conceptualizations together, we stipulate *intercultural communication is a transactional, symbolic process involving the attribution of meaning between people from different cultures.* It should be noted this definition does not suggest communication must be effective in order to be labeled intercultural. When we use the term intercultural communication, we are not implying the communication is either effective or ineffective. Effectiveness is a separate dimension, which must be addressed; but to say that two people engaged in intercultural communication is not to say they understood each other. (In Chapter 12 we examine intercultural effectiveness, which is defined as minimizing misunderstandings when people from different cultures communicate.)

There are many terms used to refer to related aspects of communication. So there is no confusion concerning how we use these terms and how they are used in the intercultural literature, we must introduce these terms. If intercultural communication refers to communication between people from different cultures, then "intracultural" communication refers to communication between people from the same culture. It should be remembered that we reserve the term culture for cultural ordering at the societal level. To illustrate, if we examine communication between two Japanese *or* between two Germans, we are looking at intracultural communication. On the other hand, if we observe communication between a Japanese *and* a German, we are looking at intercultural communication.

It should be noted here that we see the underlying communication processes in intracultural and intercultural communication as being essentially the same. The two "forms" of communication are not different in kind, only in degree. Stated differently, the variables influencing intracultural and intercultural communication are the same, but some variables have more impact on our communication in one situation than in another. For example, our ethnocentric attitude impacts on our intercultural communication more than it does on our intracultural communication. We differentiate here between intracultural and intercultural only for the sake of clarity in communicating with you, and not to suggest they are different types of communication.

Another term that needs to be clarified is "cross-cultural." While it is often used as a synonym for intercultural, the term cross-cultural traditionally implies a comparison of some phenomena across cultures. To illustrate, if we examine the use of self-disclosure in Japan *and* Germany, we are making a cross-cultural comparison. If we look at how Japanese use self-disclosure when communicating *with* Germans and how Germans use self-disclosure when communicating *with* Japanese, we are looking at intercultural communication.

If the term culture refers to societal cultures, then, as indicated above, a subculture is a subset of a culture having some different values, norms, and/or symbols that are not shared by all members of the larger culture. In other words, a subculture involves a set of ideas that arise from the larger culture but differ in some respects. With respect to our differentiation of terminology, the important subcultures are races and ethnic groups. The labels race and ethnic group are often used interchangeably—this is incorrect. A race is a group of people who are biologically similar. An ethnic group, on the other hand, is a group of people who share a common cultural heritage usually based on a common national origin or language. Jews are, therefore, an ethnic group, not a race. An ethnic group may be made up of many races, and, similarly, a race may consist of more than one ethnic group.

Even though the process of communication between people from different subcultures is essentially the same as the process of communication between people from different cultures, different terms often are used. The terms used to designate communication between people from different subcultures are not as clear as we would like, but at times it is useful to be able to differentiate the "type" of communication being discussed by using specific terms. We therefore stipulate: "interracial" communication refers to communication between people from different races and "interethnic" communication refers to communication between people from different ethnic groups. It is not this simple, however. One culture may include several races and/or ethnic groups, and one race or ethnic group may exist in different cultures. This leads to problems in labeling some forms of communication. For example, if we look at communication between a white person from the United States and a black from Ghana, are we observing interracial communication or intercultural communication? The answer, obviously, is both. As another example, what if a Jew from the United States is communicating with a Jew from Israel? Such communication is both intraethnic and intercultural. Such situations lead to conceptual confusion when we try to apply these terms.

Since the underlying processes in intracultural, intercultural, interracial, and interethnic communication are essentially the same and there is confusion as to when some of the terms are applicable, we need a way to refer to the common underlying process without differentiating among the different "types" of communication. The term intercultural communication is the most general; however, it is not adequate because it has specific connotations in the existing literature. The title of this book, *Communicating with Strangers,* hints at our solution to this problem. Anytime we communicate with people who are unknown and unfamiliar and those people are in an environment unfamiliar to them, we are communicating with strangers. The people generally viewed as the most unknown and unfamiliar are those from different societal cultures, but people from different races or ethnic groups are also unknown and unfamiliar. In addition, people from our own culture can be unknown and unfamiliar in the same sense; for example, a new groom approaching his bride's family for the first time is a stranger, according to our use of the term. In Chapter 2 we elaborate on our conceptualization of strangers; for now it is sufficient to say that when we talk about communicating with strangers, we are referring to the underlying process shared in common by intracultural, intercultural, interracial, and interethnic communication.

PLAN FOR THE BOOK

As indicated above, in the next chapter we elaborate on our conceptualization of strangers and give an overview of the process of communicating with strangers. Also in Chapter 2 we present a model of communication used to organize the material covered in Parts Two and Three of the book.

Part Two (Chapters 3-6) focuses on the conceptual filters influencing our communication with strangers. The strategy employed in this part is to introduce the relevant concepts, examine how they vary across cultures, and apply them where feasible to our communication with strangers. Specifically, in Chapter 3 we examine the cultural influences on our communication with strangers. This chapter is organized around the three components of culture introduced in Chapter 1: postulates, ends, and means. Chapter 4 focuses on the sociocultural influences on our communication with strangers, including our memberships in social groups, the role expectations we have, and how we define interpersonal relationships. In Chapter 5 we look at the categorization process, stereotypes, the attribution process, and the attitudes influencing our communication with strangers—the psychocultural influences. Chapter 6, the final chapter in Part Two, focuses on the environmental influences on our communication with strangers, including climate, geography, architecture, privacy regulation, and perceptions of the environment.

In Part Three (Chapters 7-10) we look at the encoding and decoding processes. As in Part Two, our strategy in this part is to introduce the concepts, to examine their variation across cultures, and to apply them to our communication with strangers whenever we have sufficient data. We begin by examining cultural variations in decoding, focusing mainly on perceptual processes, in Chapter 7. In Chapter 8 we look at cultural variations in verbal behavior, including language and patterns of thought; cultural variations in nonverbal behaviors are examined in Chapter 9. The final chapter in Part Three, Chapter 10, changes the focus from cultural variability to cultural universals of communication behavior.

The final part of the book, Part Four, considers selected aspects of intercultural interaction. Specifically, Chapter 11 focuses on relationships between people from different subcultures or cultures, including friendships and marital relationships. In Chapter 12 we examine the issue of intercultural effectiveness, taking into consideration how to become more effective and how to deal with ethical issues in intercultural encounters. Chapter 13 concentrates on strangers' adaptations to new cultural environments, with both adjustment and accultura- tion being considered. We conclude in Chapter 14 with a discussion of the pro- cess of becoming intercultural, which is a desirable outcome to seek as a result of our communication with strangers.

SUMMARY

The purpose of this chapter is to introduce the two major concepts, communi- cation and culture, to be used throughout the remainder of this book. In light of the eight assumptions we make about the nature of communication, we stipu- late: communication is a symbolic process involving the attribution of meaning. We reserve the term culture for the cultural ordering process associated with the societal level of social ordering. Intercultural communication, therefore, is stipu- lated to be communication between people from different societal cultures.

We take the position that the underlying process of communication between people from different cultures or subcultures is the same as the underlying pro- cess of communication between people from the same culture or subculture. Given the similarity of the underlying process and the confusion of existing terminology, we argue what is needed is a way to refer to the underlying process that all "types" of communication (i.e., intracultural, interracial, interethnic, and intercultural) have in common. Since none of the present terms are ade- quate, we introduce our notion of communicating with strangers. By commu- nicating with strangers we mean communication with people who are unknown and unfamiliar, including people from another culture and people from our own culture or subculture who are in an environment new to them.

2

An Approach to the Study of Intercultural Communication

We must never assume that we are fully aware of what we communicate to someone else. There exists in the world today tremendous distortion in meaning as men try to communicate with one another. The job of achieving understanding and insight into mental processes of others is much more serious than most of us care to admit.

Edward T. Hall

It commonly is accepted that cultural variability in people's backgrounds influences their communication behavior. This "fact" leads many scholars studying intercultural communication to view it as a unique form of communication, differing in kind from other forms of communication (e.g., communication between people from the same culture). This point of view, however, is not accepted widely. Sarbaugh (1979) points out:

> There appears to be a temptation among scholars and practitioners of communication to approach intercultural communication as though it were a different process than intracultural communication. As one begins to identify the variables that operate in the communication being studied, however, it becomes apparent that they are the same for both intracultural and intercultural settings. (p. 5)

We agree with Sarbaugh; not only are the variables the same, but the underlying communication process is also the same.

This view suggests that any approach to the study of intercultural communication must be consistent with the study of intracultural communication. It is our aim throughout the remainder of this chapter, and the remainder of this book, to lay out a perspective for the study of communication that is useful not only for understanding our communication with people from other cultures or subcultures but also for understanding our communication with people from our own culture or subculture. We first turn our attention to the linking concept in our view of communication—the concept of the "stranger" as a social phenomenon.

THE CONCEPT OF THE STRANGER

To understand communication between people from different cultures, it is necessary to recognize that when people are confronted with cultural differences (and other forms of group differences, such as racial, ethnic, or class differences) they tend to view people from the group that is different as strangers. The term stranger is somewhat ambiguous in that it is often used to refer to aliens, intruders, foreigners, outsiders, newcomers, and immigrants, as well as any person who is unknown and unfamiliar. Despite this ambiguity "the concept of the stranger remains one of the most powerful sociological tools for analyzing social processes of individuals and groups confronting new social orders" (Shack, 1979, p. 2).

The concept of the stranger comes from the German sociologist Georg Simmel's (1950, originally published in 1908 in German) classic essay "Der Fremde" ("The Stranger"). Simmel views strangers as possessing the contradictory qualities of being both near and far at the same time:

> The unity of nearness and remoteness in every human relation is organized, in the phenomenon of the stranger, in a way which may be most briefly formulated by saying that in the relationship to him, distance means that he, who is also far, is actually near. . . . The stranger . . . is an element of the group itself. His position as a full-fledged member involves being both outside it and confronting it. (p. 402)

In other words, strangers represent both the idea of nearness in that they are physically close and the idea of remoteness in that they have different values and ways of doing things. Strangers are physically present and participating in a situation and at the same time are outside the situation because they are from a different place.

Another conceptualization of the stranger is presented by Wood (1934). Wood's view of the stranger differs from Simmel's in that it is broader:

> We shall describe the stranger as one who has come into face-to-face contact with the group for the first time. . . . For us the stranger may be, as with Simmel, a potential wanderer who comes today and goes tomorrow, or he may come today and remain with us permanently. The condition of being a stranger is not . . . dependent upon the future duration of the contact, but it is determined by the fact that it was the first face-to-face meeting of individuals who have not known one another before. (pp. 43–44)

Wood, therefore, sees strangers as newly arrived outsiders.

Like Wood, Schuetz (1944) takes a broader view of the concept of the stranger than does Simmel. For Schuetz the term stranger means "an adult individual . . . who tries to be permanently accepted or at least partially tolerated by the group which he approaches" (p. 499). This conceptualization includes not only the obvious cases of immigrants and sojourners to other cultures but also people trying to join a closed club, grooms attempting to be accepted by the brides' family, recruits entering the army, or any person coming into a new and unfamiliar group. Schuetz argues that strangers lack "intersubjective understanding," or an understanding of the social world inhabited by the members of the group they approach. Parrillo (1980) succinctly summarizes Schuetz's perspective:

> Because this is a shared world, it is an intersubjective one. For the native, then, every social situation is a coming together not only of roles and identities, but also of shared realities—the intersubjective structure of consciousness. What is taken for granted by the native is problematic for the stranger. In a familiar world, people live through the day by responding to daily routine without questioning or reflection. To strangers, however, every situation is new and is therefore experienced as a crisis. (p. 3)

As Parrillo indicates, strangers may perceive their interactions in their new surroundings as a series of crises.

Herman and Schield (1960) take a similar position when they argue that the major problem strangers face in their new surroundings is "lack of security." Strangers do not have the knowledge necessary to fully understand their new environment or the communication of the people who live in it. Further, members of the host group do not possess information regarding individual strangers, even though they may have some information about the group or culture from which the strangers come. Since we do not have information regarding individual strangers, our initial impression of them must, therefore, be an abstract or categoric one (i.e., a stereotypic one). Strangers are classified on the basis of whatever information we can obtain. If the only information we have is their culture, we base our initial impression on this information. If we have additional information (their race, ethnic group, sex, class, etc.), we use that as well.

Strangers, as we conceive of them, are people who are different and unknown and have come in contact with our group for the first time. It should be obvious that "strangerhood" is a figure-ground phenomenon—a stranger's status is always defined in relation to a "host," a "native," or some existing group. For example, a person from the United States visiting another country and a person from another country visiting the United States are both strangers. A white teacher in a predominantly black school, a Native American working in a predominantly white organization, a Vietnamese refugee in the United States, a new bride visiting the groom's family, and a Chicano moving into a predominantly white neighborhood are all examples of strangers. In general, we include anyone entering a relatively unknown or unfamiliar environment under the rubric of stranger. This conceptualization, therefore, subsumes both Wood's and Schuetz's views on strangers.

Obviously, not everyone we meet for the first time is truly unknown and unfamiliar. Sometimes we are familiar with or know something about people we meet for the first time. Following Eric Cohen (1972), we can say our social interactions, not just our interactions with people we meet for the first time, vary with respect to the degree of strangeness and/or familiarity present in the interaction. Our interactions with close friends and relatives involve a high degree of familiarity, while our interactions with acquaintances and co-workers involve less familiarity and more strangeness. When we meet people for the first time, there may be any degree of strangeness and/or familiarity. For example, when we meet a close friend of our best friend for the first time, we may be somewhat familiar with that person already. In contrast, when we meet a person from another subculture of our culture (e.g., a person from another race or ethnic group), our interaction with that person usually involves more strangeness than familiarity. Because they do not share the same culture, our interactions with people from other cultures often involve the highest degree of strangeness and the least degree of familiarity.

Our use of the term stranger throughout this book refers to those relationships where there is a relatively high degree of strangeness and a relatively low degree of familiarity. Since our interactions with people from other cultures tend to involve the highest degree of strangeness and the lowest degree of familiarity, we focus on these interactions, but we also examine other interactions involving a relatively high degree of strangeness (e.g., those with members of different races or ethnic groups).

In looking at the general process of communication with strangers, we are able to overcome one of the major conceptual problems of many analyses of intercultural communication. The problem to which we refer involves the drawing of artificial distinctions among intracultural, intercultural, interracial, and interethnic communication. While some variables may take on more importance in one situation than in another (e.g., prejudice may be more important in interracial communication than in intraracial communication), each of the situations is influenced by the same variables. If the variables influencing each situation and the underlying process of communication are the same, it does not make sense to draw artificial distinctions among them. By using the stranger as a linking concept, we can examine a general process, communicating with strangers, which subsumes intracultural, intercultural, interracial, and interethnic communication into one general framework.

Prior to presenting our organizing model of communication, we must overview the process of communicating with strangers. Our focus in the next section is an elaboration of the nature of the predictions we make and their role in reducing the uncertainty present when we communicate with strangers.

AN OVERVIEW OF COMMUNICATION WITH STRANGERS

Conscious Versus Unconscious Behavior

We indicated in Chapter 1 that much of our communication behavior takes place at low levels of awareness. According to Abelson (1976), our unconscious behavior is guided by "scripts." By scripts he means "a coherent sequence of events expected by the individual, involving him either as a participant or an observer" (p. 33). Scripts, therefore, are standardized sequences of behavior we frequently experience. According to Langer (1978), we learn scripts because when we first are confronted with a situation we consciously seek cues to guide our behavior. In other words, we learn our scripts as we are socialized into our culture and various groups as children and as we enter new situations as adults. As we have repeated experiences with the same event, we have less need to attune consciously to our behavior. "The more often we have engaged in the activity the more likely it is that we rely on scripts for the completion of the activity and the less likely it is that there will be any correspondence between our actions and those thoughts of ours that occur simultaneously" (Langer, 1978, p. 39).

As indicated in Chapter 1, we become more conscious of our behavior when we enter new situations. The situations under which we are aware of our behavior, however, must be delineated more fully. Berger and Douglas (1982) list five conditions under which we are highly cognizant of our behavior:

> Briefly summarized, those conditions are (1) in novel situations where, by definition, no appropriate script exists, (2) where external factors prevent completion of a script, (3) when scripted behavior becomes effortful because substantially more of the behavior is required than is usual, (4) when a discrepant outcome is experienced, or (5) where multiple scripts come into conflict so that involvement in any one script is suspended. In short, individuals will enact scripted sequences whenever those sequences are available and will continue to do so until events unusual to the script are encountered. (pp. 46–47)

From Berger's summary of these conditions, it can be inferred we are more aware of our behavior when communicating with strangers than we are when communicating with people who are familiar.

Uncertainty Reduction

Whenever we communicate with strangers, we make predictions about the outcome of our communication behavior. Of course, we are not always aware of making these predictions. Our awareness of making predictions varies with the degree to which we are aware of alternative outcomes in a particular situation

(Miller and Steinberg, 1975). If we are aware of alternative outcomes, we are more aware of making predictions about the effects of our behavior. When we communicate with strangers, we tend to be more aware of alternative outcomes than when we communicate with someone we know, or someone who is familiar.

The predictions we make are aimed at reducing the uncertainty present whenever we communicate with strangers. In the view of Berger and Calabrese (1975), the primary concern anytime we meet someone new is uncertainty reduction, or increasing our ability to predict our behavior and that of the other person. More recently Berger (1979) modified this position, arguing that we try to reduce uncertainty when the person we meet will be encountered in the future, provides rewards to us, or behaves in a "deviant" fashion. Given that strangers, especially those from other cultures or ethnic groups, are likely to behave in a deviant fashion, it is reasonable to say we try to reduce uncertainty when we communicate with strangers more than we do when we communicate with people who are familiar.

Berger and Calabrese (1975) point out there are at least two distinct types of uncertainty present in our interactions with strangers. First, there is the uncertainty we have about how the stranger with whom we are communicating will behave. In other words, we need to be able to predict which of several alternative behavior patterns strangers will choose to employ. An illustration is the situation when we meet a person we find attractive at a party. Assuming we want to see this person again after the party, we try to think about different ways we can approach this person in order to convince him or her to see us again. The different approaches we think about are the predictions that reduce our uncertainty. The second type of uncertainty Berger and Calabrese (1975) talk about involves a retroactive explanation of strangers' behavior. Whenever we try to figure out why strangers behaved the way they did, we are engaging in explanatory uncertainty reduction. The problem we are addressing is one of reducing the number of possible explanations for the strangers' behavior. This is necessary if we are to understand their behavior and, thus, be able to increase our ability to predict their behavior in the future.

Attributional Processes

A problem closely related to uncertainty reduction is the question of how we utilize information about strangers to reach inferences about their behavior. Recent work on attribution theory is instructive concerning this process.

Jones and Nisbett (1972) argue that people ("actors" is their term) performing behavior interpret their behavior differently than do people observing it. Specifically, they suggest actors usually attribute their own behavior to situational factors, whereas observers attribute the behavior to qualities of the actors. Nisbett et al. (1973) offer two probable explanations for these divergent perspectives. The first is simply a perceptual one. The actors' attention at the moment of the action is focused on situational cues with which their behavior is coordinated. It therefore appears to actors that their behavior is a response to these situational cues. For observers, however, it is not the situational cues that are salient, but rather the actors' behavior. Observers are more likely to perceive the cause of the actors' behavior to be a trait or quality inherent in the actors. This view suggests that when we communicate with strangers our retroactive explanations of their behavior are likely to focus on characteristics of the strangers (e.g., their cultural background or group membership). The second explanation suggested by Nisbett et al. for the differential bias of actors and observers stems from a difference in the nature and extent of information possessed. In general, actors know more about their own past behavior and present experiences than do observers. This difference in information may prevent actors from interpreting their behavior in terms of personal characteristics, while allowing observers to make such an interpretation.

> If an actor insults another person, an observer may be free to infer that the actor did so because the actor is hostile. The actor, however, may know that he rarely insults others and may believe that his insult was a response to the most recent in a series of provocations from the person he finally attacked. The difference in information available to the actor and observer is, of course, reduced when the actor and observer know one another well but is always present to a degree. (Nisbett et al., 1973, p. 155)

When we are communicating with strangers, there is an increased likelihood we will attribute the cause of their behavior to one particular characteristic—namely, their cultural background or group membership. Stated differently, we are not likely to attribute the cause of others' behavior to their culture if they come from the same culture we do, but since strangers often come from another culture or ethnic group their origin or background is a plausible explanation for their behavior. (This process is discussed in detail in Chapter 5.)

Levels of Data Used in Making Predictions

Miller and Steinberg (1975) argue that we use three levels of data when we make predictions about other people's behavior. The first level of data we use is "cultural." The people in any culture generally behave in a regular fashion because of their postulates, norms, and values. It is this regularity that allows us to make predictions on the basis of cultural data. Miller and Sunnafrank (1982) elaborate:

> Knowledge about another person's culture—its language, dominant values, beliefs, and prevailing ideology—often permits predictions of the person's probable responses to certain messages. . . . Upon first encountering a stranger, cultural information provides the only grounds for communicative predictions. This fact explains the uneasiness and perceived lack of control most people experience when thrust into an alien culture: they not only

lack information about the individuals with whom they must communicate, they are bereft of information concerning shared cultural norms and values. (pp. 226–227)

Two major factors influence our predictive accuracy using cultural data. First, the more experiences at the cultural level we have, the better our predictive accuracy is. When we are confronting someone from our own culture, the experiences to which we refer are in our culture. On the other hand, when we are communicating with strangers, our accuracy depends on our experiences with their culture. If we know little or nothing about the strangers' culture, our predictions will be more inaccurate than if we know a lot about their culture. Second, errors in predictions are made either because we are not aware of the strangers' cultural experiences or because we try to predict the behavior of strangers on the basis of cultural experiences different from the ones they have had—for example, when we make ethnocentric predictions on the basis of our own cultural experiences (Miller and Steinberg, 1975).

The second level of data used in making predictions is "sociological." Sociological-level predictions are based on strangers' memberships in or aspirations to particular social groups. "Knowledge of an individual's membership groups, as well as the reference groups to which he or she aspires, permits numerous predictions about responses to various messages" (Miller and Sunnafrank, 1982, p. 227). Membership in social groups may be voluntary, or strangers may be classified as a member of a group because of certain characteristics they possess. For example, our predictions at the sociological level include those based on strangers' memberships in political or other social groups, the roles they fill, their gender, or their ethnicity. Miller and Sunnafrank (1982) argue that sociological-level data are the principal kind used to predict the behavior of people from the same culture. The major error in making predictions using sociological-level data stems from the fact that strangers are members of many groups and when we communicate with other people it is not always possible to be sure which group's norms and values are influencing their behavior (Miller and Steinberg, 1975).

The final level of data used in making predictions about the outcomes of our communication behavior is "psychological." At the psychological level predictions are based on the specific people with whom we are communicating. At this level we are concerned with how these people are different from and similar to other members of their culture and of the groups to which they belong. When predictions are based on psychological data, "each participant relates to the other in terms of what sets the other apart from most people. They take into consideration each other's individual differences in terms of the subject and the occasion" (Dance and Larson, 1972, p. 56).

For the purpose of the present analysis, we modify the labels for the three levels of data used in making predictions. Since all three levels are highly interrelated, we use labels reflecting the interrelations: cultural, sociocultural, and psychocultural. Our changing of these labels is intended only to emphasize that the three levels of data are interrelated, not to reflect a disagreement with Miller and Steinberg's (1975) conceptualization.

Categorization

Making predictions based on cultural and/or sociocultural data can be likened to "stimulus generalization," or looking for sameness when making predictions about other communicators, according to Miller and Steinberg (1975). They go on to point out, "Stimulus generalization is closely akin to abstraction: One observes a group of objects and notes aspects they have in common. . . . Stimulus generalization necessarily ignores the characteristics on which objects and events differ" (p. 24). If predictions based on cultural and/or sociocultural data can be likened to stimulus generalization, then making predictions based on psychocultural data can be likened to "stimulus discrimination," or looking for differences among communicators (Miller and Steinberg, 1975). By seeking out differences among communicators, we can reduce greatly the number of errors we make in our predictions.

Whenever we put discrete elements into groups, we are engaging in the process of categorization. All cultural groups use categories, but they "cut up the pie of experience" differently. That is, they may put the same stimuli into different categories. The categories we learn as part of our socialization into our culture and the various groups to which we belong influence the way in which we interpret the world and the predictions we make about others' behavior. Putting stimuli into categories is necessary if we are to make sense out of the uncertainty confronting us at any point in time. The process of categorization allows us to reduce highly complex bits of information to manageable proportions. If we do not categorize our experiences, we are not able to cope with our environment. Brislin (1981) points out: "After people put discrete elements into categories, they use the categories in their thinking and tend to ignore individual elements. Among category members, similarities are emphasized and differences tend to be ignored" (p. 79).

When the elements being categorized are people, we refer to the categorization process as stereotyping. As Bosmajian (1974) so accurately points out, stereotypes have acquired a very "distasteful status." "Stereotypes are," however, "absolutely necessary for thinking and communication . . . a fact which must be realized in any analysis of interaction between individuals from different backgrounds" (Brislin, 1981, p. 44).

Although a full discussion of stereotypes must be postponed until Chapter 5, for the present it should be obvious that when we make predictions about strangers using cultural or sociocultural data, our predictions are based on stereotypes. This is both necessary and unavoidable. We must recognize that we cannot communicate with people from our own or another culture (or talk about them in a book like this) without stereotypes. Stereotypes become problematical (i.e., cause us to make incorrect inferences and predictions about strangers' behavior) in the process of communication when they are held rigidly and do not allow us to perceive individual differences or to use psychocultural data to make inferences and predictions about strangers' behavior.

To summarize, our communication with strangers involves the same basic process as our communication with people who are known and familiar. Because strangers are unknown and unfamiliar, however, we tend to be more aware of our behavior when we communicate with them than of our behavior when we communicate with people who are familiar. Since strangers are, by definition, unknown, our attributions and predictions regarding their behavior must be categorical. When we first meet strangers, our initial interpretations and predictions about their behavior are based on our stereotypes. Our stereotypes may be either culturally or socioculturally based. That is, they may be based on our conceptions about how all people in the strangers' culture behave, how people in the strangers' group memberships behave (e.g., how all males or females from the strangers' culture behave), how people in the strangers' role behave (e.g., how managers are supposed to behave in the strangers' culture), or how people in particular interpersonal relationships in the strangers' culture behave (e.g., how friends in the strangers' culture behave). Based on our stereotypes, we interpret strangers' behavior and make predictions about how they will respond to us.

To the extent that our stereotypes are accurate, our inferences and cultural or sociocultural predictions of strangers' behavior are accurate. Since stereotypes are often inaccurate, however, our inferences and predictions of strangers' behavior are often inaccurate as well. To overcome these errors in inferences and predictions and to make accurate ones, we must make them relative to the strangers' culture. This requires that we not hold our stereotypes rigidly and we be able to suspend or control our natural ethnocentric tendencies. Maintaining "open" stereotypes and controlling our ethnocentrism make it possible for us to begin to make inferences and predictions about strangers' behavior based on psychocultural data, and, therefore, to open up the possibility of interpersonal relationships with strangers.

AN ORGANIZING MODEL FOR STUDYING COMMUNICATION WITH STRANGERS

The model presented in this section is designed to serve two functions. First, it helps isolate and identify the elements influencing our communication with strangers. Second, the model serves as a guide to the organization of the material presented in Parts Two and Three of the book. Our purpose in developing the model is not to describe the process of communication with strangers, but, rather, to organize the elements influencing the process so they can be discussed systematically.

The model is diagrammed in Figure 2-1. In constructing the model, we attempted to find a workable compromise between complexity and simplicity. As it stands, the model contains all of the major elements, yet is simple enough to be readily understood. The elements included in the model are encoding and decoding of messages and cultural, sociocultural, psychocultural, and environmental influences on the communication process. Each of these elements consists of several variables; for example, the cultural influences consist of postulates, ends, and means—the three components of culture introduced in Chapter 1.

In examining the model it is necessary to keep in mind that any model, out of necessity, excludes certain elements. The problem of "premature closure," as the exclusion of elements is called, is unavoidable in constructing a model. In deciding which elements to include, we used two criteria: (1) Is the element useful in explaining our communication with strangers? and (2) Is there research available on the element's influence on communication?

Since each of the elements of the model is discussed in detail in Parts Two and Three of the book, the following is intended only as an introduction. Our purpose here, therefore, is to put the material presented in the next two parts of the book into a context.

An Overview of the Model

Given our view of communication, we see encoding and decoding of communication messages to be an interactive process influenced by conceptual filters, which we categorize into cultural, sociocultural, psychocultural, and environmental factors. This is illustrated in Figure 2-1 by the way the center circle, which contains the interaction between encoding and decoding of messages, is surrounded by three other circles representing cultural, sociocultural, and psychocultural influences. The circles are drawn with dashed lines to indicate that the elements affect, and are affected by, the other elements. The two persons represented in the model are surrounded by a dashed box representing the environmental influences. This box is drawn with a dashed rather than a solid line because the immediate environment in which the communication takes place is not an isolated or "closed system." Most communication between people takes place in a social environment that includes other people who also are engaging in communication.

The message/feedback between the two communicators is represented by the lines from one person's encoding to the other person's decoding and from the second person's encoding to the first person's decoding. Two message/feedback lines are shown to indicate that anytime we communicate we are simultaneously engaged in encoding and decoding of messages. In other words, communication is not static; we do not encode a message and do nothing until we receive feedback. Rather, we are processing incoming stimuli (decoding) at the same time as we are encoding messages.

Figure 2-1. An Organizing Model for Studying Communication with Strangers

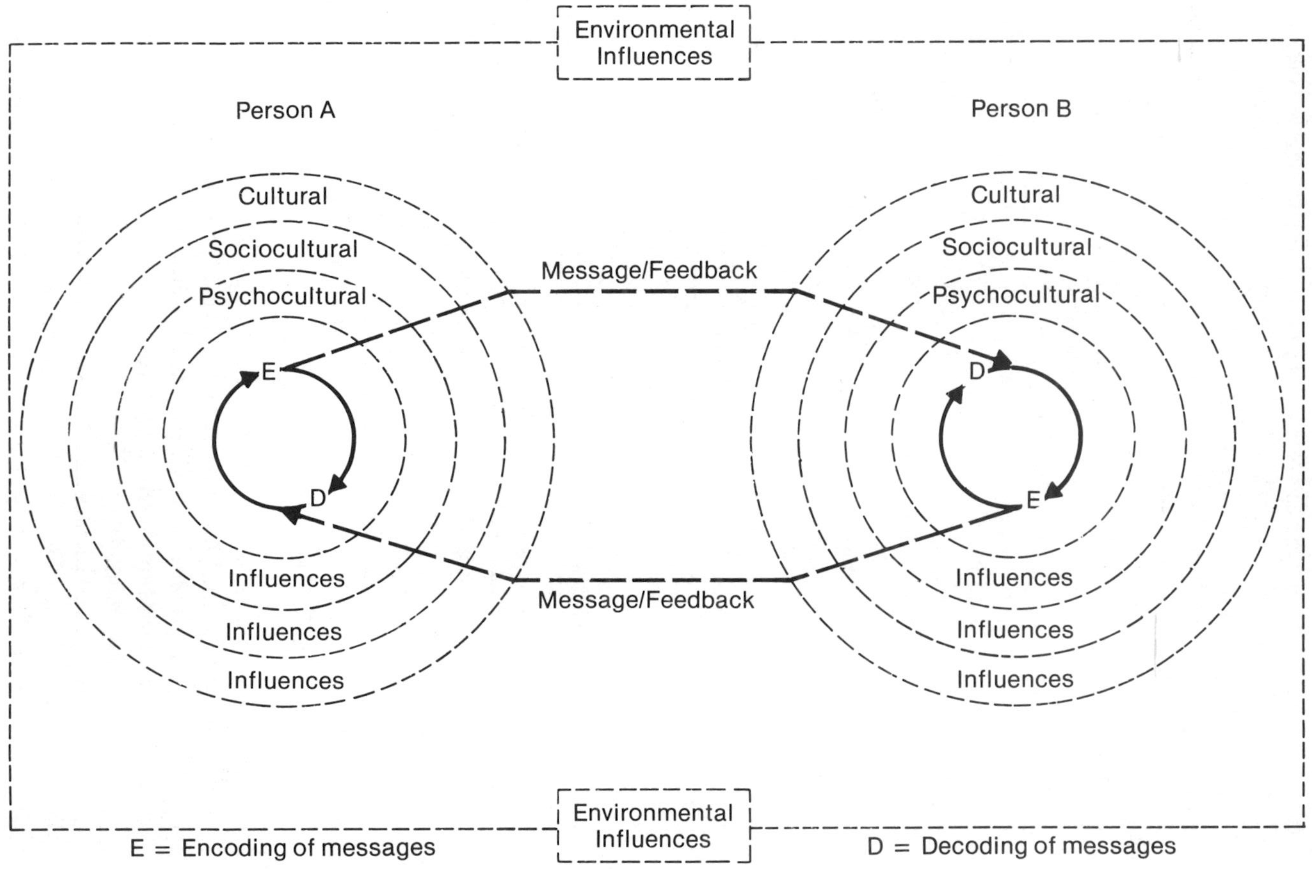

As indicated above, the cultural, sociocultural, and psychocultural influences serve as conceptual filters for our encoding and decoding of messages. By filters we mean mechanisms that delimit the number of alternatives from which we choose when we encode and decode messages. More specifically, the filters limit the predictions we make about how strangers might respond to our communication behavior. The nature of the predictions we make, in turn, influences the way we choose to encode our messages. Further, the filters delimit what stimuli we pay attention to and how we choose to interpret those stimuli when we decode incoming messages.

Encoding of Messages

Since it is impossible to transmit electrical impulses directly from one's brain to that of another person, it is necessary for us to put messages into codes that can be transmitted. Messages can be encoded into many forms, but for the purpose of our analysis two are most relevant: language (verbal codes) and nonverbal behaviors (we exclude codes such as mathematics, music, etc.). As indicated earlier, the process of encoding messages is accomplished at varying levels of consciousness.

Language is one of the major vehicles through which we encode messages. Obviously, languages can differ from culture to culture. Culture and language are closely intertwined, with each having an impact on the other. Our language is a product of our culture, and our culture is a product of our language. The language we speak influences what we see and think, and what we see and think, in part, influences our culture.

Language enables people to communicate with each other by means of rules, which are understood at varying levels. There are four levels of rules influencing language: phonemic, syntactic, semantic, and pragmatic. Phonemic rules deal with the sounds of the language and how they are combined. Syntactic rules deal with the relationship of one symbol to another or one word to another (i.e., grammar and logic), while semantic rules deal with the relationship of a symbol to its referent. Finally, pragmatic rules deal with the symbol-referent connection in a particular context. Pragmatic rules are very subtle and deeply embedded in the culture. Native speakers of a language generally have an unconscious understanding of all four levels of rules. It is possible for a non-native speaker to understand the phonemic, syntactic, and semantic rules of a language and still not be able to communicate effectively with a native speaker of the language because of a lack of understanding of the pragmatic rules. In such a situation the non-native speaker of the language may encode sentences that are correct on the surface but do not recognize differences in meaning in particular contexts. Several writers point out that in such a situation people can make fluent fools of themselves.

Not only are messages encoded verbally, but they also are encoded nonverbally. Nonverbal encoding of messages, like language, varies from culture to culture. Language is mostly a conscious activity, while nonverbal behavior is mostly an unconscious activity. That is, we generally are not aware of the messages we are encoding nonverbally through our gestures, facial expressions, or tones of voice, to name only a few. When we encounter nonverbal behaviors greatly different from our own (i.e., when communicating with strangers), however, we may become unusually conscious of those behaviors.

Decoding of Messages

To a certain extent message decoding is the opposite of message encoding. When we decode a message, our interpretation depends on what the other person says verbally, what nonverbal behavior the other person exhibits, our own encoded messages, our conceptual filters, and the context in which the message is received. In other words, how we interpret the messages encoded by strangers is a function of what they have encoded, what we had previously encoded, the context in which we are communicating, and our conceptual filters.

As indicated above, the way in which we process the incoming stimuli is partially a function of our conceptual filters. More specifically, the filters delimit the stimuli we observe and tell us how specific stimuli are to be interpreted. For example, consider strangers who are visiting Japan and are invited into a Japanese home, where it is expected that shoes be removed before entering the house. The strangers may see the Japanese family's shoes by the door but, because of their conceptual filters, not attribute any meaning to the stimuli and, therefore, walk into the house with shoes still on their feet. When the Japanese hosts become upset, the strangers will have no idea what they did wrong. The strangers' conceptual filters have delimited the stimuli to which they attribute meaning, thereby influencing the interpretations they make about the situation.

Cultural Influences

The cultural influences include those factors involved in the cultural ordering process described in Chapter 1. For the purpose of our analysis, we focus on the three components of culture described by Olsen (1978): postulates, ends, and means. Postulates, you will recall, are those things we take for granted as "the facts of life." They are the unconscious assumptions we are taught as part of our socialization into a culture. These assumptions include how the self is defined, people's relationships to one another, and their relationships to the environment and supernatural phenomena. Social (or cultural) values are shared conceptions of the desired ends of social life. They express a collective view of what is important and unimportant, good and bad. The norms and rules of a culture specify the acceptable and unacceptable means for reaching the ends of social life. It is the norms and rules of a culture that allow its members to engage spontaneously in everyday social behavior without continually having to "guess" what other people are going to do. More formally, we can say norms and rules are sets of expected behaviors for particular situations.

Our cultural postulates, ends, and means influence how we encode messages and decode incoming stimuli when we communicate with strangers. For example, consider a visit to North America by strangers from a culture with a communication rule requiring that direct eye contact always be avoided. When interacting with these strangers, North Americans will try to establish direct eye contact. If the strangers do not look them in the eye when talking, the North Americans will assume that the strangers either have something to hide or are not telling the truth, since the communication rule in North America requires direct eye contact to establish one's sincerity. A rule of North American culture, therefore, has influenced the way in which North Americans interpret the strangers' behavior. It should be noted, however, that there are some subcultures in North America (e.g., lower-class black subculture) where this rule may not be applicable.

Sociocultural Influences

The sociocultural influences are those involved in the social ordering process. As indicated in Chapter 1, social ordering develops out of our interactions with others when the patterns of behavior become consistent over time (Olsen, 1978). Three major sociocultural influences have an impact on our communication with strangers: our membership in social groups, our role expectations, and our definition of interpersonal relationships.

We are members of groups either because we are born into them or because we join them. Groups we are born into include, but are not limited to, racial and ethnic groups, families, age groups, and gender groups. Groups we join include service groups (e.g., the Lions Club), occupational groups, religious groups, and ideological groups (e.g., Democratic and Republican parties, the Ku Klux Klan), to name only a few. The various groups of which we are members enforce sets of expected behaviors (norms and rules) and have shared values and, therefore, have an impact on how we communicate with strangers.

When we communicate with another person and make our predictions based on a position that person holds in a group, we are engaging in a role relationship. The idea of position can best be illustrated by examples; positions include clerk, judge, father, mother, boss, physician, professor, student, etc. People filling one of these positions are expected to perform certain behaviors. The set of behaviors they are expected to perform is referred to as their role. Our role expectations influence how we interpret behavior and what predictions we make about people in a given role. Role expectations vary within any culture, but there is a tendency for them to vary more across cultures. If we do not know strangers' role expectations, we inevitably will make inaccurate interpretations and predictions about their behavior.

Interpersonal relationships differ from role relationships in that they involve the use of psychocultural data in making predictions. How different interpersonal relationships (e.g., acquaintance, casual friend, close friend, lover) are defined influences how we communicate with people in those relationships. That is, our definition of a given relationship influences how we interpret incoming stimuli and the predictions we make about the behavior of the other person involved. If we are not aware of how strangers define interpersonal relationships, we are likely to interpret their behavior incorrectly and to make inaccurate predictions about how they will behave.

Psychocultural Influences

The variables included under the psychocultural influences are those involved in the personal ordering process. Personal ordering, you will recall, is the process giving stability to psychological processes (both cognitive and affective). The cognitive variables influencing our communication with strangers include the categorization and stereotyping processes, as well as the attribution process. The major affective variables influencing our communication with strangers are our attitudes, particularly ethnocentrism and prejudice. Both cognitive and affective variables influence the way in which we interpret incoming stimuli and the predictions we make about strangers' behavior. Being highly ethnocentric, for example, leads us to interpret strangers' behavior from our own cultural frame of reference and to expect strangers to behave the same way we do. This invariably leads to misinterpretations of the strangers' messages, as well as inaccurate predictions about their future behavior.

Environmental Influences

As indicated in Chapter 1, the environment in which we communicate influences our encoding and decoding of messages. The geographical location, climate, and architectural setting, as well as our perceptions of the environment, influence how we interpret incoming stimuli and the predictions we make about strangers' behavior. Since strangers may have different perceptions of and orientations toward the environment, they may interpret behavior differently in the same setting. As an illustration, a North American visiting a Colombian family would expect to engage in informal interaction in the living room. The Colombian host, on the other hand, probably would define the living room as a place for formal behavior. Each, therefore, would interpret the other's behavior in light of his or her own expectations and make predictions about the other's behavior based on these same expectations. Such a situation, in all likelihood, would lead to misunderstanding.

In Hall's (1976) terminology, the environment is part of the context in which communication occurs. Environmental influences on behavior, therefore, can be expected to vary systematically across cultures, having less impact in low-context cultures and more impact in high-context cultures.

SUMMARY

Communication with people from our own culture, with people from other races or ethnic groups, and with people from other cultures shares the same underlying process. While communication in these different situations differs in degrees, it does not differ in kind. Various names are available to label communication in these different situations, but ambiguity exists as to which label is appropriate for certain situations. For example, communication between a white person from South Africa and a black person from the United States can be labeled as either intercultural or interracial communication.

Given the similarity of the underlying process of communication and the confusion in applying the various labels, we believe what is needed is a way to refer to the underlying process without referring to a particular situation. Talking about communication with strangers is a way to accomplish this end. Strangers can be conceived of as people who are unknown and unfamiliar and are confronting a group for the first time. A black student in a mainly white school, a Mexican student studying at a university in the United States, a groom meeting the bride's family for the first time, and a manager from the United States working in Thailand are all examples of strangers.

Our communication with strangers is influenced by our conceptual filters, just as their communication with us is influenced by their filters. Our conceptual filters can be placed into four categories: cultural, sociocultural, psychocultural, and environmental. Each of these influences how we interpret messages encoded by strangers and what predictions we make about strangers' behavior. Without understanding the strangers' filters, we cannot accurately interpret or predict their behavior.

PART TWO

INFLUENCES ON THE PROCESS OF COMMUNICATING WITH STRANGERS

In Part One we defined communication and culture and overviewed the process of communicating with strangers. In this part we examine, in depth, the major influences on our communication with strangers.

As indicated in Chapter 2, there are four major groups of influences on our communication with strangers: cultural, sociocultural, psychocultural, and environmental. Cultural influences are made up of the three components of culture introduced in Chapter 1: postulates, ends, and means. Sociocultural influences include those stemming from our membership in social groups, from our role relationships, and from our interpersonal relationships. Psychocultural influences involve the way we categorize objects and people, the attributions we make about others' behavior, and the attitudes we hold, particularly ethnocentrism and prejudice. Environmental influences consist of the physical environment—geography, climate, and architecture—and our perceptions of it. Each of these groups of influences impacts on the way we interpret incoming stimuli and the predictions we make about strangers' behavior.

The focus of Part Two is on examining the variables making up each group of influences and looking at how they vary across cultures. In other words, this part is designed to be cross-cultural in nature. We believe knowledge of how these influences vary across cultures is a prerequisite to effective communication with strangers. Without an understanding of the cultural variation in the variables, it is impossible to make accurate predictions about strangers' behavior or to correctly interpret incoming stimuli from them.

The four groups of influences examined in this part do not operate independently of one another; rather, each one is highly intertwined with each of the others. The culture in which we are raised, for example, has an impact on the groups to which we belong, the role relationships we learn, and the interpersonal relationships we form (the sociocultural influences), as well as on the way we categorize things and the attitudes we hold (the psychocultural influences). Further, our culture is influenced by the environment in which it exists and is affected by both the sociocultural and psychocultural factors as well. Even though we separate the four groups of influences in the four chapters in this part, you should keep in mind as you read that they are highly interrelated.

3

Cultural Influences
on the Process

*Human beings draw close to one another by their
common nature, but habits and customs keep them
apart.*

Confucian saying

The purpose of this chapter is to examine the cultural influences on our communication with strangers. The chapter is organized around the three components of culture introduced in Chapter 1: postulates, ends, and means. Postulates involve cultural ideas accepted as "the way things are." They are accepted without questioning as "the facts of life." Our discussion of postulates begins with an examination of "world view," the most general postulate existing in a culture. Next we look at "value orientations" and "pattern variables," two other important aspects of cultural postulates. The goals of organized social life, cultural ends, are the second component of culture. The ends of social life are the desired objectives or outcomes toward which the people of a culture strive. Our discussion focuses on the most basic form of cultural ends—social values. Within any culture there are prescribed and proscribed methods for reaching the acceptable ends. In other words, every culture has acceptable means to reach cultural goals. The means to reach cultural goals involve shared agreements about how people are expected to behave. Our discussion of means focuses on cultural norms and rules, those widely shared agreements about how we are expected to behave.

Before proceeding to a discussion of cultural postulates, however, we want to point out that there are two alternative approaches to examining cultural processes. One approach is to look at how a particular culture works from the inside. When using this approach, we are concerned with trying to understand the behavior of people in a culture from their point of view. Another approach to understanding culture is to compare one culture with another. When using this approach, we use predetermined categories to examine selected aspects of the cultures being studied. In other words, the objective is not to understand the cultures as their members understand them but to determine how the cultures compare with respect to some particular quality. This distinction is not new; it was originally proposed by Sapir in 1925. The distinction also is made by the linguist Pike (1966), who uses the terms "emic" and "etic" to label the first and second approach, respectively.

Our approach throughout this chapter and the subsequent chapters in Parts Two and Three is etic in nature. The focus is on looking at the various influences on our communication with strangers as they are manifested in selected cultures. These cross-cultural comparisons are necessary for understanding and improving our communication with strangers.

POSTULATES

World View

"Every social group has a world view—a set of more or less systematized beliefs and values in terms of which the group evaluates and attaches meaning to the reality that surrounds it" (Kraft, 1978, p. 407). According to Kraft, the existence of a world view (*Weltanschauung* in the original German) is observed in every known group, but members of different groups vary in the degree to which they can articulate their world views. People have a difficult time articulating their world views mainly because they are learned throughout the socialization process and tend to be unconscious. Like all postulates, world views are accepted without questioning as "the way things are."

Kraft (1978) believes a world view serves five important functions for the people of a culture. First, a world view performs an explanatory function for the members of a culture; it provides "explanations of how and why things got to be as they are and why they continue that way" (p. 408). Second, a world view performs an evaluational and validating function; that is, it provides the criteria for evaluating and validating the ends and means of the group. The third function a world view performs is psychological reinforcement. A world view provides ways for people to gain reinforcement for their beliefs in times of anxiety and crisis. This reinforcement may take the form of rituals in which the people participate or of individual activities which reinforce basic beliefs. Fourth, a world view performs an integrating function. "It systematizes and orders for them their perceptions of reality into an overall design" (p. 410). Finally, a world view provides an adaptational function for members of a culture.

In times of social change a world view gives people the means to allow them to adapt to the change that is taking place.

One way to illustrate differences in world views is to compare "Eastern" and "Western" world views. Wei (1980) suggests comparing Eastern and Western world views by looking at two specific dimensions: (1) cosmic patterns or ways of perceiving the world (Kraft's integrating function), and (2) philosophy of history (Kraft's explanatory function). The world views described below are based, out of necessity, on stereotypes. Although we believe the pictures presented are as accurate as possible, caution must be used in applying these, or any stereotypes, to individual cases.

In the West people see the cosmos as created and controlled by a "divine power." Since the cosmos is controlled by a supernatural power, there are "laws of nature" that must be followed. In contrast, the view in the East is one of a "harmoniously functioning organism consisting of an orderly hierarchy of inter-related parts and forces which, though unequal in their status, are equally essential for the total process" (Wei, 1980, p. 4). The Eastern view sees the cosmos as a self-operating system not controlled by an external source. Stemming from these general views of the cosmos are two epistemological questions: (1) What is the nature and source of knowledge? and (2) How do we come to know? In the West "the fundamental question is how I can transcend myself to reach the other, either the external inanimated world or people surrounding me? In this question there is a basic dichotomy between the knower and things to be known" (Wei, 1980, p. 5). An example of the Eastern view is seen in the Chinese orientation: "The Chinese distinguish two kinds of knowledge. The first is to investigate things, to know about . . . the second is to know the illustrious way of the universe—the tao. The first kind of knowledge is one way of achieving the second, which is the true knowledge" (Wei, 1980, p. 8).

Wei also outlines several epistemological differences between East and West in the knowing process. Specifically, he points out that in the West knowledge comes from postulation, with an emphasis on analysis through "linear" logic by syllogism and dialectic processes. In contrast, in the East knowledge comes from intuition, with an emphasis on synthesis through "spiral" logic and contemplation of the self and the universe. These differences in the knowing process have a tremendous impact on how people from the East and the West encode communication messages and perceive or interpret incoming messages. For example, linear logic causes Westerners to use a direct form of communication (i.e., "to get to the point"), while spiral logic causes Easterners to use indirect forms of communication.

Okabe (1983) illustrates the differences between Eastern and Western logic by comparing Japan and the United States:

> American logic and rhetoric value "step-by-step," "chain-like" organization, as frequently observed in the "problem-solution" pattern or in the

"cause-to-effect" or "effect-to-cause" pattern of organization. . . . By contrast, Japanese logic and rhetoric emphasize the importance of a "dotted," "point-like" method of structuring a discourse. No sense of rigidity . . . is required in the Japanese-speaking society, where there is instead a sense of leisurely throwing a ball back and forth and carefully observing each other's response. (pp. 29–30)

He goes on to point out that Westerners rely on facts, figures, and quotations to support their arguments, while Easterners like the Japanese use more subjective and ambiguous forms of support.

The second aspect of world view, philosophy of history, also evidences differences between the East and the West. The issue here is the meaning of history and the impact of specific events on history as a whole. In the West history is seen mainly as a "linear historical pattern toward progress" (Wei, 1980, p. 12). There are two different views, a "sacred" view stemming from the Judeo-Christian tradition and a "secular" view stemming from the philosophy of progress originating with Voltaire. The East, in contrast, sees history as cyclical in nature. For example, the themes of destruction and renovation are common throughout Buddhist and Hindu writings.

The differences in world views outlined above have a direct impact on our communication with strangers. Consider, for example, a business delegation from North America meeting with strangers from the East to decide whether or not their two companies should work together on a joint venture. Based only on their differing world views, it might be expected that misunderstandings will occur. The North Americans would analyze all of the "facts" and would develop a direct argument as to whether or not the two companies should do business together. The strangers, in contrast, would base their decision on a synthesis of all of the data and on their intuition as to whether or not the idea is a good one and, in addition, would discuss the issues in an indirect rather than a direct method. Obviously, if one of the groups does not understand the other's world view and adapt their communication accordingly, misunderstanding is going to occur.

Value Orientations

The second aspect of cultural postulates is value orientations. Value orientations are defined as "complex but definitely patterned . . . principles . . . which give order and direction to the ever-flowing stream of human acts and thoughts as these relate to the solution of 'common human' problems" (Kluckhohn and Strodtbeck, 1960, p. 4). The theory of value orientations is based on three assumptions: (1) people in all cultures must find solutions to a limited number of common human problems; (2) the available solutions to these problems are not unlimited but vary within a range of potential solutions; and (3) while one solution tends to be preferred by members of any given culture, all potential solutions are present in every culture.

Kluckhohn and Strodtbeck (1960, p. 11) posit five problems for which all cultures must find solutions. Posed as questions, these problems are as follows:

1. What is the character of innate human nature? (human nature orientation)

2. What is the relation of man to nature (and supernature)? (man-nature orientation)

3. What is the temporal focus of human life? (time orientation)

4. What is the modality of human activity? (activity orientation)

5. What is the modality of man's relationship to other men? (relational orientation)

As indicated above, every culture must find a solution to each of these problems. The solutions available, however, are limited for each of the problems.

Human nature orientation

As indicated above, this orientation deals with the innate character of human nature. The potential solutions to this problem appear relatively obvious: humans can be seen as innately good, innately evil, or a mixture of good and evil. It is not quite this simple, however. Humans not only can be viewed as either good or evil but also can be seen as either able to change (mutable) or not able to change (immutable). In addition, we must recognize that viewing human nature as a mixture of good and evil is not the same as viewing human nature as neutral. If we combine these various aspects, we find that there are six potential solutions to this problem: (1) humans are evil but mutable; (2) humans are evil and immutable; (3) humans are neutral with respect to good and evil; (4) humans are a mixture of good and evil; (5) humans are good but mutable; and (6) humans are good and immutable.

In applying this orientation to the United States, it is not always easy to decide which solution predominates. People in the United States inherited a view of human nature as evil but mutable from their Puritan predecessors. In this view discipline and self-control are seen as necessary if humans are to change. Some subcultures within the United States definitely adopt this solution (e.g., the Hutterites), but the predominant view in the United States is probably the view of human nature as a mixture of good and evil.

Humanity-nature orientation

There are three potential types of relations between humans and nature: mastery over nature, harmony with nature, and subjugation to nature. These solutions are relatively straightforward and are illustrated best by examples.

In industrialized societies like the United States, the mastery-over-nature view tends to predominate. This orientation involves the view that all natural forces can and should be overcome and/or put to use by humans; examples are damming rivers, moving mountains, and controlling illness through medicine.

The harmony-with-nature orientation draws no distinctions among human life, nature, and the supernatural—any one is just an extension of another. For example, the Cheyenne Indians of North America see themselves as living in harmony with nature. In their view, "human aspirations are realizable not so much through the appeasement of whimsical spirit beings and gods as through action that fits the conditions of environmental organization and functioning" (Hoebel, 1960, p. 85). This orientation also predominates in other Native American groups, such as the Navajo, as well as in many Asian cultures, including those of China and Japan.

The final solution to this problem, subjugation to nature, predominates in cultures like those of the Spanish Americans of the southwestern United States, according to Kluckhohn and Strodtbeck (1960). They cite as an example sheepherders who believe there is nothing that can be done to control nature if it threatens—neither land nor flock can be protected from storms.

Time orientation

With respect to the temporal focus of human life, it can be directed on the past, the present, or the future. The concern here is not with hours, days, weeks, months, or even years, but rather with a broader concept of time. People in any culture must, of course, come to terms with all three solutions, but, as pointed out above, one solution tends to predominate in a particular culture.

The past orientation predominates in cultures placing a high value on tradition. This orientation predominates in cultures worshipping ancestors (e.g., the Shinto religion in Japan) or emphasizing strong family ties. Also included here are cultures where there is some degree of traditionalism and aristocracy (e.g., England).

The present orientation predominates where people pay relatively little attention to what has gone on in the past and what might happen in the future. In this orientation the past is seen as unimportant, and the future is seen as vague and unpredictable. The Navajo Indians of northern Arizona, for example, have this orientation; to them only the here and now is "real," the future and the past have little reality (Hall, 1959).

The future orientation predominates where change is valued highly. In this orientation the future generally is viewed as "bigger and better," while being "old-fashioned" (the past) is scorned. Both Kluckhohn and Strodtbeck (1960) and Hall (1959) see this orientation as predominating in the United States. (The time orientation is discussed further in Chapter 9.)

Activity orientation

As with the previous two orientations, there are three ways in which human activity can be handled: doing, being, and being-in-becoming. The predominant orientation in the United States is doing. A doing orientation involves a focus upon those types of activities which have outcomes external to the individual that can be measured by someone else. Activities must be tangible. In appraising a person, people in the United States tend to ask questions like "What did he do?" or "What has she accomplished?" According to this orientation, if you are sitting at your desk thinking, you are not doing anything because your thoughts cannot be externally measured.

The being orientation is almost the extreme opposite of the doing orientation. This orientation involves "a spontaneous expression of what is conceived to be 'given' in the human personality" (Kluckhohn and Strodtbeck, 1960, p. 16). An excellent example of this is the Mexican fiesta, which, according to Kluckhohn and Strodtbeck, reveals "pure" impulse gratification.

The final activity orientation, being-in-becoming, is concerned with who we are, not what we have accomplished. The focus of human activity is on striving for an integrated whole in the development of the self. The best example of this orientation may be Zen Buddhist monks who spend their lives in contemplation and meditation to fully develop the self. This view also was manifested in the self-improvement movement of the 1960s and 1970s in the United States, as, for example, Maslow's (1970) self-actualized person is in a constant state of being-in-becoming.

Relational orientation

There are three potential ways in which humans can define their relationships to other humans: individualism, lineality, and collaterality. As we might expect, individualism is the predominant orientation in the United States. This orientation is characterized by the autonomy of the individual; or, in other words, individuals are seen as unique, separate entities. In this orientation individual goals and objectives take priority over group goals and objectives.

The lineality orientation, on the other hand, focuses on the group, with group goals taking precedence over individual goals. The crucial issue in the lineality orientation, according to Kluckhohn and Strodtbeck (1960), is the continuity of the group through time. Specific individuals are important only for their group memberships. One example of this orientation is the aristocracy of many European countries.

Collaterality, the third relational orientation, also focuses on the group, but not the group extended through time. Rather, the focus is on the laterally extended group (an individual's most immediate group memberships in time and space). The goals of the group take precedence over those of the individual.

In fact, in this orientation people are not considered except vis-à-vis their group memberships. One example of this orientation is the Japanese identification with the company for which they work or the university from which they graduated. (This relational orientation also is discussed in Chapter 7.)

Applying the orientations

At this point you may be saying to yourself, "Those are interesting abstract ideas, but what do they have to do with communication?" While a complete discussion of their application must be postponed, we can begin to look at how value orientations can be used to understand our communication with strangers.

Two cultures that appear relatively similar on the surface are those of England and the United States. While there are surface similarities, there are also basic differences in value orientations, which can cause misunderstandings between people from the two cultures. For the purpose of illustration, consider the time dimension. In the United States the future orientation tends to predominate, while in England the past orientation does. "Indeed, some of the chief differences between the peoples of the United States and England derive from their somewhat varying attitudes toward time. Americans have difficulty understanding the respect the English have for tradition, and the English do not appreciate the typical American's disregard for it" (Kluckhohn and Strodtbeck, 1960, p. 15). As another example, we can look at the relational orientation. People in the United States see themselves as individuals first and members of groups second, while people in many high-context cultures like Japan see themselves as members of groups first and foremost (either lineal or collateral orientation). When people with these two orientations come into contact, especially in the business world, there are often misunderstandings. Consider a manager from the United States in Japan whose subordinates (all Japanese) negotiate a very large business deal. The tendency in the United States would be to decide which individual is responsible for the deal and to reward him or her in some way. The manager from the United States would, therefore, naturally seek out an individual to reward. Assuming he or she locates an individual in the department and proceeds to reward that individual, what might the consequences be for the person selected? Many writers on Japanese business argue this person might be ostracized from his or her work group because of being singled out. By being singled out the person has assumed a self-definition outside of his or her membership in the group. In Japan the group, not the individual, would be rewarded.

These two brief examples illustrate how understanding the abstract concept of value orientations can help in understanding specific cultural differences, as well as misunderstandings that might occur when communicating with strangers.

Pattern Variables

Another view of cultural postulates is presented by Parsons (1951). Parsons's presentation of postulates centers around his concept of "pattern variables." A pattern variable is defined as "a dichotomy, one side of which must be chosen by an actor before the meaning of a situation is determinate for him, and thus before he can act with respect to that situation" (Parsons and Shils, 1951, p. 77). In other words, pattern variables are mutually exclusive choices individuals make prior to engaging in action. These choices are made both consciously and unconsciously; however, they are generally made unconsciously since they are learned during the socialization process at an early age.

Affectivity-affective neutrality

The affectivity-affective neutrality orientation is concerned with the nature of the gratification that we seek. Do we look for immediate gratification from the situation at hand (affectivity) or do we delay gratification into the future by expressing self-restraint (affective neutrality)? Affectivity is associated with emotional responses throughout Parsons's writings. On the other hand, affective neutrality is associated with people responding from a more cognitive (nonemotional) level. The United States typically is characterized as having an affective neutrality orientation, while Latin American cultures usually are characterized as showing an affectivity orientation. People from the United States, therefore, are more likely to base decisions on cognitive information, while people from cultures with an affectivity orientation are more likely to base their decisions on emotional responses.

Self-orientation-collective orientation

Are we oriented toward ourselves or toward the group to which we belong? If a self-orientation is chosen, we put our personal interests above those of our group and seek out private goals. A collective orientation, on the other hand, involves a focus on the interests of the group over those of the individual. Interaction is oriented toward contributing to the group's welfare, rather than to individual glory. This orientation is similar to Kluckhohn and Strodtbeck's (1960) relational problem, with the lineal and collateral orientation being collapsed into the collective orientation. The predominant orientation in the United States is obviously self-orientation. In contrast, the collective orientation is prevalent throughout Asian and Arab cultures. People from cultures in which self-orientation predominates define themselves in terms of individual accomplishments, while individuals from cultures in which the collective orientation predominates define themselves in terms of their group memberships and the groups' accomplishments.

Universalism–particularism

This orientation is concerned with modes of categorizing people or objects. The categorization of people or objects in terms of some universal or general frame of reference is a universalistic orientation. The categorization of people or objects in specific categories is a particularistic orientation. Universalistic interaction generally follows a standardized pattern, while particularistic interaction is unique to the situation. Given this, we expect low-context cultures like the United States to be characterized by a universalistic orientation, while a particularistic orientation tends to predominate in high-context cultures like those in Asia. People from cultures in which a universalistic orientation predominates communicate with strangers in the same way in a variety of situations, while people from cultures in which a particularistic orientation predominates communicate with strangers differently in different situations.

Diffuseness–specificity

The universalism–particularism orientation as pattern variable is concerned with how we categorize people or objects. The diffuseness–specificity orientation is concerned with how we respond to people or objects. If a person or an object is responded to in a wholistic manner, a diffuseness orientation is displayed. On the other hand, if a particular aspect of a person or an object is responded to, a specificity orientation is used. In high-context cultures there is a tendency for a diffuseness orientation to predominate, while the specificity orientation tends to prevail in low-context cultures like the United States. When people from a culture in which a diffuseness orientation predominates interact with a waiter or waitress, for example, they respond to the waiter or waitress as a whole person, not just to his or her role. In contrast, people from cultures in which the specificity orientation predominates respond to the waiter or waitress only in a more role-specific way.

Ascription–achievement

Are objects or people treated in terms of qualities ascribed to them or in terms of qualities they have achieved? With an ascription orientation a person is judged on qualities inherent in them (e.g., gender or family heritage). The prevalent orientation in the United States is achievement, while that in many other cultures (e.g., India) is ascription. People from cultures in which an ascription orientation predominates base their sociocultural predictions about others' behavior on the groups into which the others were born (gender, age, race, ethnic group, caste, etc.). People from cultures in which an achievement orientation predominates, on the other hand, base their sociocultural predictions on group memberships others have achieved through their own efforts (occupational group, social class, etc.).

Instrumental–expressive orientation

What is the nature of the goals we seek in our interactions with others? Are our interactions a means to another goal (instrumental), or are our interactions an end in and of themselves (expressive)? In the expressive orientation interactions are valued because they are important, not because they will lead to anything else. Instrumental interactions, in contrast, are valued only because they help the person reach another goal. The instrumental orientation is the predominant pattern in the United States, while the expressive orientation predominates in many other cultures (e.g., Arab or Latin American cultures). People from cultures in which an expressive orientation predominates tend to value friendships for their own sake more than do people from cultures in which an instrumental orientation predominates.

Applying the pattern variables

The six pattern variables presented above can be used to analyze cultural differences. One specific illustration of such use is Lipset's (1963) comparison of Great Britain, Canada, Australia, and the United States. The results of his study indicate "the United States emphasizes achievement, egalitarianism, universalism, and specificity. Canada is lower than the United States on all of these dimensions. Great Britain in turn ranks lower than Canada. Australia was found more egalitarian but less achievement-oriented, universalistic, and specific" (Zavalloni, 1980, p. 89). Thus, although these cultures appear very similar on the surface, their underlying orientations toward action are significantly different. A person from one culture who does not recognize the differences in underlying orientations influencing strangers inevitably makes errors in predicting the strangers' behavior. To make accurate predictions about strangers' behavior, we must understand their postulates, the things they take for granted.

ENDS

Values involve relationships "among abstract categories with strong affective components and implying a preference for certain types of actions" (Triandis, 1972, p. 16). Values, therefore, are the desired objectives or ends of social life.

Following Manheim (1936), values are classified as either ideological or utopian. Ideological values are those that support, justify, or explain the existing social order. Utopian values, on the other hand, evaluate or suggest change in the existing social order. The values of the youth counterculture of the 1960s can be seen as utopian values. A value can, of course, begin as a utopian value, become widely accepted over time, and thus become an ideological value. One example of this is racial equality in the United States. This value originally was held by only a small portion of the population but over time became widely accepted, and today it is an ideological value.

The nature of ideological values can be illustrated by looking at the values predominating in the United States. Vander Zanden (1965) argues there are seven principal values operating in the culture of the United States:

1. Materialism. Americans are prone to evaluate things in material and mone-tary terms. . . . We tend to get quite excited about things as opposed to ideas, people, and aesthetic creations.

2. Success. . . . Part of the American faith is that "There is always another chance" and that "If at first you do not succeed, try, try again." If we our-selves cannot succeed, then we have the prospect for vicarious achievement through our children.

3. Work and Activity. . . . Work and activity are exalted in their own right; they are not merely means by which success may be realized; in and of themselves they are valued as worthwhile.

4. Progress. A belief in the perfectibility of society, man, and the world has been a kind of driving force in American history. . . . Americans tend to equate "the new" with "the best."

5. Rationality. Americans almost universally place faith in the rational ap-proach to life. We continuously search out "reasonable," "time-saving," and "effort-saving" ways of doing things.

6. Democracy. "Democracy" has become almost synonymous with "the Ameri-can way of life." . . . We extol the Declaration of Independence with its in-sistence that "all men are created equal" and "governments (derive) their just power from the consent of the governed."

7. Humanitarianism. . . . Philanthropy and voluntary charity have been a char-acteristic note of America. More recently, more attention has been given to numerous programs for social welfare, with government playing an active role. (pp. 67–69)

Obviously, all of these values are not held by every person living in the United States. They are, however, values which tend to be held by a majority of the people and, therefore, can be considered characteristic of the United States.

As a contrast to these American values, consider Arab values derived from the Bedouin culture (desert dwellers). While only a small percentage (about 10%) of present-day Arabs are Bedouins, contemporary Arab culture holds the "Bed-ouin ethos as an ideal to which, in theory at least, it would like to measure up" (Patai, 1976, p. 73). According to Patai, the five values predominating in the Bedouin culture are hospitality, generosity, courage, honor, and self-respect.

The value of hospitality is aimed at meeting a more general goal of strengthening the group. This value requires a family to receive and give asylum to anyone who comes and requests it. While the actual practice of hospitality varies in villages and urbanized areas, it is still a value held by the vast majority of Arabs (Patai, 1976).

The second value, generosity, is tied very closely with the rules of Islam and the Muslim duty of *zakat* (paying a part of one's wealth to the poor). "Lavish generosity in traditional Arab society counterbalances the accumulation of wealth and the development of extreme riches and poverty" (Patai, 1976, p. 87).

Courage "means essentially the ability to stand physical pain or emotional strain with such self-control that no sound or facial expression betrays the trial one is undergoing" (Patai, 1976, p. 89). It is sometimes difficult to distinguish this value from the concept of bravery, which requires that Arabs be willing to give their life for the group, according to Patai.

In the Arab world honorable behavior is that "which is conducive to group cohesion and group survival, that which strengthens the group and serves its interest; while shameful behavior is that which tends to disrupt, endanger, impair, or weaken the social aggregate" (Patai, 1976, p. 90). Also, "Arab ethics revolve around a single focal point, that of self-esteem or self-respect. The most important factor on which the preservation of this self-esteem depends is the sexual behavior of the women for whom the Arab is responsible: his daughters and sisters" (p. 96).

The preceding lists of values in the cultures of the United States and Arab countries illustrate how different value systems often stem from different postulates. Values in the United States, for example, stem from individualism, affective neutrality, universalism, achievement, specificity, and instrumental relations. Arab values, in contrast, stem from a collective orientation, particularism, ascription, diffuseness, and expressive relations.

One example of a cross-cultural comparison of values is Triandis and his associates' (1972) study of values in the United States, Greece, India, and Japan. Their study reveals several interesting differences. The values of the United States revealed in the study include self-confidence, individual progress, good adjustment, status, peace of mind, and achievement. The study suggests that Greeks value affiliation, societal well-being, and *philotimos* (a Greek word with no direct English translation, but suggesting a person who follows the norms of the culture). The Indians in the study value increased status of the individual, glory, and societal well-being, while the Japanese value serenity, aesthetic satisfaction, contentment, advancement, and good adjustment.

Zavalloni (1980) summarizes results of several other cross-cultural studies with student populations, which suggest that students in the United States are activist and self-indulgent in their values and are not subject to social restraint as much as the students in the other cultures examined. Indian students value a strong emphasis on self-control and social restraint, while Japanese students are more oriented toward their society and its people than are the other groups, as well as respecting inward directedness. Chinese students value withdrawal, self-sufficiency, and enjoyment in action, and Arab students report valuing group participation and self-control, but not carefree enjoyment or contemplation.

Before moving on to the third component of culture, we must briefly mention another approach to the study of cultural values. We have cited examples of the traditional social science approach to the study of values. This, however, is not the only approach that can be used to compare values across cultural boundaries. Another approach is to examine the literature and mythology of cultures in order to understand their values. Edith Hamilton (1960) points out: "The golden deeds of a nation, however mythical, throw clear light upon its standards and ideals. They are the revelation that cannot be mistaken for the conscience, of what they think men should be like. Their stories and their plays tell more than all their histories" (p. 14). One example of this approach is McGranahan and Wayne's (1954) comparison of 45 popular dramas from North America and Germany. North American plays generally carried a message of virtue, while the lesson in the German plays was that worldly conflicts are won by using power and ruthlessness. The percentage of times that four specific themes appeared in the plays examined was as follows: for North America, love, 60%; morality, 36%; idealism, 4%; and power, 2%; for Germany, love, 31%; morality, 9%; idealism, 9%; and power, 33%.

By knowing the values of strangers when we communicate with them, we can increase our ability to predict their behavior. Values tell us the ends people strive for in their lives. As an illustration of how values can be used in predicting strangers' behavior, consider a North American male student meeting a female Arab exchange student and her brother for the first time. Assuming the North American student understands the Arab values specified above, he will know the male Arab sees it as his responsibility to protect his sister's virtue while the two are in the United States. The North American male would, in all likelihood, then take care in his interactions with the Arab female to be sure there was no sexual innuendo in his behavior. On the other hand, if the North American student does not understand Arab values, he might predict the Arab male would respond like a brother in the United States. Being attracted to the sister, he might, therefore, "make a pass" at her in front of her brother, thereby accidentally insulting the brother. In general, we can say knowledge of strangers' values can increase our accuracy in interpreting and predicting their future behavior and, therefore, increase the likelihood of effective communication.

MEANS

The third broad category of cultural ideas is the means to achieving the acceptable ends of social life. The means consist of the proscriptions and prescriptions for acceptable behavior. When the standards of acceptable behavior have moral or ethical connotations, we refer to them as norms, and when there are no moral or ethical connotations in the standards, we refer to them as rules (Olsen, 1978).

Norms

There are innumerable definitions of norms in the social science literature. For example, norms are defined as "rules of conduct," "blueprints for behavior," and "cultural expectations." Comparing existing definitions, Gibbs (1965) finds three attributes of a norm: "(1) a collective evaluation of behavior in terms of what ought to be; (2) a collective expectation as to what behavior will be; [and] (3) particular reactions to behavior including attempts to apply sanctions or otherwise induce a particular kind of behavior." Norms, therefore, can be defined as socially shared guidelines for expected and accepted behaviors, violation of which leads to some form of sanction. The sanctions can vary from a disapproving look to ostracism from the group to death.

Social life is possible to the extent we take into account the existence of other people and their expected responses to our behavior. When the expectations are shared by a group of people, we can say a norm exists. Once norms are formed and we have internalized them, we tend to follow them whether or not we want to. Birenbaum and Sagarin (1976) put it this way:

> . . . most people are aware that rules exist in all areas of life and take them into account when engaged in or anticipating interaction with other people. This awareness is part of the organized character of social life. . . . even when people dislike or reject a rule, it may be extremely difficult for them not to obey it, for much everyday life involves opportunities to demonstrate social competency, a factor that may override the will to disobey. Often obedience to the rule is simply reflexive, whereas transgression is effortful. (p. 4)

Two aspects of Birenbaum and Sagarin's position deserve brief elaboration. First, these writers are using the terms "rules" and "norms" interchangeably. This is consistent with many people writing on norms, but there are some who use the terms differently. Olsen (1978), for example, believes norms have an ethical or moral connotation that is lacking in rules. Rules, according to Olsen, are developed for reasons of expediency, because they allow people to coordinate their activities more easily. To illustrate, Olsen cites rules such as driving on the same side of the road to keep traffic running smoothly and requiring citizenship and registration in order to vote. (As noted above, we distinguish between norms and rules here.)

The second aspect of the above quotation requiring comment is Birenbaum and Sagarin's argument that obedience to norms and rules is reflexive. What must be kept in mind is that obedience to a norm or rule can only be reflexive if you grow up in the culture where the rule exists and internalize it from a very early age. If a person socialized into one culture is living in or visiting another culture, obedience to the norms and rules of the host culture probably is effortful, and transgression may be reflexive.

Sumner (1940) divides norms into three categories: folkways, mores, and laws. Sumner views folkways as those pervasive everyday activities widely accepted by the people of a culture. Folkways include, but are not limited to, such actions as the way we greet others, the way we dress, the way we eat, the way we smell, the way we say good-bye, and other such actions that are widely accepted. Since folkways do not have moral or ethical connotations, they are more accurately considered rules rather than norms by our terminology. Mores, according to Sumner, are those norms expressing strong moral demands on an individual's behavior; they are the norms believed necessary for collective action. Examples of mores include commandments derived from religious doctrine, incest taboos, and rules about what is acceptable to eat (e.g., in the United States it is unacceptable to eat the meat of dogs, cats, and people). The final category of norms discussed by Sumner is laws. Laws are norms codified by a political entity such as a nation, state, or city. A law may be derived from either the folkways or the mores of a culture.

The violation of any norm brings some form of sanction on the person committing the violation. The sanctions vary from a disapproving glance to the loss of life. The sanctions imposed for violation of a folkway are through interpersonal channels. For example, if you were to "slurp" your soup in public in the United States, you probably would receive only disapproving glances from the people who heard you (of course, they may also make comments to their friends about your impolite behavior). On the other hand, if you do not slurp your soup in some cultures, you may receive disapproving glances. Similarly, if you were to wear informal clothes (e.g., your best jeans) to a black-tie dinner, people would look at you disapprovingly and make comments about your lack of appropriate attire, but they would not use more severe sanctions.

The violation of mores, in contrast to that of folkways, brings about more severe sanctions. An extreme example of a mos (singular of mores) in the United States is that we do not eat people (there is a prohibition on cannibalism). If people find out that you are a cannibal, they will, in all likelihood, stop talking to you (you will be ostracized).

Violations of laws obviously bring about legal sanctions. These sanctions, of course, can vary from a verbal reprimand from a judge to the death penalty.

The people of a culture are aware of some of the norms guiding their behavior and unaware of many others. Even if people are aware that the norm exists, however, they probably cannot articulate all of the specific behavioral expectations associated with the norm. This lack of awareness is illustrated by something as simple as a handshake. Shaking hands is a norm when greeting people for the first time in the United States; but what are the rules for shaking hands? Can you tell a person who has never shaken hands before, for example, someone from Mars, all of the rules necessary for him or her to shake hands "correctly"? Many people would say that you grip the other person's extended hand and pump up and down. But is it that simple? What would you do if you met a person for the first time and she or he extended the left hand? That obviously isn't appropriate because we shake hands with the right hand. What if the other person extends the right hand but does not hold on to your hand (i.e., uses a "limp" grip)? Is this acceptable? No, probably not. What if the person uses the "correct" grip with the right hand and when you shake hands doesn't stop, but continues to pump up and down, up and down. How would you feel? Comfortable? Uncomfortable? Probably uncomfortable because the rule is that we pump our hands a few (one or two) times and stop. We could go on, but by now you get the point that shaking hands is not as simple as it initially seems. It is a complex process with many subtle expectations. We may not be able to explain all of the expectations, but we know when they are violated.

One way to become aware of norms guiding our behavior is to have them violated. When we interact with people from the same culture, our expectations generally are not violated often because people of the same culture share similar expectations. When we communicate with strangers, however, our behavioral expectations may be violated with much greater frequency because strangers probably learned a different set of norms in their culture. When our expectations are violated, we may react to the other person negatively; this is a "normal" reaction. There is also the possibility of positive outcomes, however. For example, when our expectations are violated, we can gain tremendous insight into the norms of our culture and how they influence our behavior. In addition, we come to see alternative behavioral patterns, which we might prefer. In other words, confronting cultural differences offers the possibility of personal growth and/or cultural change. (We discuss this process in detail in Chapter 14.)

Rules

As indicated above, rules differ from norms in that rules do not have moral or ethical connotations. According to Noesjirwan (1978):

> Rules provide a statement of expected or intended behaviour and its outcome. As such, rules provide a number of related functions that serve to order social life and render it meaningful. Rules provide a set of mutual expectations, thus rendering the behaviour of each person predictable and understandable to the other. . . . The rules partly serve to define the meaning a situation has, and to define the meaning that any given action has within a situation. (pp. 305–306)

Rules, therefore, perform many of the same functions that norms do in establishing coordinated activities among individuals.

Cushman and Whiting (1972) point out there are two basic types of rules: (1) constitutive rules, which specify an action's content, and (2) procedural rules, which specify the appropriate procedures for carrying out the action. In general, rules specify shared patterns of expectations and are reducible to the following form: in situation X, Y is permitted or required.

Rules vary along four dimensions: (1) level of understanding, (2) rule clarity, (3) rule range, and (4) rule homogeneity or consensus (Cushman and Whiting, 1972). Both constitutive and procedural rules can vary with respect to level of understanding. According to Cushman and Whiting, the greater the need for coordination in human activity, the greater is the degree of accuracy in understanding of the rules. Given Hall's (1976) description of low-context and high-context cultures, it can be argued there is a greater need for coordination of activity in high-context cultures than in low-context cultures and, therefore, there is a correspondingly greater degree of accuracy in the understanding of rules in high-context cultures than in low-context cultures.

In addition to varying with respect to level of understanding, rules vary with respect to the specificity of the actions required or permitted in a situation in which a rule applies and in terms of the span of situations in which particular actions are permitted or required (the range of rules). When rules have a large range and a low degree of specificity, Cushman and Whiting (1972) contend, habitual communication behavior emerges. Given Hall's (1976) distinction between low-context and high-context cultures, it can be inferred that rules are more specific and have more range in high-context cultures than in low-context cultures. Stated differently, rules are more specific with respect to the behaviors permitted or required in a situation in high-context cultures than in low-context cultures. Further, rules tend to be less situation-specific (have a large range) in high-context cultures than in low-context cultures, where the same rule may apply to more limited situations.

As indicated above, rules also vary with respect to the degree of consensus there is about them. "The homogeneity of a rule system refers to the degree to which accurate understanding on standard usage are evenly distributed among participants in a communication system" (Cushman and Whiting, 1972, p. 233). Given the nature of high-context cultures, they tend to be more homogeneous than are low-context cultures like the United States. Because of the homogeneity of their culture, members of a high-context culture are more likely to exhibit coordinated activity than are members of a low-context culture.

When people using different rules interact, misunderstanding often occurs. An example of this can be seen in the analysis by Byers and Byers (1972) of student-teacher interaction in integrated classrooms. These researchers find that white teachers and white students use one rule for establishing contact in the classroom, while black students use another, noncomplementary rule. Byers and Byers conclude black students' attempts to establish contact "are not timed to catch the pauses or general 'searching the scene' behavior of the teacher" (p. 23).

Sigman (1980) makes the same point when he argues "each of the cultural participants brings to the intercultural interaction different rules for the form and function of behavior, assumptions about the behavior of others, and notions about the degree of mutability of their own rules via negotiations" (p. 44).

Noesjirwan (1978) demonstrates how rules can be seen to vary systematically across cultures. In her study of Indonesia and Australia she finds little systematic variation in 69 different rules, or value statements, while there are many between-culture variations in the same statements. To illustrate, her study reveals different rules for dealing with other people in waiting rooms and at bus stops. The rule in both situations in Indonesia requires one to talk to any other person present. In contrast, the rule for Australians in both situations requires one to ignore any other person present.

Argyle (1982) isolates several areas where rules tend to vary across cultures. These include rules with respect to "bribery," "nepotism," gift giving, buying and selling, eating and drinking, and seating guests. While this list obviously is not all inclusive, it illustrates the various areas where cultural rules exist.

This brief overview of rules should suffice to demonstrate that to communicate effectively with strangers we must attempt to understand their rules. The importance of understanding a stranger's rules is illustrated by Noesjirwan (1978): "Given a knowledge of the rule/value structure of the two cultures it becomes possible to predict, among other things, the likely sources of misunderstanding and conflict between those cultures, and the likely difficulties in adjustment faced by a person of one culture moving to the other" (p. 314). Should you find yourself moving from one culture to another (i.e., you are a stranger in a new culture), probably the first rule you should try to ascertain is the one regarding how members of the new culture are to communicate with strangers.

Norms and Rules on Conflict

The norms and rules concerning when conflict is acceptable and how it is to be resolved are among the most important ones influencing our communication with strangers. Conflict between individuals serves as a "barrier" to interpersonal communication. "A barrier to interpersonal communication," according to Tafoya (1983), "is anything that prevents, restricts, or impedes the convergence of meaning, by words or gestures, between two or more persons in a social setting" (p. 213).

One dimension of conflict that differs cross-culturally is the basis (reason) for the conflict. According to Olsen (1978), conflicts arise from either "instrumental" or "expressive" sources. Expressive conflicts arise from a desire to release tension, usually generated from hostile feelings. In contrast, instrumental conflicts stem from a difference in goals or practices. Ting-Toomey (1982) believes members of low-context cultures "are more likely to perceive conflict as instrumental rather than expressive in nature," while members of high-context cultures "are more likely to perceive conflict as expressive rather than instrumental in nature" (p. 7). The rationale for this position is based on differences in the forms of logic and perception used in the two types of cultures. Namely, low-context cultures tend to use analytic, "linear" logic, while high-context cultures tend to use wholistic, "spiral" logic (Ting-Toomey, 1982).

A second dimension on which conflicts tend to differ across cultures is the conditions under which they occur. Ting-Toomey (1982) argues that in low-context cultures conflict is likely to occur when an individual's expectation of appropriate behavior is being violated. In contrast, conflict is more likely to occur in high-context cultures when the group's normative expectations of behavior are being violated. The reason for this difference lies in the role of context in providing information in the two types of cultures. In high-context cultures context plays a crucial role in providing meaning to communication messages, while in low-context cultures context plays a less crucial role because more information is provided in the message. The more important the context is, the more often violation of collective normative expectations leads to conflict. The less important the context is, the more often violation of individual expectations leads to conflict.

The third dimension of conflict varying across cultures is the attitude of the participant toward dealing with the conflict. Ting-Toomey (1982) takes the position that people in low-context cultures "are more likely to possess a confrontational, direct attitude toward conflicts," while people in high-context cultures "are more likely to possess a non-confrontational, indirect attitude toward conflicts" (p. 9). This argument is supported by Barnlund's (1975) research with college students from Japan and the United States. A direct approach to conflict in low-context cultures probably stems from the doing orientation and the use of linear logic in low-context cultures. On the other hand, members of high-context cultures have a strong desire for group harmony and tend to use indirect forms of communication and, therefore, tend to prefer a nonconfrontational approach to conflict.

The final dimension of conflict that varies across cultures is the communication style individuals use for dealing with the conflict. Glenn, Witmeyer, and Stevenson (1977) outline three persuasive styles used to resolve conflicts: factual-inductive, axiomatic-deductive, and affective-intuitive. The factual-inductive method begins with the important "facts" and inductively moves toward a conclusion. This is the predominant style in the United States, according to Glenn and his associates. The axiomatic-deductive style begins with a general principle and deduces the implications for specific situations, and the affective-intuitive style is based on the use of emotional or affective messages. These two styles predominate in the Soviet Union, according to Glenn and his associates. Ting-Toomey (1982) argues that members of all low-context cultures, not just people in the United States, tend to use the factual-inductive approach. In addition, she suggests the axiomatic-deductive style also is used by members of low-context cultures. In contrast, Ting-Toomey believes members of high-context cultures "are more likely to use affective-intuitive styles in conflict" (p. 11).

If we know the conditions under which conflict arises in the strangers' culture, the strangers' attitude toward conflict, and the style of communication they are likely to use in resolving conflict, we can increase our ability to correctly interpret and predict strangers' behavior in a conflict situation. The more accurate our interpretations and predictions, the greater is the likelihood of successful resolution of the conflict.

SUMMARY

In this chapter we examined the three major cultural influences on our communication with strangers: postulates, ends, and means. Each of these three components has an impact on the way we see the world and communicate with others.

Cultural postulates are the things we take for granted as the "facts of life." We tend to be unaware of the postulates guiding our behavior because we learned them as children. When we confront different postulates in our communication with strangers, we may become more aware of those guiding our behavior. By understanding the postulates guiding strangers' behavior, we can increase our ability to accurately interpret and predict their behavior, thereby decreasing the likelihood of misunderstandings.

Values are the desirable ends of social life. In contrast to our unawareness of postulates, we tend to be more aware of our values and their influence on our behavior. The values we hold come not only from our culture but also from the various groups of which we are members. Knowledge of strangers' values also can help us to make more accurate cultural and sociocultural predictions about their behavior.

The norms and rules of our culture (the two types of means) tell us the prescribed and proscribed methods for achieving our values. Since norms and rules tend to vary systematically across cultures, our behavioral expectations tend to be violated with greater frequency when we communicate with strangers than when we communicate with people who are known. Knowing the norms and rules guiding strangers' behavior, as well as those guiding our own behavior, can help us to communicate more effectively with them.

4
Sociocultural Influences on the Process

Generally, in every situation the person seems to know what group he belongs to and to what group he does not belong. He knows more or less clearly where he stands, and this position largely determines his behavior.

Kurt Lewin

Our communication with strangers is influenced not only by our culture but also by the social relationships we form within our culture. The purpose of this chapter is to examine the sociocultural influences on the intercultural communication process. The influences we examine include our memberships in social groups, the nature of our role relationships, and our expectations in interpersonal relationships. The groups to which we belong, the roles we fill, and how we define interpersonal relationships are each influenced by the culture in which we live, and, in addition, each influences how we encode and decode communication messages.

MEMBERSHIPS IN SOCIAL GROUPS

Membership and Reference Groups

Every individual is a member of many different social groups. Our membership affiliations—family, social class, racial group, ethnic group, sex, occupational group, and nationality—are those groups to which we actually belong. If we are conscious of belonging to a group or social category, we refer to that group as a *membership group.*

According to Janis and Smith (1965), there are several factors that lead us to maintain our associations with our membership groups. First, there are the positive rewards we obtain from memberships in groups, including affection and friendship. Second, we all desire to avoid the social isolation that can take place without close group ties, while at the same time we desire to obtain the status and prestige associated with membership in certain groups. Finally, there are restraints acting upon us to keep us in certain groups, even if we prefer to leave. For example, people cannot choose their race or ethnic group.

It is necessary to draw a distinction between those groups to which we actually belong and those groups to which we would like to belong. When we look to another group for guidance in determining our behavior, that group is referred to as a *reference group.* Sarbin and Allen (1968) define a reference group this way:

> This term designates a group which a person values. It is often used to explain behavior oriented toward audiences not physically present. A reference group may be a membership or nonmembership group, a single other person, . . . a category of people, or even nonexistent groups or categories of people, for example, the future generation, God, ancestors. (p. 532)

In other words, a reference group is a group to which we look for guidance in how to behave. The closer our values coincide with those held by a particular group, the greater is the likelihood we will view the group as a reference group (Sarbin and Allen, 1968).

One of the largest membership groups to which we belong is our nation. A nation usually is defined in terms of historical, political, social, and economic events shared by a group of people. Such a conceptualization ignores the consideration of the degree of consensus of the people about their membership in the group, or nation. The historian Emerson (1960) proposes a more social-psychological definition of nation: "The simplest statement that can be made about a nation is that it is a body of people who feel they are a nation; and it may be that when all the fine-spun analysis is concluded this will be the ultimate statement as well" (p. 102).

A second type of group to which we all belong is a social class. The concept of social class is used in many different ways in the social science literature. No single definition does full justice to the nuances found under this rubric. For our purposes, however, Hodges's (1964) conceptualization suffices:

> . . . a social class is much more than a convenient pigeonhole or merely arbitrary divisional unit—like minutes, ounces, I.Q. points or inches—along a linear continuum. It is a distinct reality which embraces the fact that people live, eat, play, mate, dress, work, and think at contrasting and dissimilar levels. These levels—social classes—are the blended product of shared and analogous occupational orientations, educational backgrounds, eco-

nomic wherewithal, and life experiences. Persons occupying a given level need not be conscious of their class identity. But because of their approximately uniform backgrounds and experiences and because they grew up perceiving or "looking at things" in similar ways, they will share comparable values, attitudes, and life styles. (p. 13)

The social class to which we belong is, therefore, a membership group. This class, however, may not be our reference group. If we look to another social class for guidance in our behavior, that social class becomes our reference group.

All people are members of one of two other membership groups—a majority group or a minority group. The easiest way to differentiate between these two types of groups is to examine the characteristics of minority group membership. According to Schaefer (1979), there are five factors characterizing minority group status. First, members of minority groups are treated differently from members of a majority group. This inequality usually takes the form of segregation, prejudice, and discrimination. Second, members of minority groups have either physical or cultural characteristics that make them stand out from the majority group. Third, because minority groups stand out, membership in them is not voluntary. Fourth, members of a minority group tend to associate with and marry other members of their group. Finally, "members of a minority group are aware of their subordinate status, which leads to strong group solidarity" (Schaefer, 1979, p. 8).

The eminent sociologist Louis Wirth distinguishes between two types of minority groups. According to Wirth (1945), *racial groups* possess "racial marks, . . . the most visible and permanent marks with which we are afflicted" (p. 347). On the other hand, *ethnic groups* possess distinctive linguistic, religious, cultural or national characteristics. The distinction between racial and ethnic groups is often not as clear as would be desirable from a conceptual standpoint; therefore, it is often a difficult distinction to make. The distinction is blurred further because several writers argue that the concept of race should be dropped from both popular and scientific use on humanitarian grounds. One proponent of this position is the anthropologist Ashley Montagu. In one of his earlier works, *Man's Most Dangerous Myth,* Montagu (1952) suggests a broad definition of ethnic group, which encompasses the concept of race:

> An ethnic group represents one of a number of populations, which together comprise the species *Homo sapiens,* but individually maintain their differences, physical or cultural, by means of isolating mechanisms such as geographic and social barriers. These differences will vary as the power of the geographic and social boundaries vary. Where these boundaries are of low power, neighboring ethnic groups will integrate or hybridize one another. Where the barriers are of high power, such ethnic groups will tend to remain distinct from each other or replace each other geographically or ecologically. (pp. 87–88)

More recently, Montagu (1972) suggests in *Statement on Race* that substituting the term ethnic group for race would help avoid the "negative" connotations associated with racial terms and lead to increased investigation and discussion.

In-Groups and Out-Groups

As part of our socialization into our membership groups, we are taught we should avoid interacting with certain other groups of people because of their ethnic heritage, race, social class, color, religion, or occupation. The groups we are taught to avoid are referred to as *out-groups*. The groups of people with whom we are taught to associate, in contrast, are referred to as *in-groups*. This tendency to draw a distinction between in-groups and out-groups is so strong, contend Brewer and Campbell (1976), that it is "universal" among humans.

There are at least two consequences of the formation of in-groups and out-groups that must be noted here. First, there is a tendency for us to expect other members of our in-groups to behave and think similarly to the way we do (Tajfel, 1969a). Second, as members of in-groups, we have a tendency to put our own groups in a favorable light when they are compared to out-groups (Brewer, 1979). Both of these consequences impact on the way we categorize and use information about strangers.

Our in-groups are not necessarily limited to our families, or racial or ethnic groups. When dealing with people from other cultures, we may define the in-group as people from our own culture and the out-groups as people from other cultures. In such an instance, the tendency is for us to maximize the advantage of people in our culture and judge the behavior of people in the other culture (the out-group) in terms of our cultural standards.

Levine (1965) points out that the images in-group members have of out-groups are passed on to children from adults. He goes on to argue:

> . . . the images of an out-group that adults pass on to children are affected by the amount of direct experience the adults have had with members of the out-group and by the amount of conspicuous difference (in physical features, dress, language, and occupational specialization) between the in-groups and the out-groups. (p. 49)

Not only are images of out-groups passed on to children from adults; they also are reinforced by peer group interactions.

Our membership and reference groups constitute our in-groups, and the groups we tend to avoid, our out-groups. As an illustration of how this unconscious distinction between in-groups and out-groups influences our communication with strangers, consider the situation that arose with the massive influx of Indochinese refugees to many areas of the United States after the Vietnam War. The refugees tended to relocate to areas of the United States in groups. The groups of refugees usually included people with many different occupations, social classes, educational levels, and English-language proficiencies. The refugees, therefore, belong to many different membership groups, e.g., families, occupational groups, and even ethnic groups. Individual refugees may have different reference groups, however. Two refugee physicians, for example, may look to different groups for guidance in their behavior, one looking to the refugee group and his or her status within it and the other looking to the local host medical community. This would lead the two people to engage in different behaviors vis-à-vis the local community in which they live, the first physician avoiding locals as much as possible and the second seeking them out at every opportunity. The local residents of the area in which the refugees live probably would not see the different membership and reference groups of the refugees; rather, they probably would see all refugees as one out-group. Local people also would tend to assume all locals have the same attitude toward the refugees as they do. In their interactions with the refugees, the locals would tend to put the refugees down in order to make the locals appear in a more favorable light, thus leading to discrimination against the refugees. Perceiving all refugees as members of one out-group would lead locals to misinterpret incoming stimuli from refugees and make inaccurate predictions about many individual refugees. If a local physician met the two refugee physicians referred to above, for example, he or she probably would treat them the same, at least initially, and therefore not recognize their different motivations toward the local community.

Social Identity

Tajfel (1972, 1974, 1978) takes an intergroup approach to discussing the development of our social identity, which is one part of our self-concept. Following Kelly (1955), Tajfel (1972) begins by assuming we constantly strive to define ourselves vis-à-vis the world in which we live. One of the major cognitive "tools" used in this process is social categorization. According to Tajfel (1978), social categorization is "the ordering of social environment in terms of groupings of persons in a manner which makes sense to the individual" (p. 61), for example, men and women, blacks and whites. The strategies used in social categorization are learned through socialization into the various social groups to which we belong. Once we become aware of belonging to one or more social groups, our social identity begins to form. According to Tajfel (1978), social identity is "that *part* of an individual's self-concept which derives from his knowledge of his membership in a social group (or groups) together with the value and emotional significance attached to that membership" (p. 63). Thus, we identify and evaluate ourselves in terms of the groups to which we belong and the characteristics of those groups (e.g., their status, skin color, gender, ability to reach goals). Our group memberships can contribute either positive or negative aspects to our social identity. For the group membership to contribute positive aspects to our social identity, our group (in-group) must favorably compare to other relevant groups (out-groups). A positive social identity is therefore ensured by our interpreting the social environment and behaving in such a manner that the in-group is positively evaluated when compared with out-groups.

Intergroup-Interindividual Behavior

The fact that we are all members of many different social groups raises a question important in understanding our communication with strangers: how do we distinguish between when we are communicating with strangers mainly as individuals and when we are communicating with strangers mainly as representatives of their cultural or group memberships? Tajfel (1978) addresses this question by presenting a continuum of intergroup-interindividual behavior; he distinguishes between these two forms of communication as follows:

> These differences can be conceived as lying on a continuum, one extreme of which can be described as being "purely" intergroup. What is meant by "purely" interpersonal is any social encounter between two or more people in which all interaction that takes place is determined by the personal relationship between the individuals and by their respective individual characteristics. The "intergroup" extreme is that in which all of the behavior of two or more individuals towards each other is determined by their membership in different social groups or categories. (p. 41)

Tajfel's distinction is similar to Miller and Steinberg's (1975) discussion of making predictions based on cultural, sociological, or psychological data (see Chapter 2 for a review). The "pure" form that Tajfel calls interindividual behavior is the case in which *all* predictions are made using psychological data. On the other hand, "pure" intergroup behavior takes place when *all* predictions are made on the basis of sociological and/or cultural data. In other words, "pure" intergroup behavior takes place when *no* individual differences are recognized.

Tajfel (1978) argues it is impossible to conceive of "pure" interindividual behavior, no instance of it can be found. "It is impossible to imagine a social encounter between two people which will not be affected, at least to some minimal degree, by their mutual assignments of one another to a variety of social categories about which some general expectations concerning their characteristics and behavior exist in the mind of the interactants" (p. 41). This is true, according to Tajfel, even for husbands and wives and close friends. On the other hand, it is possible to conceive of an example of "pure" intergroup behavior. Tajfel (1978) cites an example of a bomber crew on a mission against an enemy population. In this case the bomber crew is involved in "pure" intergroup behavior because they are not distinguishing the enemy as individuals. If you watch "M*A*S*H," you may recall the episode "Dear Sigmund" in which a U.S. bombardier limps into the 4077th for medical aid. While Hawkeye is administering to his wounds, the flyer talks about how the war does not inconvenience him much. All he does is strap himself into his seat in the plane, fly over the enemy, push a button, and drop his bombs, returning to his wife in Tokyo every weekend. Hawkeye then asks the bombardier if he has ever seen the enemy, and the flyer says he has not. The bombardier is, therefore, engaged in a "pure" form of intergroup behavior. During his stay at the 4077th, however, the bombardier is put to work carrying the wounded into the operating room. During one trip into the operating room, he notices a young Korean child who is about to undergo surgery. He asks Hawkeye what happened to the child. Hawkeye tells him that a bomb exploded in the child's village. The bombardier then asks whether it was one of "ours" or one of "theirs." Col. Potter responds by saying it doesn't make any difference whose bomb it was. The bombardier declares that it makes a difference to him. Hawkeye counters by saying it doesn't make any difference to the child. At this point the bombardier begins to see the Koreans, on whom he has been dropping bombs, as individuals. Since he now recognizes individual differences, however slight, in the members of the other group, the bombardier's subsequent behavior will not be "pure" intergroup behavior.

ROLE RELATIONSHIPS

The Concept of Role

According to Sarbin and Allen (1968), the concept of role, "a term borrowed directly from the theater, is a metaphor intended to denote that conduct adheres to certain 'parts' (or positions) rather than the players who read or recite them" (p. 489). In other words, a role is a set of behavioral expectations associated with a particular position in a group. Examples of positions include—but obviously are not limited to—professor, student, father, mother, physician, lawyer, judge, police officer, clerk, and customer. The behaviors you expect professors, for example, to perform are considered their role.

In discussing the concept of role, Sarbin and Allen (1968) point out three kinds of questions to guide our study:

1. Is the conduct appropriate to the social position granted to or attained by the actor? That is, do his performances indicate that the actor has taken into account the ecological context in which the behavior occurs? In short, has he selected the correct role?

2. Is the enactment proper? That is, does the overt behavior meet the normative standards which serve as valuational criteria for the observer? Is the performance to be evaluated as good or bad?

3. Is the enactment convincing? That is, does the enactment lead the observer to declare unequivocally that the incumbent is legitimately occupying the position? (p. 490)

Obviously, what is classified as appropriate conduct and proper enactment may vary across cultures.

Cross-cultural variations in role can be illustrated by the role of manager. In the United States it is the manager's responsibility to make decisions, possibly after receiving input from subordinates. In Japan decisions are not made this way. Rather, decisions are usually initiated by the workers concerned and a consensus emerges as the discussions move up the hierarchy to the appropriate person (i.e., a manager). A Japanese manager working in the United States (a stranger), therefore, may have problems in working with his subordinates. The subordinates will, in all likelihood, make predictions about and interpret the stranger's behavior based on the expectations they have for managers (the role in the United States), assuming they have no knowledge of Japanese managerial techniques. The Japanese manager, in turn, probably will make predictions about his subordinates and interpret their behavior based on expectations he learned in Japan. When the subordinates do not initiate decisions, the manager will see them as not enacting their role competently. Similarly, the subordinates probably will see the manager as not enacting his role convincingly. Both attributions will be a result of not understanding cultural differences in role expectations.

Occupational Prestige

When we are looking at role behavior, we are focusing specifically on the behavior of the person filling the position. A closely related concept worth noting before continuing with our discussion of roles is occupational prestige. This concept refers to the amount of prestige associated with the social positions called occupations. Although specific role behavior may vary tremendously across cultures, there is a surprising amount of similarity in the prestige attributed to different occupations across cultures. Ramsey and Smith (1960) point out:

> Studies of occupational prestige have revealed striking similarities between one culture and another, between one subculture and another, and at different times within the same culture. Except for minor variations, the following regularities in ideas of occupational ranking are found: (a) white-collar jobs are accorded higher prestige than blue-collar and agricultural work; (b) occupations requiring no training rank lower than those requiring manual skill and apprenticeship, while both of these are accorded lower prestige than occupations for which a high formal education attainment is required; and (c) the few differences observed in the cultural comparisons make sense in cultural terms. (p. 475)

Thus, people traveling from one culture to another may be granted the same relative degree of prestige in the culture they are visiting as they are in their home culture. It must be kept in mind, however, that people in the host culture may not expect the same specific behaviors from people in a given occupation. The role expectations may be different, or they may be similar.

Cross-Cultural Differences in Role Relationships

The issue with which we are concerned in this section involves the dimensions along which role relationships differ across cultures. We can isolate at least four dimensions along which role relationships differ across cultures: (1) the degree of personalness of the relationship, (2) the degree of formality expected in the participants' behavior, (3) the degree of hierarchy present in the relationship, and (4) the degree of deviation allowed from the "ideal" role enactment. Even though these four dimensions can be isolated for the purpose of discussion, it should be noted that they are highly interrelated and at times the distinctions become blurred.

The degree of personalness

One area where there are often different behavioral expectations across cultures is in the degree of personalness expected in a role relationship. An illustration is a Kenyan student's reaction to waiters in the United States: "Waiters extend courtesy to get a bigger tip or because the manager is around. They are very impersonal; it's just a job to them" (Feig and Blair, 1975, p. 31). In other words, the Kenyan student was expecting waiters to see him not just in the role of customer but also as a person.

Differences in expected degree of personalness are illustrated further by a study of North Americans in Athens and their Greek co-workers completed by Triandis (1967). Triandis found that Greeks perceive North American behavior in organizations as " 'inhumanly' legalistic, rigid, cold, and overconcerned with efficiency" (p. 21). Even though Greek organizations are highly complex bureaucracies, "decisions are often taken on the basis of friendship and following strictly personal norms. . . . Greeks cannot understand the distinction between 'work behavior' and 'friendship behavior' " (p. 21). Thus, Greeks tend to place a high degree of importance on personalness in role relationships. A similar tendency is described for Mexican bank employees by Zurcher (1968).

Differences in the degree of personalness expected in role relationships are further illustrated by DeVos (1978) when he compares roles in Japan and the United States:

> Americans consider the ideal personal relationship to include considerable capacity for individuals to relate directly to one another in intimate non-hierarchical contact. This contact is defined as occurring between "selves" rather than individuals playing roles defined by status considerations. The Japanese tradition, in contrast, subordinates concern with the self to role expectations. To illustrate, the traditional Japanese concept of "sincerity"

sees the sincere individual acting in accordance with his role expectations, *not* in accordance with his own personal subjective feelings. In a contrary sense, for an American to be "sincere" is to behave in accord with his feelings rather than acting only from the standpoint of what might be expected of him in the exercise of a given role. Indeed, the person who acts in accordance with role expectations at the expense of feelings would be seen as insincere and dissimulating. (p. 10)

DeVos's comparison should not be taken as suggesting there is not a personal component to Japanese role relationships. The degree of personalness in some Japanese role relationships can be illustrated by the *sempai-kohai* relationship. Although the direct translation of this relationship is senior-junior (or boss-subordinate), it really corresponds to a mentor-protégé. Pascale and Athos (1981) compare the relationships as follows:

Extensive research into the nature of boss-subordinate relationships in the West . . . reveals that an American boss wants to know three things about those who work for him: (1) can they be trusted?; (2) are they competent?; and (3) are they consistent, or dependable? . . . The subordinate likewise weighs the clues that provide him data on his boss: (1) does he have integrity?; (2) is he competent?; and (3) is he open?—does he tell subordinates what they need to know in order to get the job done? . . . In Japan, the *sempai* (senior) expects the *kohai* (junior) to understand *him.* If the *sempai* doesn't always perform well, the *kohai* is expected to compensate for him and not to judge him except as a total human being. The *sempai,* in turn, is expected to display a wider breadth of understanding than normally exists in Western enterprises. (p. 138)

Thus, there is a relatively high degree of personalness present in certain Japanese role relationships.

The dimension of the degree of personalness expected in role relationships is related directly to Parsons's (1951) pattern variable of diffuseness or specificity (discussed in Chapter 3). Specifically, an expectation of impersonalness stems from a specificity orientation, the tendency to respond to specific aspects (i.e., the role) of another person. In contrast, an expectation of personalness stems from a diffuse orientation, the tendency to respond to others as total persons.

Differences in the degree of personalness or impersonalness in role expectations may become a barrier to the development of intimate relationships with strangers we meet or may cause misunderstandings in role relationships we might have as strangers in unfamiliar environments (e.g., serving as a manager for a corporation in another culture). For example, consider a North American businessperson with an impersonal orientation negotiating a contract with a stranger who has a personal orientation. The North American businessperson will expect to meet the stranger and get down to business after a very short period of informal conversation, that is, will deal with the stranger only as a businessperson.

In contrast, the stranger will expect to get to know the North American businessperson as a person before getting down to business. These different role expectations will, in all likelihood, lead to misunderstanding if neither of the two understands the other's role expectations.

Degree of formality expected

Role relationships also differ considerably with respect to the degree of formality expected in the relationship. Feig and Blair (1975) illustrate this by quoting a Turkish woman talking about the student-teacher relationship; she says, "You're supposed to fear the teacher like you fear Allah. When he comes into the class, all stand up. When you meet him on the street, you bow" (p. 39). Iranians display a similar attitude, according to Feig and Blair: "a professor who allows himself to be treated without the utmost respect or one who confesses ignorance on a subject is not generally taken seriously by Iranian students. 'The average student,' said one man, 'loses respect for a teacher when he is too friendly and common with his pupils'" (p. 83). The formality of student-teacher relationships in some cultures is summarized aptly by an Egyptian proverb, "Whoever teaches me a letter, I should become a slave to him forever."

As suggested above, the degree of formality or informality of our role expectations may cause misunderstandings when we communicate with strangers. To illustrate this, we can use the same example cited earlier when we discussed the degree of personalness or impersonalness—a North American businessperson negotiating a business contract with a stranger from another culture. The North American businessperson probably has an informal orientation (i.e., he or she begins to use people's first names immediately after being introduced to them). For the purpose of the example assume the stranger comes from a culture at the other extreme of this dimension, where role relationships always are considered to be formal. When these two people sit down to negotiate their contract, the North American businessperson will begin to call the stranger by his or her first name and the stranger will call the North American by his or her last name. The stranger probably would perceive the host as overly casual in transacting business affairs. In contrast, the North American businessperson, in all likelihood, would tend to see the stranger as overly stiff. Such attributions must influence the degree of trust each would have in the other and could potentially be a major stumbling block in the negotiations.

Degree of hierarchy

Another area where there are considerable differences in the nature of role relationships is the degree of hierarchy present in the relationship. To illustrate this, we can look at role relationships in Vietnam. Social relations, including role relationships, between Vietnamese are influenced by Confucianism. As Liem

(1980) points out, Confucianism is a doctrine of social hierarchies that "defines, by rigid rules, the attitudes which each member of the society should have" (p. 15). With respect to the employer-employee relationship, Liem says:

> The Vietnamese employee considers his employer as his mentor. As such, the latter is expected to give guidance, advice, and encouragement, and the former is supposed to execute orders, to perform his task quietly, and not to ask questions or have doubt about the orders. Because of his concept of the relationship, the Vietnamese employee does not voice his opinion to the boss, he just listens to his orders. (p. 16)

Obviously, such an expectation differs from the employer-employee relationship in Western cultures.

Asian cultures are not the only cultures having hierarchical role relationships; many African cultures also have similar role expectations. For example, the "clientship" relationship of the Kanuri culture in the Bornu province of Nigeria involves a wide-ranging hierarchical relation between a "patron" and a "client." Tessler, O'Ban, and Spain (1973) describe the relationship as follows:

> The term clientship refers to the diffuse relationship between two individuals (adult males), one of whom is considered the superior or patron and the other the subordinate or client. It is a diffuse relationship because the patron may demand a wide range of services from the client, while the client may expect a wide range of considerations from his patron. . . . These relationships are established explicitly to foster the immediate and long-term ambitions of both individuals involved. . . . Theoretically, each person in Bornu is the client of someone else. . . . However, in the common day-to-day perceptions of Kanuri, some people are simply not thought of as *being* clients; rather they are seen as *having* clients. . . . In general two types of client relationships may be distinguished: the apprentice-master relationship and the "simple" dependence relationship. For both, the relationship is entered into on a voluntary basis after initiation by the subordinate and with the agreement of the superior. . . . they both "agree with" or are satisfied with the behavior of the other. The stress on behavior in such agreements reflects their mutual trust in the willingness and ability of each to meet the role expectations of the other. (pp. 144–146)

Before moving on, it should be noted that the hierarchical nature of social relations in general, and role relationships in particular, often is reflected in the language of the culture. For example, in Japanese different verb endings are used depending on whether you are talking to people of equal status, higher status, or lower status. Thus, any time people speak in Japan, they are placing themselves into the social hierarchy.

As an illustration of the potential misunderstandings that can occur in our communication with strangers because of this dimension of role expectations, consider the example of a female North American student (the stranger) studying at an Asian university. In the United States or Canada there is some degree of hierarchy in the student-teacher role relationship, but it is a much lesser degree than exists in Asian universities, where students are expected to take notes on what the professor says and not ask challenging questions. If the North American student does not understand this expectation, she probably will carry over her expectations of the student-teacher role relationship in the United States or Canada and question the ideas presented by the Asian professors in their lectures. If the professors avoid answering the questions or tell the student to look the answers up for herself, the student may perceive the professors as lacking knowledge of their fields. The professors, on the other hand, may see the student as a troublemaker because she is not engaging in proper conduct for the role of student.

Degree of deviation allowed from the ideal role enactment

There are almost always discrepancies between the ideal role enactment and the actual behavior engaged in by people performing the role. Some cultures allow more deviance from the ideal role than do other cultures. Mosel (1973) suggests we can talk about those cultures that allow a lot of deviance from the ideal role as having "loose" social structures. On the other hand, according to Mosel, cultures that do not allow much deviance can be said to have "tight" social structures. Mosel argues that if we consider "loose" and "tight" as the ends of a continuum, we can say Thailand has a loose social structure and the United States is loose but not as loose as Thailand. On the other hand, Japan has a tight social structure, and India is also on the tight end, while Germany is about in the middle of the loose–tight continuum. In other words, more deviance from the ideal role enactment is tolerated in the United States and Thailand than in Japan and India.

Mosel (1973) points out a relationship between the looseness or tightness of the social structure and the predictability of behavior. He believes behavior is much more predictable in a tight social structure than in a loose social structure. The degree of certainty we have about how another person will behave, therefore, decreases as we go from a culture with a tight social structure to one with a loose social structure. If there is little variation from the ideal role enactment, as is true in a tight social structure, then the behavior of the people occupying roles should be predictable with a relatively high level of accuracy.

To illustrate the idea of a loose social structure, we can look at a North American businessman working in Thailand (this example is drawn from *The Bridge,* Summer, 1979, p. 19). After spending some time in Thailand, the North American businessman discovers that the deadlines he imposed for his Thai subordinates are not being met. The employees verbally agree to complete the work on time; in other words, they agree to meet the supervisor's role expectation. When it is time to turn in their work, however, they fail to do so and the North American becomes increasingly upset with this behavior. In order to understand the problem, the businessman talks about it with several Thai supervisors. Each of the Thai supervisors tells the North American the same thing, *Mai pen rai,* a Thai saying meaning roughly, "Don't worry about it; it doesn't really matter." This example suggests that a tremendous amount of variation from the ideal role is tolerated in Thai culture. While it is not of direct concern here, it is worth mentioning the cultural origins of this attitude. There are two Thai values that appear to influence the looseness of the social structure. On the one hand, Thais value "group harmony," the preserving of good feelings among members of the group at all costs. On the other hand, they also value "individualism" or "noninvolvement," a view which says that a person is only responsible to himself or herself and what he or she does is no one else's concern. Thais, therefore, tend to reject discipline and specific guidelines for their behavior, including ideal role prescriptions. At the same time, however, they strive to keep their interpersonal relationships pleasant, an attitude reflected in the saying *Mai pen rai.* To prevent anger from coming to the surface, Thais must ignore the little disagreements they have with other people.

A tight social structure is illustrated by Japan. In the Japanese culture there are several role relationships that allow very little deviation from the ideal. The tightness of the Japanese culture is seen in the concepts of *on* (and its reciprocal, *ongaeshi*) and *giri. On* and *ongaeshi* involve a reciprocal set of obligations between a superior and a subordinate. *"On* is a beneficence handed down from one's superior. It institutes an obligation (*ongaeshi*) to the superior on the part of the person who receives its benefit. By its very nature, *on* always connotes a hierarchical relation between two specific actors" (Beardsley, 1965, p. 94). Although the superior-inferior aspect of the *on-ongaeshi* relationship is not explicitly stated, it is accepted by all parties. According to Beardsley (1965), the person filling the superior role may be one of four types: (1) "a class superior," for example, an employer; (2) "a kin superior," for example, a person's grandparent or parent; (3) "an age-status superior," for example, a teacher; and (4) "a superior in a limited situation," for example, the person who arranges one's marriage. Once an *on-ongaeshi* relationship is begun, the inferior has an obligation for loyalty to the superior for as long as the relationship lasts, with little or no deviation being permitted.

Giri involves a reciprocal relationship in which each party is expected to repay an obligation in the same manner as it was created. In other words, a *giri* relationship does not necessarily set up an inferior-superior relationship between the persons involved. This type of relationship is illustrated by the exchange of services among neighbors when a member of the family dies. The neighbors provide services to the family of the bereaved during the period of mourning. In turn, the family receiving the services repays in kind at a later date when any neighbor needs assistance. A *giri* relationship also applies in a gift-giving situation. If someone gives you a gift, you are expected to return an equal gift at a later date (for example, return fruit for flowers). A *giri* relationship can be converted to an *on* relationship, however, if an equal gift is not returned. As an illustration, consider a situation where a family gives small gifts to a professor at a university. If the professor does not return all of the *giri*, an *on* relationship is established. When it comes time for the son of the family to get into the university, the professor will be obligated to return *on* and assist the son in gaining admission. The obligation would not have occurred if the professor had returned all of the *giri.*

The concept of tight versus loose social structure is related closely to Hall's (1976) notion of high-context and low-context cultures. In high-context cultures most of the information is found in the context and not in the communication message transmitted. On the other hand, in low-context cultures most of the information is found in the communication message rather than the context. High-context cultures require more conformance in behavior and, therefore, allow less deviation in role performance (i.e., have a tight social structure in Mosel's terminology). Since most of the information is in the message in low-context cultures, more deviance from the ideal role enactment is permissible. Low-context cultures, thus, tend to have looser social structures. We do not mean to say it is impossible for a low-context culture to have a tight social structure or for a high-context culture to have a loose social structure. Rather, we believe these combinations are probably "exceptions to the rule."

INTERPERSONAL RELATIONSHIPS

Categories of Interpersonal Relationships

How do you communicate with strangers, with acquaintances, with casual friends, with close friends, with members of your family, with a lover? Obviously, your communication with a particular person depends on the category in which you place him or her. You probably would not talk to a person who is only an acquaintance in the same way you would talk to a close friend. How we define our relationship with another person influences how we choose to encode our messages to that person and how we decode messages coming from that person.

The way people categorize types of interpersonal relationships varies across cultures. The type of behavior expected of people in the same category (e.g., friend) may also vary across cultures. To begin our discussion of interpersonal relationships, we examine two recent studies of the types of interpersonal relationships. As we indicated above, people put their relationships with others into numerous categories. The categories used include, but are not limited to, strangers, acquaintances, colleagues, chums, friends, buddies, close friends, best friend, and lover.

One study of the dimensions of interpersonal relationships comes from Wish, Deutsch, and Kaplan (1976). They examine 45 different types of relationships between people in the United States. The results of their research suggest that people tend to use four dimensions to distinguish among different types of relationships: (1) cooperative-friendly to competitive-hostile, (2) equal to unequal, (3) intense to superficial, and (4) socioemotional-informal to task-oriented–formal. The fourth dimension, socioemotional-informal to task-oriented–formal, is related to the distinction we have made between interpersonal and role relationships and to the degree of personalness or impersonalness within role relationships. The second dimension, equal to unequal, is similar to the degree of hierarchy in role relationships discussed earlier in this chapter. The cooperative-friendly to competitive-hostile dimension is important but not addressed here because of lack of cross-cultural data. Of primary concern here is the intense to superficial dimension. Another way of looking at this dimension is to think of it as addressing the issue of the degree of intimacy present in a relationship.

Recent research by Knapp, Ellis, and Williams (1980) suggests that North Americans draw distinctions among many different types of relationships, especially on the dimension of intimacy. These researchers asked subjects to rate 62 different relationship terms on a nine-point intimacy scale (1 = intimate, 9 = nonintimate). The ratings can be exemplified as follows: lover, 1.50; boy/girlfriend, 2.31; best friend, 2.48; close friend, 3.05; friend, 3.83; chum, 4.24; pal, 4.88; colleague, 5.89; and acquaintance, 6.96. These examples illustrate not only the variation in categories people in the United States impose upon their relationships, but also the tremendous variation in the degree of intimacy perceived in these relationships. As we suggested above, the categories are important because "the way we choose to label something often provides us with expectations and perceptual orientations which we deem appropriate to that label" (Knapp, Ellis, and Williams, 1980, p. 262).

In contrast to the categorization of interpersonal relationships in the United States, consider the Japanese scheme. According to Nakane (1974), the Japanese distinguish among only three different categories of people: "(1) those people within one's own group; (2) those whose background is fairly well-known; and (3) those who are unknown—the strangers" (p. 124). As one would expect, the style of communication in the first group, which includes not only family members but also co-workers, is generally informal; however, "as a personal relationship becomes more distant, the style becomes more formal, employing more honorific expressions" (p. 125).

Nakane (1974) contends that communication with people within one's own group is generally very effective (i.e., there is little "miscommunication"). This is at least partly due to the stability of people's reference groups in Japan where individuals may live in the same place and work for the same company all of their lives. Since individuals spend the majority of their lives within the same group, they are more concerned with how others react.

With people in the second group communication is more formal than with people in the first group. According to Nakane (1974), "more universal forms of Japanese etiquette" are used (p. 127). This second category includes an indefinite number of people who are not actually known personally, for example, people who went to the same university or grew up in the same rural town. Even though the people may not be known, their backgrounds are. Nakane cites an example that illustrates communicating with a person in this group. In the example she tells of visiting another university (one she had not been to before) to give a series of lectures. When she arrived, she met an unknown professor who greeted her by saying, "You must be Professor Nakane. I am also from Tokyo. Please do come into my office." They went to the professor's office, had tea, and talked. This was only possible, according to Nakane, because the professor belonged to Nakane's second group, they went to the same university (Tokyo University). Because the professor's background was known, Nakane could make reliable predictions about his behavior.

The third category of people in Japan, strangers, are totally unknown. According to Nakane (1974), Japanese "do not feel the necessity of applying any particular code of etiquette" to strangers (p. 128). "Japanese rarely greet or smile at a stranger, even if they share the same table in a crowded restaurant" (p. 128). Contact with strangers is avoided because there is no way to predict how they might behave. Strangers are, to a certain extent, "nonpersons." When in a train crowded with strangers, for example, Japanese act as though the other people are not there. If one bumps into strangers, there is no reason to say "excuse me," because strangers are "nonpersons."

Carr (1973) describes a very similar pattern of interpersonal relationships among Chinese. According to Carr, Chinese divide people into two categories: (1) people they don't know—strangers; and (2) people they know intimately. As with the Japanese, there are different rules for interacting with people in each of the categories. In dealing with strangers, the Chinese are cautious. Carr suggests strangers are not seen as human; if people have contact with strangers, the strangers are not recognized as people. Asking strangers to excuse you for bumping into them, according to Carr, is like saying "excuse me" to a chair. The Chinese term used to refer to people who are known intimately is *kwan-hsi*, roughly translated as a connection between people. A *kwan-hsi* relationship is not necessarily a friendship in the Western sense of the term, it is more of a contract. The Chinese *kwan-hsi* relationship is similar to the Japanese *on-ongaeshi* relationship. Both involve high levels of familiarity, as well as a high level of obligation, according to Carr.

The emphasis in East Asia is on the form of behavior, not on its content (Carr, 1973). In other words, behavior is judged by the manner in which it is performed. For example, in archery it is less important to hit the target than it is to use the correct form in drawing the bow and releasing the arrow. This also carries over to interpersonal relationships. In judging people who have been assigned a task, the question is not whether or not they complete the task, but rather how they go about trying to complete it. Did they act sincerely?

The interpersonal behavior patterns discussed above are due, at least in part, to the level of context present in Japanese and Chinese cultures. Because of the contexting process, people in high-context cultures such as Japan and China draw greater distinctions between "insiders" and "outsiders" than do people in low-context cultures such as the United States has. Hall (1976) points out that people in high-context cultures expect the person to whom they are talking to know what is on their mind. People in high-context cultures will talk indirectly about what is on their mind, giving the other person all of the necessary information except the "crucial" piece. Figuring out the final piece and putting it all together are the responsibility of the other person. Obviously, only insiders can effectively perform these expected functions. Strangers invariably would find themselves frustrated in a situation like this.

The cross-cultural differences in the categorization of interpersonal relationships discussed above can cause misunderstandings in our communication with strangers and in our communication when we are strangers in unfamiliar environments. For example, consider the misunderstandings that might occur when North Americans are strangers in Asia. As indicated above, Asians tend to avoid contact with strangers because their behavior is not predictable. The strangers from North America have a different approach to people who are unknown and unfamiliar: don't avoid them; approach them and try to get to know them. In other words, the strangers are applying a different communication rule for dealing with people who are unknown. Applying this rule in Asia might lead only to frustration, however. Since the North Americans are strangers, Asians would tend to see them as "nonpersons," and the rules of etiquette would not apply to interactions with them. These different rules would lead each party to make faulty attributions about the other's behavior. The strangers, in all likelihood, would see the Asians as standoffish and impolite, while the Asians might see the strangers as overly aggressive and impolite. Only by becoming aware of each other's expectations regarding different categories of relationships can the two parties begin to correctly interpret and make more accurate attributions about each other's behavior.

Comparing Relationships in Specific Cultures

Our discussion of interpersonal relationships so far has focused on differences in how relationships are categorized and some of the implications of different categorization schemes. We now turn our attention to interpersonal relationships in specific cultures. When reading the following material, you should keep in mind that it is, out of necessity, stereotypical. As we discuss in Chapter 5, caution should always be used in applying stereotypes to individual cases.

Feig (1980) contrasts patterns of friendship in North America and Thailand:

Americans contrast a "fair weather friend" with "a friend in need (who) is a friend indeed." Thais draw a similar distinction between "eating friends" and "friends to the death." Eating friends, like fair weather friends, feast with you when you can feast with them then swiftly disappear if you fall upon hard times. . . . Since both peoples, as noted earlier, prize a certain mobile, independent existence, their relationships usually do not involve the deep reciprocal set of rights and duties that are characteristic of friendships in more communal societies. . . . Thais are often reluctant to impose on their friends, at least for rather routine favors. One Thai explained that they are taught not to ask, but to give to those who ask; to be self-sufficient, and never impose on others, but to be kind and ready to help at all times. . . . One way in which American friendships differ to a certain extent is that they tend to be more compartmentalized, centering around an activity, an event or shared history. A person can thus have one friend to play bridge with, another to discuss politics with, and a third to go socializing with. . . . An American can thus fragment the personality to some degree and view the other person (and himself) as a composite of distinct accomplishments and interests. . . . Thais, on the other hand, tend to react to the totality of other individuals and thus probably wouldn't form friendships with someone whose preferences in many areas of life they didn't approve of. (pp. 33–34)

Thus, in Parsons's (1951) terminology, Thai friendships tend to be diffuse, while North American friendships tend to be specific. Feig goes on to suggest that another difference between North American and Thai friendships involves what happens when a disagreement leads to an argument. Since verbal arguments are so rare in Thailand (due to the value placed on group harmony), a disagreement between two people will be taken much more seriously than it would be in North America. According to Feig, two Thais may not be able to continue a friendly relationship after an argument; they may become enemies.

Thus, while there are a few similarities between friendships in Thailand and North America, there are also important differences. North Americans traveling to Thailand probably would expect to see differences because the Thais speak a different language and there are obvious cultural differences. What happens, though, when North Americans travel to a country such as Australia? On the surface Australia appears very similar to Canada and the United States. The surface similarities (e.g., language and architecture) may lead North Americans traveling in Australia to believe the patterns of interpersonal relationships are also similar. This, however, is not the case.

According to Renwick (1980), one area in which the United States and Australia differ is with respect to their attitudes toward friendship. He believes the differences are at least partially due to different histories:

Emerging from their particular heritage are the Australians' fundamental beliefs that one has a responsibility for his or her neighbor and that loyalty to one's friends is not only appropriate, it is essential. An Australian assumes a natural, basic commitment to his fellows. As a friendship develops, an Australian makes and expects deeper commitments, whether they are simply understood or expressed directly.

Most Americans, on the other hand, while placing a high value on being "friendly," tend to take less seriously than Australians their relationships with, and loyalty to, particular friends, often valuing more highly a wide circle of friends. Such preferences enable Americans to move in and out of relationships more easily and frequently than do Australians. (pp. 16–17)

Thus, one of the differentiating characteristics between friendships in North America and Australia involves the fact that Australians expect relationships to include both high levels of familiarity and commitment, while North Americans do not necessarily expect both to be present.

According to Renwick (1980), the importance of Australian friendships is expressed in the term "mateship," which suggests a feeling of "we're in this thing together." The Australian mateship is an end in itself. In Parsons's (1951) terminology such an orientation is labeled as expressive. On the other hand, friendships among North Americans often are seen as a means to an end, or reflecting an instrumental orientation in Parsons's terminology. In North America interpersonal relationships often are used to attain some other external objective. Renwick goes on to suggest that Australians are more likely to offer assistance to a stranger than are North Americans.

In some cultures, such as that of North America, friendships tend to form "around work, children, or political opinions—around charities, games, various occasions for sharing food and alcohol, etc." (Glenn, 1966, p. 270). Because their friendships usually are formed around an activity, North Americans tend to form friendships that are not as "deep" as friendships in some other cultures. For example, Russians form deep bonds with others, and once such a bond is formed they feel "an obligation of almost constant companionship, and the rejection of any reticence or secretiveness among friends" (Glenn, 1966, p. 270). Russians, contends Glenn, tend to embrace the whole person rather than selected parts of the person, as is often the case in North America. In Parsons's terminology these tendencies reflect orientations of diffuseness and specificity, respectively.

Henrick Smith, who won the Pulitzer Prize for his news coverage from Moscow for *The New York Times,* describes Russian friendships in his book *The Russians* (1976):

Among family and friends, they become the wonderful, flowing, emotional people of Tolstoy's novels, sharing humor and sorrow and confidences, entering into a simple but profound intimacy that seems less self-centered and less self-conscious than one generally finds in the West. Precisely because their public lives are so supervised and because they cannot afford to be open and candid with most people, Russians invest their friendships with enormous importance. Many of them, in cities at least, are only-children whose closest friends come to take the place of missing brothers and sisters. They will visit each other almost daily, like members of the family. Their social circles are usually narrower than those of Westerners, especially Americans who put such great stock in popularity, but relations between Russians are usually more intense, more demanding, more enduring, and often more rewarding. (pp. 143–144)

Friendships in the French culture share certain aspects with friendships in Russia and North America. They are specialized like friendships in North America; however, according to Glenn (1966),

> . . . they also tend to be organized in patterns of long duration, often with an expectation of family friendships extending over more than one generation. Where Americans are competitive even within the group of friends, for Frenchmen as for Russians, friendship excludes competitiveness; the coexistence of cooperation with competition, so natural to Americans, appears incomprehensible to French and Russian informants. (p. 271)

Glenn goes on to suggest that French friendships possess a contradiction, which stems from the demand for long, close friendships and, at the same time, privacy and independence.

Several of the preceding comparisons of friendship patterns reflect the comments of people from many cultures when they meet North Americans, especially people from "traditional" cultures. People from traditional cultures often view friendships in the United States as lacking the depth and permanence expected of friendships in their home culture. These people often report that the ease with which North Americans can be approached is misleading; it leads to an expectation of deep and permanent friendships, which often do not follow. On the other hand, the North American may feel annoyed because of the expectations of a visitor who is hardly known.

SUMMARY

Our communication with strangers is influenced by the groups to which we belong, the roles we fill, and how we define interpersonal relationships. Our membership groups and our reference groups both have an impact on the values, as well as the norms and rules, we learn. As part of our socialization into these groups, we are taught to avoid people from certain other groups (our out-groups). The orientation we learn toward out-groups causes us unconsciously to try to put our own group in a more favorable light when it is compared to them. This tendency in turn often leads us to make inaccurate attributions and predictions about the behavior of strangers from the out-group.

In addition to our group memberships, our role expectations also influence our communication with strangers. We learn what behavior is expected in different roles as we are socialized into our culture and membership groups. Since roles tend to vary across cultures, it is necessary to know strangers' role expectations if we are to understand and accurately predict their behavior.

Like our expectations regarding roles, our definitions of different types of interpersonal relationships influence our communication; for example, we expect strangers, acquaintances, casual friends, close friends, and lovers to behave differently. Not only do the categories of relationships vary across cultures, but the behaviors associated with the same relationship (e.g., friend) also differ cross-culturally. If we are to communicate effectively with strangers, we must understand the way they categorize relationships and the expectations they have for people in each category. Without this knowledge we cannot correctly interpret or make accurate sociocultural predictions about the strangers' behavior.

5

Psychocultural
Influences
on the Process

One of the greatest stumbling blocks to under-
standing other peoples within or without a particu-
lar culture is the tendency to judge others' behavior
by our own standards.

James Downs

In the preceding two chapters we examined those influences on our communication with strangers due to our socialization within a culture and the social relationships we form within our culture. Our analysis would be incomplete if we did not go one step further and examine processes occurring within individuals. The focus of this chapter is, therefore, on those influences we have labeled psychocultural: cognitive processes and attitudes.

Cognitive processes include a wide range of activities, including how we perceive the world around us, how we classify it, and how we give it meaning. For the purpose of the present analysis, we have chosen to divide our discussion of cognitive processes between two chapters. The division is somewhat arbitrary, but necessary when looking at the individual elements of the model separately. The material to be covered in this chapter focuses on how individuals classify the world around them and the impact of this classification on the attribution of meaning. More specifically, this chapter examines the categorization process, stereotyping, and attributional processes. The second part of our discussion of cognitive processes is presented in Chapter 7, which focuses on cultural variations in perception and patterns of thought.

The second section of this chapter is devoted to attitudinal influences on our communication with strangers. Rather than examine a large number of attitudes that may have a minor impact on the process, we examine two critical attitudes, ethnocentrism and prejudice, in depth.

COGNITIVE PROCESSES

The Categorization Process

In Chapter 2 we pointed out that whenever we put discrete elements into groups, we are engaging in the process of categorization. The human brain requires categories in order to process information and think. Categorization cannot be avoided; it is necessary for an orderly life. As Neisser (1976) argues, preexisting structures (i.e., categories) are necessary if any information is to be acquired. A category is "a *set of specifications* regarding what events will be grouped as equivalent—rules respecting the nature of the critical cues required, the manner of their combination, their inferential weight, and the acceptance limits of their variability" (Bruner, 1957, p. 133). Categories, therefore, form the basis for normal prejudgment and the predictions we make when we communicate.

The categorization process we use is not the same throughout our lifetime. Bruner's theory of cognitive growth illustrates how the categorization process changes as children mature (see Bruner, Oliver, and Greenfield, 1966). According to Bruner, children's conceptual development involves a shift in the attributes they use to determine whether or not things are alike. Initially, very young children tend to use perceptual qualities such as shape, color, and size in defining things as alike. As they develop intellectually, children begin to look at what things do or what people can do with things (functional attributes) in classifying things as alike. At about the same time children begin to use a common name for the things classified as similar. Bruner also points out that along with these changes, children's categorization also progresses from what are initially loose groupings (in which several different characteristics are used in the classification) to groupings based on one common feature.

According to Brislin (1981), eight dimensions are used in our formation of categories. First, we form categories on the basis of differences that are easily observed. Second, categories are formed when we overgeneralize information with which we are already familiar. Third, we form some categories because the categories are functional; for example, the category serves the function of keeping in-group members away from out-groups. Fourth, categories are formed because they increase the in-group's positive image of itself. Fifth, we form categories by projecting our own feelings; for example, we often assume everyone behaves about the same way as we do. Sixth, categories are formed because we sometimes hold beliefs in common with others. Seventh, we form categories in order to highlight desirable and undesirable traits of in-groups and out-groups.

Finally, Brislin points out we form categories because we perceive information to be important or personally relevant. Any category we form may be based on one or more of these eight dimensions.

Once categories are formed, what effects do they have on us? The work of Bruner, Goodnow, and Austin (1956) suggests an answer to this question. Bruner and his associates identify five functions of the categorization process. First, the use of categories reduces a highly complex environment to manageable size, so that we can cope with it. Second, the categorization process enables us to identify what various stimuli are; for example, it allows us to differentiate between tigers and house cats. Third, since the use of categories allows us to identify stimuli as members of a class, it reduces the necessity for us to be constantly learning what new stimuli are. Fourth, the use of categories enables us to predict appropriate and inappropriate behavior in advance. Finally, the categorization process allows us to relate one class of events to another class of events. Bruner, Goodnow, and Austin also point out we tend to categorize stimuli as fast as possible, so we can better predict what behavior is appropriate in the situation in which we find ourselves.

It should be obvious from the above that whenever we categorize objects, animals, plants, or people, we are focusing on similarities among the stimuli and playing down any differences that may exist. In saying this, we do not mean to imply categorization is a simple unidimensional process. Rather, as Cole and Scribner (1974) point out,

> there is a whole multiplicity of processes by which we deal with environmental variability, reducing or holding differences constant and establishing similarity or equivalence as a basis for action or thought. These processes may vary with the attributes of the things in question, the context in which the act of classifying occurs, and the skills and knowledge we possess (p. 100)

In other words, the way we categorize objects, plants, animals, people and behavior (the different classes of categories) varies, depending on the thing we are categorizing, where we are categorizing it, and the level of our skill in classifying things.

Stereotypes

The term stereotypes comes from Walter Lippman's classic book *Public Opinion.* Lippman refers to stereotypes as "pictures in our heads." More recently stereotypes have come to "refer to any categorization of individual elements *concerned with people* which mask differences among those elements" (Brislin, 1981, p. 44). Stereotypes, therefore, are a subset of the more general process of categorization.

Like other forms of categorization, stereotypes are necessary for us to make sense of our social environment and communicate with each other. Argyle (1969) argues, "One of the main processes involved in person perception is the assignment of people to categories and the application of the relevant categories" (p. 133). It should not be assumed, however, that a stereotype is the only factor used in forming an impression of another person. Grant and Holmes (1981) point out, "Observers use stereotype information to form an impression of an ethnic group member regardless of his or her traits. However, they do not appear to ignore trait information that is unrelated to the person's ethnic group stereotype. Rather, their impressions of such a person include all the stereotype traits and these unrelated traits" (p. 114).

Stereotypes are not just simple pictures of groups of people; rather, they are complex, multidimensional images. In fact, according to Vassiliou, Triandis, Vassiliou, and McGuire (1972), stereotypes vary along six dimensions:

1. *Complexity.* The number of traits assigned to the other group.

2. *Clarity.* (a) *Polarization* of the judgments on each trait dimension, that is, the extent to which people from one group assign non-neutral values of the trait to people from another group. (b) *Consensus,* that is, agreement among people in assigning the trait to another group.

3. *Specificity-Vagueness.* The extent to which the traits are specific or vague (abstract).

4. *Validity.* The extent to which the stereotypes correspond to substantially realistic assignment of traits.

5. *Value.* The favorability of the assigned traits.

6. *Comparability.* The extent to which the framework of the perceiver is involved in the stereotyping so that a comparison is made between autostereotype (group looking at self) and heterostereotype (one group looking at another). (pp. 90-91)

↗ Normative & Nonnormative Stereotypes ↘

All stereotypes vary along each of these dimensions. When stereotypes involve substantially realistic assignments of traits to a group of people (i.e., are valid), Bogardus (1959) refers to them as "sociotypes."

Vassiliou et al. (1972) present one of the few attempts to develop a theory to explain stereotype formation when no strong preconceptions are already held. The theory presented by these writers differentiates between normative and non-normative stereotypes formed by members of the in-group prior to contact with the out-group. A normative stereotype is a "cognitive norm for thinking about a group of people" (p. 112) based on information gained from education, the mass media, and/or historical events. For example, a normative stereotype about Iranians developed in the United States during the hostage crisis of 1979-1981.

This stereotype formed on the basis of the image of Iranians presented in the mass media and the historical events being reported. A nonnormative stereotype, on the other hand, is not formed on the basis of information from such sources. When one group does not have a normative stereotype about another group with whom "friendly" relations exist, the members of the group begin thinking about the other group as being "like us." In other words, nonnormative stereotypes are purely projective in nature. To illustrate, North Americans tend to have little information about Greeks; therefore, if they have had no previous contact with Greeks, they are likely to project their image of themselves and see Greeks as very similar to themselves. If friendly relations do not exist, Vassiliou et al. argue, the stereotype of the out-group formed by the in-group will then be a normative one.

The formation of stereotypes as outlined above assumes no previous contact between the in-group and the out-group. One obvious question needs to be addressed: what impact does contact have on stereotypes that are already formed? Vassiliou et al. (1972) argue, "Contact has the effect of changing the stereotypes to match the sociotypes; that is, it increases the validity of the stereotypes" (p. 114). It should be noted, however, that although contact has a tremendous impact on nonnormative stereotypes, it has a lesser impact on normative stereotypes. More specifically, contact increases the clarity of nonnormative stereotypes but has little or no effect on the clarity of normative stereotypes. Further, contact with members of the out-group increases the complexity and specificity of the in-group's stereotype of them.

As indicated earlier, stereotyping is the categorization process involved when we are categorizing people. The stereotypes we hold have a direct impact on our communication with strangers. Our initial predictions about strangers' behavior must, out of necessity, be based on the stereotypes we have about the strangers' culture, race, or ethnic group. To the degree that our stereotypes are accurate, we can make accurate cultural level predictions about strangers' behavior. If our stereotypes are inaccurate, we cannot make correct attributions about strangers' behavior. Further, if we rigidly hold our stereotypes and are not willing to question them, we can never reach the point where we know strangers as individuals (i.e., we can never make psychocultural predictions about their behavior), and our attributions about an individual stranger's behavior will continue to be incorrect.

Attributional Processes

The impetus for much of the research on attributional processes stems from Jones and Davis's (1965) theory of correspondent inferences. In this theory attribution is seen as a largely rational activity through which perceivers integrate information from the behavior of actors and the surrounding circumstances. As we pointed out in Chapter 2, Jones and Nisbett (1972) propose that actors performing a behavior interpret it in different terms than do people observing the behavior. More specifically, they argue actors usually attribute their own behavior to situational factors, while observers tend to attribute the behavior to qualities of the actors.

Nisbett et al. (1973) suggest two probable reasons for the differences in actors' and observers' attributions about the actors' behavior. The first reason is a perceptual one. At the moment of action the actors' attention is focused on the situational cues with which their behavior is being coordinated. In contrast, the observers' attention at the moment of action is focused on the actors, not on the situation. The second reason for the differential bias stems from a difference in the nature and extent of the information possessed by actors and observers. Specifically, the actors know more about their own past and present experiences than do the observers. Thus, the actors may be prevented from interpreting their behavior in terms of personal characteristics, while at the same time allowing the observers to make such an interpretation.

It should be obvious that attributions made about behavior are often in error. There are two "causes" for errors in attribution. One cause is the divergent perspectives used by actors and observers in interpreting behavior. Since they use different perspectives, there can never be perfect agreement between them as to what behavior means. The second cause stems from the fact that "the world more often than not provides a person with stimulation that does not clearly fit the definition of any one class or label, but rather stands at the boundary of a particular label's applicability: it can be labeled with equal or near equal appropriateness by more than one term" (Wallach, 1959, p. 1). In other words, the second cause stems from the fact that a particular stimulus can be categorized in more than one way.

Two other types of potential errors in the attribution process can be identified. One potential error stems from our tendency to stop looking for different interpretations of behavior (either our own or that of another person) once a relevant and reasonable interpretation of the behavior has been found (Taylor and Fiske, 1975). Another error has been referred to as the "principle of negativity" by Kanouse and Hanson (1972). These writers believe we have a tendency to overemphasize negative information about other people's behavior. The principle of negativity is an example of what Ross (1977) calls the "fundamental attribution error." This error involves the idea that observers consistently overestimate the force of actors' traits in determining their behavior and underestimate the force of situational factors.

Jones and Davis's (1965) theory of correspondent inferences is based on the assumption that observers know what the behavior they are observing means. This assumption, however, is questionable when we communicate with strangers. Detweiler (1975) points out:

> . . . the process of cross-cultural attributions should not be the same as within-culture attribution. There are unique factors which may yield differ-

ent attributions inter-culturally than intra-culturally. First, it is important to recognize that attributions are based upon our knowledge of cultural expectations. Hence, it is hypothesized that whether or not the actor is from one's own culture or a different culture should have a major impact on the inference process. Second, to the degree that this cultural difference is recognized by the observer, inferences will be limited. (pp. 593-594)

Thus, the model proposed by attribution theorists may need modification for intercultural encounters. In examining the nature of intercultural attributions, Jaspers and Hewstone (1982) conclude:

(1) Behavior of members of other groups perceived as out-of-role and unexpected from the perspective of one's own group is more likely to lead to person attribution.

(2) Since social categorization in terms of cultural differences is probably very salient in such situations, the person attribution will be associated with the perceived differences in culture.

(3) The same behavior which gives rise to person attribution cross-culturally may lead to a situational attribution within a particular group or culture because social categorization does not covary with the behavior, but is constant. (p. 139)

To illustrate the nature of intercultural attributions, we can use an example presented by Triandis (1975). This example is drawn from the files of George Vassiliou, a Greek psychiatrist, and involves a segment of interaction between a North American supervisor and a Greek subordinate. Triandis describes the interaction between a superior, who wants employees to participate in decisions, and a subordinate, who expects to be told what to do, as follows (pp. 42-43):

Behavior	Attribution
American: How long will it take you to finish this report?	*American:* I asked him to participate.
	Greek: His behavior makes no sense. He is the boss. Why doesn't he tell me?
Greek: I do not know. How long should it take?	*American:* He refuses to take responsibility.
	Greek: I asked him for an order.
American: You are in the best position to analyze time requirements.	*American:* I press him to take responsibility for his own actions.
	Greek: What nonsense! I better give him an answer.
Greek: 10 days.	*American:* He lacks the ability to estimate time; this time estimate is totally inadequate.

American: Take 15. Is it agreed you will do it in 15 days?

American: I offer a contract.
Greek: These are my orders. 15 days.

In fact the report needed 30 days of regular work. So the Greek worked day and night, but at the end of the 15th day, he still needed one more day's work.

Behavior	Attribution
American: Where is my report?	*American:* I am making sure he fulfills his contract. *Greek:* He is asking for the report. (Both attribute that it is not ready.)
Greek: It will be ready tomorrow. *American:* But we had agreed that it would be ready today.	*American:* I must teach him to fulfill a contract. *Greek:* The stupid, incompetent boss! Not only did he give me wrong orders, but he does not even appreciate that I did a 30-day job in 16 days.
The Greek hands in his resignation.	The American is surprised. *Greek:* I can't work for such a man.

The above illustrates how people from different cultures may make different attributions about the same behavior. Research by Detweiler (1975) also suggests that the attribution process is influenced by whether or not the observer recognizes that the behavior in question can have more than one meaning. The recognition of multiple interpretations of behavior is influenced by the width of the observers' categories, according to Detweiler. Detweiler distinguishes among narrow, moderate, and wide categorizers. "For a narrow categorizer to place an object in a category, that object must be very equivalent to the other objects in that category. Conversely, once an object is placed in a category, the narrow CW [category width] would be unwilling to acknowledge discrepancies among category members" (p. 593). Wide categorizers, on the other hand, allow greater discrepancies when placing two objects in the same category. Detweiler's research supports the position that observers who use narrow categories tend to evaluate the behavior of people from other cultures from their own cultural frame of reference. Narrow categorizers also tend to see culturally dissimilar actors as responsible for negative outcomes. In contrast, observers who use wide categories do not always attribute responsibility for negative outcomes to culturally dissimilar individuals; rather, they tend to withhold attributions because they feel they do not have enough information on which to base an evaluation. Thus, narrow categorizers tend to fall victim to the fundamental attribution error more often than do wide categorizers.

There is more of a tendency for the fundamental attribution error to occur when one is communicating with strangers than when one is communicating with people who are familiar. This error occurs with such regularity Pettigrew (1978) refers to it as the "ultimate attribution error." According to Pettigrew, undesirable acts occurring in intergroup situations generally are attributed to innate personal characteristics of strangers, with situational and role requirements being overlooked. In contrast, desirable behaviors generally are attributed to either situational and role requirements or motivational qualities of strangers and not to innate personal characteristics. Brislin (1981) supports Pettigrew's assertion. He also goes on to point out negative information is more influential when attributing traits to members of out-groups than is positive information.

ATTITUDINAL INFLUENCES ON THE PROCESS

More than 100 definitions of the term *attitude* can be found in the social psychological literature. Although no two of these definitions are exactly the same, "there appears to be a general consensus that an attitude is a learned predisposition to respond in an evaluative (from extremely favorable to extremely unfavorable) manner toward some attitude object" (Davidson and Thompson, 1980, p. 27). In other words, attitudes predispose us to behave in a positive or negative manner toward various objects or people.

Components of attitude

Attitudes generally are conceptualized as having three components: cognitive, affective, and conative (McGuire, 1969). The cognitive component involves our beliefs about the attitude object. A belief, according to Rokeach (1972), "is any simple proposition, conscious or unconscious, inferred from what a person says or does, capable of being preceded by the phrase 'I believe that'" (p. 113). Examples of beliefs include "blacks are musical," "the Irish are heavy drinkers," and "the Japanese are ambitious." The affective component of an attitude involves our emotional or evaluative reaction to the attitude object. Thus, the affective component refers to our subjective evaluation of the positive or negative aspects of the attitude object. The conative component of an attitude involves our behavioral intentions toward the attitude object. This may involve, for example, an intention to avoid members of the out-group.

Before turning to an examination of specific attitudes influencing our communication with strangers, we need to discuss briefly the functions attitudes serve for the people who hold them. By functions we mean what attitudes do for people who hold them, or in other words, the uses of attitudes. Katz (1960) proposes four general functions any attitude can serve:

General Functions of attitudes:

1. *The utilitarian or adjustment function.* We hold some attitudes because they are useful in our culture; they lead to the attainment of rewards.

2. *The ego-defensive function.* We hold some attitudes because they allow us to protect our self-image (ego). These attitudes allow us to avoid admitting uncomfortable things about ourselves.

3. *The value-expressive function.* We hold some attitudes because we want to express those parts of our lives that are important to us.

4. *The knowledge function.* We hold some attitudes because they allow us to structure or organize incoming stimuli in a way that makes sense to us.

Ethnocentrism

Ethnocentrism: The attitude

The word ethnocentrism is derived from two Greek words: *ethnos,* or nation; and *kentron,* or center. This suggests that ethnocentrism occurs when our nation is seen as the center of the world. In common usage, however, the concept is applied more broadly. In his classic book *Folkways,* William Graham Sumner (1940) defines ethnocentrism as

> . . . the technical name for the view of things in which one's own group is the center of everything, and all others are scaled and rated with reference to it. . . . the most important fact is that ethnocentrism leads people to exaggerate and intensify everything in their own folkways which is peculiar and which differentiates them from others. It therefore strengthens the folkways. (p. 13)

In other words, ethnocentrism refers to our tendency to identify with our ingroup (e.g., ethnic or racial group, culture) and to evaluate out-groups and their members according to its standards. Because of ethnocentrism, we tend to view our own cultural values and ways of doing things as more real, or as the "right" and natural values and ways of doing things. The major consequence of this view is our in-group's values and ways of doing things are seen as superior to the out-groups' values and ways of doing things.

The above should not be taken to suggest ethnocentrism is always deliberate. Often the expression of ethnocentrism is a function of how we are socialized. For example, people born and raised in the United States are taught many subtle cues suggesting the United States is the center of the world. Consider the major league baseball championship series played between the winners of the two leagues. Is it called the United States Series? No, obviously not; it is called the World Series, implying that no other nation has baseball teams (granted there are now Canadian teams in the World Series, but no Japanese, Korean, or Mexican teams). Another example of the tendency for people in the United States to view their country as the center of the world is in the use of the term "American." We must remember that citizens of the other members of the Organization of American States (OAS) from North, Central, and South America are also "Americans."

The existence of ethnocentrism is not limited to recent historic times or to the United States. The early Greeks used the term *barbarikos* (barbarians) to refer to those people living around them who did not speak Greek. Because they did not speak Greek, the ancient Persians and Egyptians were considered by the Greeks to be inferior. In current times many languages have a word with very similar meaning. For example, the Japanese word *gaijin* means foreigner, a person who is not Japanese, and is often used with a condescending overtone.

Anthropologists document the existence of ethnocentric attitudes in almost every culture they study. As Klass and Hellman (1971) point out, ethnocentrism often is expressed in the way people draw their maps:

> There is nothing unusual about this type of thinking: the Chinese, who called their country the Middle Kingdom, were convinced that China was the center of the world, and similar beliefs were held by other nations— and still are held. The British drew the Prime Meridian of longitude to run through Greenwich, near London. Europeans drew maps of the world with Europe at the center, Americans with the New World at the center. (p. 61)

Functions and dysfunctions of ethnocentrism

Ethnocentrism is related closely to the attitude of nationalism. Rosenblatt (1964) believes both attitudes arise from a comparison of in-groups with out-groups. The attitudes differ, however, in that ethnocentrism focuses on cultural patterns of behavior, while nationalism focuses on a nation's political ideology. According to Rosenblatt, high levels of nationalism and ethnocentrism both serve several functions that maintain the integrity of the in-group. These include:

Advantages of Ethnocentrism:

1. GROUP SURVIVAL—Groups with high ethnocentrism and high nationalism are more likely to survive the threats of external forces.

2. TANGIBLE PAYOFFS—Administrative efficacy is promoted (e.g., power in policy making decisions, division of labor, promotion of group welfare).

3. INCREASED HOMOGENEITY—Groups will have more homogeneous attitudes, greater cohesiveness, and increased conformity.

4. GREATER VIGOR AND PERSISTENCE—Problems affecting the group are addressed with persistence and energy.

5. GREATER EASE OF STRIVING AGAINST OUTSIDERS—Relations against outgroups are executed with greater ease because of strong commitments to group maintenance.

6. DECREASED SOCIAL DISORGANIZATION—Intragroup organization increases.

7. INCREASED TENURE OF LEADERS—Leaders are more likely to remain in the leadership position.

8. NEW DISSENSION—Intragroup conflicts arise frequently amid the strain toward homogeneity.

9. MISPERCEPTION OF OUTGROUPS—Attributions to outgroup members are not accurate because of misperceptions.

10. FACILITATION OF LEARNING—Learning correct ingroup behavior is easier when the pressures to conform are pervasive. (Rosenblatt, 1964, summarized in Burk, 1976, pp. 21-22)

High levels of ethnocentrism and nationalism are functional when they satisfy needs in the lives of group members and when the in-group is strengthened or becomes more cohesive, according to Burk (1976). Using Katz's (1960) terminology, an ethnocentric attitude serves all four functions. The utilitarian function involves the notion that if we are highly ethnocentric, we tend to conform to our culture and, thus, be in a better position to obtain its rewards. Ethnocentrism also helps us to protect ourselves from uncomfortable things about ourselves (e.g., we can put down parts of another culture, thereby elevating the qualities of our own). An ethnocentric attitude also serves a value-expressive function. Specifically, this attitude allows us to express our values as the true and correct ones to hold. Finally, ethnocentrism serves the knowledge function; it allows us to structure a set of beliefs about people in other cultures based on our own culture.

High levels of ethnocentrism and nationalism are also dysfunctional. Burk (1976) argues that the extremes of these attitudes are dysfunctional when they lead to hostility and conflict with out-group members. "When the ingroup feeling develops to the extent that the members of a particular society feel their way of life is so superior to all others that it is their duty to change other people to their way of thinking and doing (if necessary by force), then this attitude becomes a menace" (Holmes, 1965, p. 347). Thus, high levels of ethnocentrism and nationalism are one cause of wars. In the words of Catton (1961), "it is not asserted that ethnocentrism is *the* cause of war; it is only being hypothesized that ethnocentrism is *a* factor which enables homo sapiens to engage in war despite rational considerations to the contrary" (p. 205).

The preceding discussion of dysfunctions is focused on the group level of analysis. On the individual level, a high level of ethnocentrism is also dysfunctional with respect to successful communication with strangers. Specifically, a high level of ethnocentrism leads to misperception of members of out-groups; this misperception causes us to make inaccurate attributions about strangers' behavior. In other words, a high level of ethnocentrism leads us to interpret strangers' behavior using our own cultural frame of reference, thereby possibly distorting the meaning of the strangers' behavior. If we do not understand strangers' behavior, effective communication is probably impossible.

Ethnophaulisms

When high levels of ethnocentrism exist, the members of the in-group communicate their hostile view of the out-group through name-calling and slurs, or ethnophaulisms. Ehrlich (1973) specifies three types of ethnophaulisms: (1) ethnic names used as mild disparagement (e.g., "Irish confetti," "Jewbird"); (2) explicit group devaluations (e.g., "luck of the Irish," "Jew him down"); and (3) disparaging nicknames (e.g., "Polack," "jungle bunny," "honky"). If you are familiar with the television program "All in the Family," you will recognize that Archie Bunker used all of these three types of ethnophaulisms.

Although the use of ethnophaulisms is an important aspect of our communication with strangers, little research on such use exists. Research by Palmore (1962) indicates that all racial and ethnic groups use ethnophaulisms and they usually express unfavorable stereotypes. His study also reveals that when ethnophaulisms are directed toward other races, physical characteristics generally are highlighted. On the other hand, when ethnophaulisms are directed toward people from the same racial group, highly visible cultural differences usually are highlighted. Further, the number of ethnophaulisms we use is closely related to the degree of our ethnocentrism and the use of ethnophaulisms can intensify our ethnocentrism. Palmore concludes, "We may discover that ethnophaulisms are essential for the existence of such forms of ethnocentrism as chauvinism, perjorative stereotypes, scapegoats, segregation, and discrimination" (p. 445).

A consequence of ethnocentrism: Communicative distance

The attitudes we hold influence the way we speak to other people. The speed with which we talk or the accent we use may be varied in order to generate different feelings of distance between us and strangers with whom we communicate (i.e., to make the distance seem smaller or greater). Peng (1974) uses the concept of "communicative distance" to explain this linguistic diversity:

> A communicative distance cannot be measured directly. It is not even visible. But we can be sure of its presence when we hear certain words or expressions. In other words, our awareness of a communicative distance in the midst of a conversation depends to a large extent on certain linguistic devices which serve, from the speaker's point of view, to set up the communicative distance, or from the hearer's point of view, to let the hearer know that it has already been set up by the speaker. (p. 33)

Lukens (1978) expands Peng's conceptualization of communicative distance to cover "ethnocentric speech," which is reflected in three communicative distances: (1) the distance of indifference, (2) the distance of avoidance, and (3) the distance of disparagement. Lukens goes on:

In essence, speech in accordance with the three communicative distances may be used: (1) to demonstrate lack of concern for persons of other cultures and reflect an insensitivity to cultural differences (the distance of indifference), (2) to avoid or limit the amount of interaction with outgroups (the distance of avoidance), and (3) to demonstrate feelings of hostility towards outgroups and to deride or belittle them (the distance of disparagement). (p. 41)

Lukens associates each of the three distances with a different level of ethnocentrism (low, moderate, and high, respectively).

The distance of indifference, according to Lukens (1978), is the speech form used to "reflect the view that one's own culture is the center of everything" (p. 42). This distance, therefore, reflects an insensitivity to strangers' perspectives. One example of the speech used at this distance is "foreigner talk," the form of speech used when talking to people who are not native speakers of a language. It usually takes the form of loud and slow speech patterns, exaggerated pronounciation, and simplification (e.g., deletion of articles). Downs (1971) points out, "We tend to believe that, if we speak slowly enough or loudly enough, anyone can understand us. I have done this myself quite without realizing it, and others have tried to reach me in the same way in Japanese, Chinese, Thai, Punjabi, Navajo, Spanish, Tibetian, and Singhalese" (p. 19).

According to Lukens (1978), the distance of avoidance is established in order to avoid or minimize contact with members of an out-group. One technique commonly used to accomplish this is the use of an in-group dialect. "The emphasizing of an ethnic dialect and other linguistic differences between the ingroup and outsiders may be purposefully used by ingroup members to make themselves appear esoteric to the outgroup thus lessening the likelihood for interaction" (p. 45). At this distance members of the in-group also may use terms of solidarity. Feelings of cultural pride and solidarity are increased through the use of such terms as "black power," "black is beautiful," and "red power." In establishing this distance, jargon common to the in-group is used extensively.

The distance of disparagement, according to Lukens (1978), reflects animosity of the in-group toward the out-group. It arises when the two groups are in competition for the same resources. This level is characterized by the use of perjorative expressions and ethnophaulisms. Lukens indicates that at this distance imitation and mockery of speech styles are characteristic.

Communicative distances and cultural relativism

Before concluding our discussion of ethnocentrism, we want to point out one shortcoming of Lukens's (1978) conceptualization of communicative distances. While we agree that the three levels of communicative distance are manifested in speech patterns and are based on differing levels of ethnocentrism, we believe the trichotomy is incomplete as it now stands.

In Chapter 1 we implied that the attitude of ethnocentrism is only "one side of the coin," the other side being the attitude of cultural relativism. Cultural relativism, as you recall, involves the view that all cultures are of equal value and the values and behavior of a culture can only be judged using that culture as a frame of reference. Often ethnocentrism and cultural relativism are discussed separately, are seen as two distinct attitudes. In contrast, we believe ethnocentrism and cultural relativism are opposite sides of the same coin. If we adopt this view, a high level of ethnocentrism and a high level of cultural relativism can be seen as opposite end points of an attitudinal continuum. We can label at least five different points on the continuum: high ethnocentrism, moderate ethnocentrism, low ethnocentrism/low cultural relativism, moderate cultural relativism, and high cultural relativism. Each of these five points should be reflected in a different level of communicative distance. Luken's (1978) analysis addresses the first three, but not the last two.

The level of moderate cultural relativism reflects none of the characteristics of Lukens's three distances. Rather, this level reveals a sensitivity to cultural differences. The speech at this level reflects our desire to decrease the communicative distance between ourselves and strangers. This distance might best be labeled the *distance of sensitivity.* The level of high cultural relativism reflects our desire to minimize the distance between ourselves and strangers. This distance involves an attitude of equality, one where we demonstrate we are interpreting the language and behavior of strangers in terms of their culture. This distance might best be labeled the *distance of equality.*

Prejudice

Prejudice: The attitude

The term prejudice stems from the Latin word *praejudicium,* which, according to Allport (1954), means a precedent, or "a judgment based on previous decisions and experiences" (p. 7). From this beginning the meaning of the term prejudice has gone through several transformations. First, it acquired the connotation of a judgment formed before a due examination of the facts, or what might be called a premature judgment. Next, points out Allport, prejudice acquired a connotation of favorableness or unfavorableness accompanying the prejudgment. Although prejudice can involve either a pro or a con bias, ethnic prejudice generally is negative. With this view, Allport defines negative ethnic prejudice as "an antipathy based on a faulty and unflexible generalization. It may be felt or expressed. It may be directed toward a group as a whole, or toward an individual because he is a member of that group" (p. 10). Obviously, the generalization on which the prejudice is based may be a stereotype.

People who are highly prejudiced tend to ignore information not consistent with their faulty and inflexible generalization. Allport (1954) presents an excellent example of the process used by a highly prejudiced person when confronted with contradictory information:

> *Mr. X:* The trouble with Jews is that they only take care of their own group.
>
> *Mr. Y:* But the record of the Community Chest campaign shows that they give more generously, in proportion to their numbers, to the charities of the community, than do non-Jews.
>
> *Mr. X:* That shows they are always trying to buy favor and intrude into Christian affairs. They think of nothing but money; that is why there are so many Jewish bankers.
>
> *Mr. Y:* But a recent study shows that the percentage of Jews in the banking business is negligible, far smaller than the percentage of non-Jews.
>
> *Mr. X:* That's just it; they don't go in for respectable business; they are only in the movie business or run night clubs. (pp. 13–14)

Thus, highly prejudiced people tend to alter their beliefs to justify their attitude when confronted with contradictory information. Allport refers to this process as rationalization.

What if people changed their minds after being confronted with accurate information? Allport (1954) argues "errors of prejudgment" are different from prejudice. If people do not change a prejudgment when given new information, they are prejudiced; however, if they rectify an erroneous prejudgment on the basis of the new information, they are not prejudiced, according to Allport.

Many writers discuss the attitude of prejudice as a dichotomy—a person is either prejudiced or not prejudiced. We believe such a view oversimplifies the discussion. Prejudice, like any other attitude, can best be conceptualized as varying by degrees or amounts. This means every person has some degree of prejudice. Brislin (1979) takes a similar view when he specifies six forms of prejudice: (1) red-neck prejudice, (2) symbolic prejudice, (3) tokenism, (4) arm's-length prejudice, (5) real likes and dislikes, and (6) the familiar and unfamiliar.* In Brislin's conceptualization, the six forms of prejudice range from high (red-neck prejudice) to low (familiar and unfamiliar).

Red-neck prejudice exists when members of an in-group believe members of an out-group are inferior according to some standard imposed by the in-group. Symbolic prejudice involves the members of an in-group having negative feelings about members of an out-group because they perceive the out-group as threatening their basic values. Tokenism also involves negative feelings about the out-group; however, at this level the in-group members do not want to admit to themselves they are prejudiced. According to Brislin (1979), people who hold a level of prejudice of tokenism engage in positive intergroup behaviors that are actually unimportant. Arm's-length prejudice involves members of the in-group engaging in positive behaviors toward members of the out-group under some

---

*Brislin uses the term racism rather than prejudice for the first two types. We changed the label because racism, as it usually is used, denotes prejudice aimed only at a racial group.

circumstances, but holding them at arm's length under other circumstances. Brislin contends that usually people who hold this attitude act friendly to members of out-groups in semiformal situations (e.g., casual friendships, formal dinners), but act more unfriendly in more intimate situations (e.g., dating, conversing with neighbors). Prejudice in the form of real likes and dislikes, according to Brislin, involves members of an in-group having negative feelings about members of an out-group because the members of the out-group actually engage in behaviors they dislike. Brislin believes this category is necessary because people do have real likes and dislikes that can be expressed without basing their judgments on group membership. Brislin's final form of prejudice, the familiar and unfamiliar, reflects a low level of prejudice. When members of one group come into contact with those from another group, they are inevitably uncomfortable and, therefore, prefer to interact with people of their own group (such interaction is more comfortable and less stressful). Brislin suggests, and we agree, that such an attitude reflects a low level of prejudice but is still prejudice.

Functions of prejudice

Prejudice, like ethnocentrism, is functional for people who hold the attitude. Brislin (1979) examines the functions of prejudice using Katz's (1960) scheme. The first function prejudice performs is to help us either to avoid punishment or to obtain rewards in our culture (utilitarian function). Brislin (1979) presents an example of this function when he points out "people want to be well liked by others in their culture. If such esteem is dependent upon rejecting members of a certain group, then it is likely that people will indeed reject members of the outgroup" (p. 29).

The second function prejudice performs is to protect us from information that might damage our self-image (ego-defensive function). To illustrate how prejudice fulfills this function Brislin (1979) refers to people who are not successful in their chosen occupation. If they are highly prejudiced, they can blame their lack of success on members of the out-group (who may be seen as a bunch of cheaters), rather than admit to any personal inadequacies.

Another function that prejudice performs is to allow us to express important aspects of our lives (value-expressive function). An example of this can be drawn from religion. As Brislin (1979) points out, people of one religion may react negatively toward members of another religion "because they see themselves as standing up for the one true God (as defined by their religion)" (p. 30).

The final function that prejudice serves is to assist us in organizing the world around us (knowledge function). Prejudice allows us to behave in accordance with the categories we have constructed, rather than on the basis of the actual incoming stimuli. In his book *The Social Animal,* Aronson (1972) provides an excellent example of how highly prejudiced people interpret incoming stimuli so that they are consistent with their attitude:

Prejudiced people see the world in ways that are consistent with their prejudice. If Mr. Bigot sees a well-dressed, white, Anglo-Saxon Protestant sitting on a park bench sunning himself at three o'clock on a Wednesday afternoon, he thinks nothing of it. If he sees a well-dressed black man doing the same thing, he is liable to leap to the conclusion that the person is unemployed — and he becomes infuriated, because he assumes that his hard-earned taxes are paying that shiftless good-for-nothing enough in welfare subsidies to keep him in good clothes. If Mr. Bigot passes Mr. Anglo's house and notices that a trash can is overturned and some garbage is strewn about, he is apt to conclude that a stray dog has been searching for food. If he passes Mr. Garcia's house and notices the same thing, he is inclined to become annoyed, and to assert that "those people live like pigs." Not only does prejudice influence his conclusions, his erroneous conclusions justify and intensify his negative feelings. (p. 174)

Thus, the attributions we make about strangers are influenced by the attitudes we hold about the groups to which they belong.

Prejudice and discrimination

From the above it should be obvious that prejudice is an attitude, a predisposition to behave in a certain way. It should not be confused with its behavioral counterpart, discrimination. Williams (1947) defines discrimination as "the degree that individuals of a given group who are otherwise formally qualified are not treated in conformity with these nominally universal institutionalized codes" (p. 39). In other words, discrimination involves behaving in such a way that members of an out-group are treated disadvantageously.

What is the relationship between prejudice and discrimination? Do highly prejudiced people always discriminate? Do people with a relatively low level of prejudice always engage in nondiscriminatory behavior? If attitudes always guided behavior, then the answer to these two questions would be a simple yes; however, attitudes are not the only factor influencing behavior. A simple yes, therefore, is not sufficient.

Merton (1957) presents a model of the possible relationships between prejudice and discrimination. His model suggests it is conceivable for people who have low levels of prejudice to discriminate under certain circumstances. Merton's model reveals four types of relationships:

1. *The prejudiced discriminator, or "active bigot."* For this group of people there is consistency between attitudes and behavior. Prejudiced discriminators openly express their beliefs about out-groups and openly practice discriminatory behavior.

2. *The prejudiced nondiscriminator, or "timid bigot."* This group's behavior is not consistent with their attitudes. Timid bigots believe many of the

stereotypes about out-groups and also feel hostility toward them, but do not express their beliefs. Timid bigots do not express their beliefs because of their desire to conform and not to violate social norms or laws. If there was no law or social pressure, timid bigots would discriminate.

3. *The nonprejudiced discriminator, or "fair-weather liberal."* Like timid bigots, fair-weather liberals do not behave in accordance with their attitudes. Probably the key word for this group of people is expediency. When people around them discriminate or talk in a prejudicial manner, fair-weather liberals will take the expedient course of action and keep quiet. The major reason for the inconsistency in attitudes and behavior is the social norms of the situation.

4. *The nonprejudiced nondiscriminator, or "all-weather liberal."* There is no inconsistency between the attitudes and behavior of all-weather liberals. Merton argues that this group of people are likely to discuss the issues of prejudice and discrimination with others and will not keep quiet when faced with people who discriminate or talk in a prejudicial manner.

Contact with Strangers and Attitude Change

In the two preceding sections we have discussed two of the major attitudes influencing our communication with strangers. The next issue that needs to be addressed involves the question of whether the attitudes of ethnocentrism and prejudice, once developed, are set for life or if contact with strangers changes attitudes.

The major assumption of the early studies concerning contact with strangers was that contact tends to produce better intergroup attitudes and social relations. There is, however, conflicting evidence on the exact nature of the effect of contact with strangers on intergroup attitudes. Many studies support the assumption that contact with strangers reduces prejudice and increases favorable attitudes, but there is also evidence that contact may not reduce prejudice and that it can even increase tension and cause violence. Because of the divergent nature of these findings, Sherif and Sherif (1953) argue, "In any discussion on the effects of contact on intergroup attitudes, we must specify: what *kind* of contact? contact in what capacity?" (p. 221). This view is reinforced by Amir and Garti (1977): "Clearly, the outcome of ethnic contact depends upon conditions prevailing at the time of the contact, and conditions of both situational and personal nature" (p. 58).

In his review of the kind of contact leading to favorable attitude change, Allport (1954) enumerates four situational factors of critical significance. According to Allport, prejudice is reduced and conflict is minimized when two groups: (1) possess equal status in the contact situation, (2) seek common goals, (3) are cooperatively dependent on each other rather than in competition, and

(4) interact with the positive support of law and custom (pp. 250-270). In a closely related analysis, Cook (1957) presents three similar dimensions for evaluating the contact situation and its potential for positive attitude change: (1) the opportunity that the contact situation offers for personal interaction, (2) the relative status levels of the participants, and (3) the nature of the social norms with respect to contact with strangers.

Since the writings of Allport and Cook, other factors have been found that affect the outcomes of contact with strangers. Based on a thorough review of the literature, Amir (1969) expands the list to include six factors:

> Some of the favorable conditions which tend to reduce prejudice are (a) when there is equal status contact between the members of the various ethnic groups, (b) when the contact is between members of a majority group and *higher* status members of a minority group, (c) when an "authority" and/or social climate are in favor of and promote the intergroup contact, (d) when the contact is of an intimate rather than a casual nature, (e) when the ethnic intergroup contact is pleasant or rewarding, (f) when the members of *both* groups in the particular contact situation interact in functionally important activities or develop common goals or superordinate goals that are higher ranking in importance than the individual goals of each of the groups. (p. 338)

In addition, findings from a study by Amir and Garti (1977) suggest one additional variable is important in influencing the outcomes of contact. Amir and Garti find changes in attitudes to be related to previous contact with strangers. Specifically, only people without previous contact display attitude change as a result of contact with strangers.

The answer to the question posed at the beginning of this section, therefore, is that our attitudes of ethnocentrism and prejudice are not set for life—they can and do change based on our communication with strangers. We can become less ethnocentric and prejudiced if we have contact with strangers under the favorable conditions outlined by Amir (1969). This suggests that if we have contact with strangers under unfavorable conditions (e.g., nonrewarding, superficial contact with strangers of lower status) we must consciously analyze the interaction so it does not increase our prejudice and ethnocentrism. We do not mean to suggest that being ethnocentric and prejudiced is "bad." Holding these attitudes is natural and unavoidable. Rather, we are suggesting that in order to effectively communicate with strangers we must understand their behavior, and in order to understand their behavior we must be able at least to suspend, or to control, our ethnocentrism and prejudice.

SUMMARY

The way we categorize objects and events, the stereotypes we develop, and the attitudes we hold are learned as part of our socialization into our culture and the various groups of which we are members. In turn, how we categorize things, including people, and the attitudes we hold have a major impact on our communication with strangers.

The stereotypes we hold provide the initial predictions we make about strangers' behavior at both the cultural and sociocultural levels. To the degree that our stereotypes are valid, we will be able to make accurate predictions about strangers' behavior. Also, if we are not willing to question our stereotypes, we will never be able to make psychocultural predictions about strangers. In other words, if our stereotypes are rigidly held, we will never get to know strangers as individuals.

Because cultural differences usually are very salient in our interactions with strangers, we tend to attribute the cause of strangers' behavior to cultural traits. While such a tendency may, at times, be warranted, often it is not. Strangers often behave the way they do because of situational demands or individual traits. Attributing strangers' behavior to their culture, therefore, can lead us to misinterpret their behavior and to make inaccurate predictions regarding the future behavior of either the same strangers or other strangers from the same culture.

The stereotypes we form and the attributions we make are related closely to the attitudes we hold. The two major attitudes influencing our communication with strangers are prejudice and ethnocentrism. High levels of either of these attitudes lead us to misinterpret strangers' behavior. Being very ethnocentric, for example, impels us to interpret strangers' behavior using our own cultural standards. This tendency inevitably causes us to misinterpret strangers' behavior and to make inaccurate predictions about their behavior, thereby increasing the likelihood of misunderstandings. Since it is natural for everyone to be prejudiced and ethnocentric to some degree, we must consciously control our attitudinal responses if we are to effectively communicate with strangers.

6
Environmental
Influences
on the Process

*Living organisms can be understood only when
they are considered as part of the system within
which they function. This is particularly true of us
human beings because all aspects of our lives are
profoundly influenced by an immense diversity
of physical and cultural forces which shape our
bodies, our behaviors and the social structure to
which we must relate in order to become fully
human.*

René Dubos

The purpose of this chapter is to complete our examination of the major influences on our communication behavior. In the preceding three chapters we looked at the cultural, sociocultural, and psychocultural influences on our communication with strangers. In this chapter we examine the environmental influences on our communication behavior.

The environment in which interaction occurs obviously influences the communication taking place. These influences, however, are generally outside of our awareness. The environmental impact on behavior is so strong Lewin (1936) includes it as one of the two factors in his definition of behavior: $B = f(P,E)$, where B = behavior, P = person, and E = environment. In other words, Lewin believes the behavior in which we engage is a function of us and the person with whom we are communicating, as well as of the environment within which the interaction takes place. In Lewin's analysis the environment is divided into the physical environment and the psychological environment, or what people think about the physical environment. Both aspects of the environment influence communication. To illustrate the influence of the psychological environment, we need only look at the research on the impact of different types of rooms on behavior. According to Saarinen (1948), when we enter a room, we rarely feel indifferent about it. Research by Mintz (1956) suggests prolonged exposure to an "ugly" room brings about such reactions "as monotony, fatigue, headache, sleep, discontent, irritability, hostility, and avoidance of the room" (p. 466). On the other hand, exposure to a "beautiful" room brings about "feelings of comfort, pleasure, enjoyment, importance, energy, and a desire to continue [the] activity" (p. 466).

The physical setting in which communication occurs defines what is proper. Obviously, such settings as an office behind closed doors, an elevator, a living room, a bedroom, and a formal dining room suggest different forms of communication within any particular culture. People within a culture are taught during the socialization process what it is appropriate to talk about in each of these different settings. As Deutsch (1954) observes, "it is evident that behavior settings are 'coercive' primarily because there exist shared frames of reference of collective action as to what is appropriate behavior in a given behavior setting or with a given behavior-object" (p. 194). (The preceding should not be taken to suggest the same communication cannot occur in different settings, because it can and does.) The setting in which the communication occurs also performs the additional function of defining boundaries about how to interpret messages. The same message transmitted in different settings can have two entirely different meanings. For example, a physician asking a member of the opposite sex to remove his or her clothes means one thing in the physician's office, but an entirely different thing in a bedroom; only the context tells the receiver how to interpret the message. A "social act is always interpreted in relation to some normative context" (Deutsch, 1961, p. 398).

With respect to communication with strangers, the physical setting takes on increased importance for at least two reasons. First, what is appropriate behavior in a particular setting can differ across cultures. In some cultures (e.g., the United States), for example, being in the living room of a home calls for informal conversation, while in other cultures (e.g., Colombia) being in the living room calls for formal behavior. Second, when we communicate with strangers, the strangers are often in a physical setting unfamiliar to them. The strangers, therefore, may not know what behavior is expected in that setting.

Given the above distinction, we divide our discussion of the environmental influences on our communication with strangers into two categories: physical and psychological. The physical environment, as we are using the term, includes geography, climate, landscape, and architecture. The psychological environment includes our perceptions of the physical environment, our perceptual and cognitive beliefs about the environment, and how we use the environment when we interact with one another.

PHYSICAL ENVIRONMENT

Geography and Climate

Few anthropologists would disagree "with the general statement that environment is an important conditioner of culture" (Meggers, 1954, p. 801). But how does the environment influence the development of culture? Meggers argues, "The primary point of interaction between a culture and its environment is in terms of subsistence, and the most vital aspect of environment from the point of view of culture is its suitability for food production" (p. 802). In other words, the geography in which a culture exists influences how the people obtain food. Since food can be imported, people in a culture are not limited to the food they can produce. The geographical location of a culture also has other influences. "It would seem almost obvious that mountains or flat terrain, barren or fertile land, and the availability of resources, particularly of water, would affect human institutions and thereby alter the forms of social behavior" (Barnlund, 1968, p. 512).

Another factor in the physical environment closely associated with geography is climate, including temperature and humidity. Climatic factors have subtle influences on behavior. For example, it often is pointed out that the murder rates in the United States increase during the summer months when the temperature and humidity rise. Climate also influences the frequency and the form of the interactions taking place in a culture. Some cultures, for example, exist in climates so hot and muggy that it is impossible to do business during certain parts of the day. People from a more moderate climate must make adjustments if they are to cope with the differences.

Architecture and Landscape

Those aspects of the environment constructed by the human population of a culture provide an additional influence on communication behavior. To borrow an analogy from the theatre, the architecture and landscape, combined with the geography and climate, provide the stage for the human players. "The streets of Calcutta, the avenues of Brazilia, the Left Bank of Paris, the gardens of Kyoto, the slums of Chicago, and the canyons of lower Manhattan provide dramatically different backgrounds for human interaction" (Barnlund, 1968, p. 512). The physical structure of buildings, as well as the way they are decorated, is influenced by culture and also influences the interaction occurring within them. Winston Churchill often is quoted as saying, "We shape our buildings, and afterwards our buildings shape us." A conversation on the same topic held in an adobe house in New Mexico and a Japanese house in Kyoto will, in all likelihood, not be the same. Many aspects of architecture and landscape vary across cultures; however, we focus here on the aspect most central to people's lives—housing.

Rapoport (1969) argues that while the physical environment influences the way houses are designed and constructed, the design of houses also is influenced by the culture in which they are built. Human shelter varies from buildings with one room to structures with several hundred. Not only do the physical aspects of houses (e.g., construction material, size, shape, layout of rooms) differ across cultures, but how the house and its parts are defined and perceived also varies. For example, is the house a place where visitors are entertained, or is it reserved for only close friends and family? Do certain rooms in the house have a single function (e.g., sleeping), or is the same room used for several different functions (e.g., sleeping, eating, and entertaining guests)? There is obviously tremendous variation in the construction and perception of houses within any one culture; however, there are many similarities that remain relatively constant. These similarities may not be obvious until houses based on other cultural assumptions are confronted. In order to illustrate cross-cultural variations in housing, we look at Japanese, Arab, German, and Latin American homes.

Most houses in the United States distinguish particular rooms to fill specific functions (e.g., eating in the dining room, sleeping in the bedroom). The traditional Japanese home, in contrast, does not make these distinctions. The same room often is used for dining, entertaining, and sleeping. This is accomplished through the use of very little furniture in Japanese homes. Rooms are separated by sliding walls (those made with rice paper are called *shoji*), rather than by fixed walls as in the United States. Thus, in a Japanese home people cannot generally go into their own room and lock the door to be alone. Floors in a Japanese home are covered with straw mats (*tatami*); therefore, people remove their shoes upon entering a house.

What furniture there is in a Japanese home usually is found in the center of the room rather than around the edges as in the United States. The multipurpose room usually has one single low table, which is used for many purposes (e.g., studying, eating). Rather than sitting in chairs by the table, Japanese sit on cushions that can be moved easily when it is time for the room to change its function. For example, when it is time to sleep, the table and cushions are removed, thick sleeping mats (*futons*) are laid out, and the room becomes a bedroom.

While the Japanese tend not to make the distinctions made in the United States among dining room, living room, and bedroom, they do make a distinction between the bath and toilet. In the United States the bath and toilet are found in the same room, while in Japan the two rooms are separate. The bath (*ofuro*) is only for bathing (becoming clean), not for the "dirty" function of using the toilet (*otearai*).

In contrast to Japanese homes, Arab homes tend to have a lot of space, very high ceilings, and unobstructed views (Hall, 1966). The desire for an unobstructed view is so strong that one way to "get even" with neighbors is to obstruct the view from their home. Hall (1966) points to a structure built by a person in Beirut that is several stories high but only four feet wide. The house is referred to as the "spite house" by local residents because it was built for the purpose of punishing neighbors by blocking their view of the Mediterranean.

Like people in the United States, but unlike the Japanese, Arabs tend to entertain guests in their homes. The amount and type of contact guests have in a house, however, is determined by their relationship with the family. In a "typical" Arab home all rooms look alike, with the function of each room decided by the family, but one room usually is set aside for entertaining guests. In this room the family displays heirlooms, souvenirs, and the best furnishings (Condon and Yosef, 1975). Guests who are not longtime friends usually are entertained only in this room and may never see any other part of the house. By entertaining guests in the most formal part of the home and introducing them only to selected family members, "the guest is honored and the family status is reflected" (Condon and Yosef, 1975, p. 160). As guests become accepted by the family, they may see other parts of the house. Indicators of this change in status, according to Condon and Yosef, are increases in the length of visits and meeting family members of the opposite sex. (Arabs may be friends for years without meeting family members of the opposite sex).

German homes differ somewhat from the other houses discussed here in that they tend to be surrounded by hedges and fences in order to ensure privacy, a pervasive value in German life (Condon and Yosef, 1975). "The ideal German home has a foyer or entryway that leads visitors into the house without exposing them to specific rooms and a resultant loss of privacy for the family members" (Condon and Yosef, 1975, p. 165). The most formal room in the house is the living room (*Wohnsimmer*), which is used for entertaining guests. Unlike children in the United States, German children who are old enough to greet guests are expected to come into the living room when a guest arrives and remain for the length of the visit, speaking only when spoken to.

A "typical" German home, like a "typical" German office, is characterized by large furniture and heavy doors (Hall, 1966). The large furniture, according to Hall, is used so guests will not be tempted to move the furniture and change the order of the room. A heavy door performs two functions. First, because of its weight, the door serves a soundproofing function when closed, thus fulfilling the German desire for privacy. Second, since the door is typically closed, in both homes and offices, it preserves the "integrity of the room and provides a protective boundary between people" (Hall, 1966, p. 136).

The final type of house to be examined here is the Latin American home, more specifically, Colombian homes in Bogotá. The "typical" middle-class Colombian home is built much closer to the street than is the "typical" North American home, according to Gorden (1974). Generally, the front yard is very small, while the backyard is large and enclosed with a high fence. Each house abuts the houses on both sides of it. In other words, there is no yard space between houses; only double walls separate houses. This pattern of constructing houses is obviously different from the common one in North America, but the two different patterns appear to be aimed at the same goal—privacy. Gorden observes: "Privacy in the United States is obtained by increasing the open space between a person and his neighbor, while in Bogotá it is achieved by abutting walls with no doors or windows" (p. 16).

Colombians tend to invite kinfolk into their homes, but not co-workers or neighbors. People may work side by side for years, and live near each other, but never see the inside of each other's homes. The house, according to Gorden (1974), "is more strictly a family thing in the sense of a tendency to exclude nonrelatives and to include relatives beyond the nuclear family" (pp. 22–23).

The various rooms in a Colombian home have different functions than do the same rooms in a North American home. The living room, for example, in a Colombian home is a formal room not used for family gatherings. On the other hand, a bedroom may be used for family gatherings and entertaining friends. In discussing problems North Americans had when living with Colombian host families, Gorden (1974) points out:

> Some misunderstandings between the American guest and the Colombian host hinge upon the basic difference in their assumptions regarding the function of a bedroom. Both cultures accept the bedroom as a place to sleep, to make conjugal love, and to read, but beyond that there is little agreement. The American thinks of it (particularly when he is in a foreign country) as a place to retreat, to find privacy, to study, to listen to records. The Colombian host families did not agree on all these things. The senora thinks of her bedroom as being a place to socialize with her friends, to watch television with members of the family and with friends. (p. 51)

North Americans taking refuge in their bedroom, therefore, often are perceived as "aloof" by the Colombian host family.

PSYCHOLOGICAL ENVIRONMENT

As we indicated earlier, the psychological environment refers to our perceptual and cognitive beliefs about the physical environment and how we use the physical environment where we interact with one another. Ittelson (1973) argues there are at least five levels at which we relate to the surrounding environment: (1) we have feelings about the environment, (2) we are oriented spatially within the environment, (3) we categorize phenomena in the environment, (4) we organize the environment in terms of relationships among its features, and (5) we manipulate the environment. Each of these levels can influence our behavior. Some writers, in fact, believe the psychological environment is more important than the physical environment in influencing behavior. For example, the renowned biologist René Dubos (1981) observes:

In addition to the influences that reach us from the outside—the world external to us—there are other influences that exist in the individual mind of each of us and that constitute our private conceptual environment. Whether primitive or poorly informed, or sophisticated and learned, each one of us lives as it were in a private world of his own. In fact, the conceptual environment may be more important than the external environment because it affects all aspects of our lives. (p. 31)

Although there is very little cross-cultural research on differences in psychological environments, there is some relevant work that can be examined. In this section we look at three aspects of the psychological environment: postulates as they relate to the environment, perceptions of privacy, and the use of time.

Postulates

In Chapter 3 we introduced Kluckhohn and Strodtbeck's (1960) conceptualization of value orientations. One of the value orientations involves the perceived relationship between humans and the environment. In this conceptualization there are three possible relationships between humans and the environment: (1) people are subjugated to nature, (2) people exist in harmony with nature, and (3) people dominate nature.

The mastery-over-nature view tends to predominate in industrialized societies with a Judeo-Christian heritage. According to this view, humans are not just another object in the world, but a special type of being of divine origin (Ittelson, Proshansky, Rivlin, and Winkel, 1974). Because of their special status, humans are obligated to control, alter, and shape the environment. In other words, all natural forces can and should be overcome and put to the use of human beings. Nature is controlled through the use of technology and radical agriculture (e.g., putting bridges over rivers, damming up rivers to collect water, digging wells, moving mountains). This view tends to predominate in most Western cultures. In contrast, most Eastern cultures are characterized by the harmony-with-nature view. In most Eastern philosophies humans are seen as an intrinsic element in nature, with no real separation of human life, nature, and the supernatural—each is seen as an extension of the others. People are to be treated as a part of nature in the same sense that animals and plants are. An excellent example of this view is given by Turnbull (1961) in his classic book *The Forest People*. Turnbull points out that the Pygmies of Zaire see the forest in which they live as a living thing of which they are just one part. He illustrates this point by quoting one Pygmy: "The forest is a father and mother to us, and like a father and mother it gives us everything we need, food, clothing, shelter, warmth, . . . and affection. Normally everything goes well, because the forest is good to its children. But when things go wrong, there must be a reason" (p. 92).

These differences in the perceived relationship between people and their environment have an impact on the way people communicate, especially when a person from one culture is working as an agent for social change in another culture (e.g., a Peace Corps volunteer from the United States in a culture that has a harmony-with-nature orientation). For example, people in some cultures would not understand why one would want to build a dam to stop the flow of water in a river; in their view this is not natural since it would destroy the harmony with the river.

Privacy

The concept of privacy is intertwined closely with our perceptions of the environment. Altman (1975) defines privacy as the "selective control of access to the self or to one's group" (p. 18). Thus, privacy is a mechanism that allows us to control our interaction with others. Altman differentiates between desired privacy, "how much or how little contact is desired at some moment in time," and achieved privacy, "the actual degree of contact that results from interaction with others" (p. 10). To the extent desired and achieved privacy match, we have controlled the interaction.

From the above definition it should be obvious that there is more than one type of privacy. Westin (1970) outlines four types of privacy: solitude, intimacy, anonymity, and reserve. Solitude, according to Westin, is when we are alone and cannot be observed by others, while intimacy occurs when a dyad or small group of people separate themselves from others to be alone. When we are "lost in a crowd," not expecting to be recognized by others, Westin says we are anonymous. The final type of privacy, reserve, involves "the creation of a psychological barrier against unwanted intrusion" (Westin, 1970, p. 32).

In the United States privacy often is regulated through the use of closed doors. A closed door—whether it leads to a bedroom, den, office, or bathroom—sends the message "leave me alone!" (Altman, 1975). People in the United States, according to Altman, tend to use other physical barriers (e.g., fences, hedges) in addition to doors as enforcers of privacy. This is not necessarily the case in some other cultures. Hall (1966) observes that people in England do not tend to have private offices; instead, they conduct their business in open spaces. Privacy is achieved by speaking softly and by directing one's voice carefully, not by closing doors.

Privacy in many cultures is regulated psychologically, rather than through the use of an environmental barrier. To illustrate, Geertz points out that in Java it is impossible to regulate privacy through manipulation of the environment because the people do not put up physical barriers between themselves and outsiders. To North Americans, therefore, it often appears that there is no privacy at all in a Javanese household. This is not the case, however. Geertz describes the situation as follows:

. . . people speak softly, hide their feelings and even in the bosom of a Javanese family you have the feeling that you are in a public square and must
behave with appropriate decorum. Javanese people shut people out with a
wall of decorum, . . . with emotional restraint, and with a general lack of
candor in both speech and behavior. It is not, in short, that the Javanese do
not wish or value privacy; but merely that because they put up no physical
or social barriers against the physical ingress of outsiders into their household life they must put up psychological ones and surround themselves with
barriers of a different sort. (Cited in Westin, 1970, p. 16)

Thus, Javanese privacy regulation can be described as "reserve," using Westin's
four categories.

Altman (1975) and Altman and Chemers (1980a) argue that while the specific mechanisms for privacy vary across cultures, every culture has some method
for regulating it. Privacy regulation can, therefore, be considered a "cultural
universal," according to these writers.

Privacy also is regulated through the use of territory. The concept of territory, as it is used in social science, is very similar to its everyday usage (e.g., "my
turf"). "Territorial behavior is a self/other boundary-regulation mechanism that
involves personalization of or marking of a place or object and communication
that it is 'owned' by a person or group" (Altman, 1975, p. 107). In other words,
territorial behavior is the personalizing of an area in order to regulate communication. Perception of what constitutes "owned" territory obviously can vary
across cultures. Hall (1966) illustrates this by comparing the use of territorial
boundaries in Germany and the United States. For example, if you are standing
on the porch of a house with the screen door closed, you are considered to be
"outside" the house in the United States. Similarly, if you "poke" your head
into the door of an office, you still are considered to be outside the office. In
Germany the person in both of these situations is considered to be "inside,"
or within the other person's territory. Germans, according to Hall, consider
people to be inside their territory if they can *see* inside; if you can see, you are
intruding.

One final aspect of privacy that must be mentioned briefly is the issue of
crowding. Crowding is different from density. Density of population involves
the concentration of people within a certain geographical area (e.g., the number
of people per square mile). It is a physical indicator with no psychological meaning. Crowding, on the other hand, is a psychological phenomenon; it is the subjective feeling associated with too little space. Following Altman's definition
of privacy, "crowding occurs when a privacy regulation system malfunctions,
such that more social contact occurs than was originally desired" (Altman and
Chemers, 1980a, p. 374). Altman and Chemers argue that when crowding is perceived, psychological stress is generated. This stress, in turn, motivates us to
make increased attempts to return to the desired level of social interaction.

Although there is yet no research across cultures comparing responses to crowding, a few general observations can be made. People in some cultures have developed coping mechanisms for dealing with high levels of population density. For example, the Japanese have a very high population density (a population approximately one half of that of the United States in a geographical area about the size of Montana), which requires the development of sophisticated coping mechanisms. One of these mechanisms is to treat people who are encountered in public but who are unknown as "nonpersons," that is, as if they were not there. This is accomplished through the use of psychological methods of privacy regulation rather than physical methods.

One major problem in communicating with strangers occurs when a person from a culture using physical methods of privacy regulation visits, lives, or works in a culture using psychological methods of privacy regulation. A North American visiting Japan, for example, invariably feels crowded and evaluates the people as being "pushy" or having no concern for others, when in fact they just have a different privacy regulation system.

Temporality

The final aspect of the psychological environment to be discussed here is the temporal nature of social life. In Chapter 3 we introduced Kluckhohn and Strodtbeck's (1960) time orientation. According to this view, one of three orientations toward time tends to predominate in a culture: past, present, or future. The past orientation predominates in cultures placing an emphasis on tradition, while the present orientation predominates when people pay relatively little attention to the past and to what might happen in the future. A future orientation predominates when change is valued highly and the future is seen as "bigger and better." Although all of these orientations may exist in any one culture, one of them does tend to be predominant. Like all cultural postulates, a people's orientation toward time tends to be unconscious, taken for granted, or outside of their awareness until a different cultural system is confronted.

In addition to their time orientation, cultures develop temporal patterns of life. These patterns define when it is appropriate to do certain things (e.g., sleep, eat, arrive for meetings), as well as how many things it is appropriate to do at the same time. Hall (1959) distinguishes between monochronic and polychronic time patterns. Monochronic time involves compartmentalization; people compartmentalize their time and schedule one event at a time. In contrast, polychronic time does not involve compartmentalization; people tend to engage in several activities at the same time. Hall equates the use of monochronic time with cultures characterized by low levels of involvement among people and the use of polychronic time with cultures characterized by high levels of involvement among people. Cultures like those of the United States and most of Europe, which are characterized by low levels of involvement among their people, tend to have compartmentalized time schedules. On the other hand, cultures like those of Latin America and of the Arab states, which are characterized by high levels of involvement among their people, tend to use polychronic time patterns in which several activities are scheduled for the same time. Members of the United States Foreign Service assigned to an Arab country for the first time are bound to feel "insulted" when they arrive for a meeting with their Arab counterpart and find several other people in the counterpart's office doing business at the same time. There is, however, no reason to feel insulted; they have just encountered a different time pattern.

Another aspect of culture varying across cultures involves the time of arrival for appointments. Hall (1959) differentiates five time intervals for arriving late for appointments: (1) "mumble something" period, (2) slight apology period, (3) mildly insulting period, (4) rude period, and (5) downright insulting period. In the United States, for example, if you are 5 minutes late for an appointment, you mumble something about why you were late and that is sufficient. If you are 10 to 15 minutes late, you would probably make a slight apology to the person with whom you have the appointment. If you are 45 to 60 minutes late for an appointment, you are being downright insulting (and probably should get down on your knees and beg for forgiveness). Other cultures are not as time conscious as the United States. In Latin American and Arab cultures time is treated differently. It is not unusual for a person to be 45 minutes late for an appointment; however, this period is not considered an insult but is seen as falling into the "mumble something" category. A North American who has an appointment to do business in Latin America often finds this "cavalier" attitude toward time frustrating; similarly, a Latin American doing business in North America finds the more "rigid" time schedule frustrating.

SUMMARY

The environment and our perceptions of the environment influence our communication with strangers, as well as our communication as strangers. The physical environment—including geography, climate, landscape, and architecture—has an impact on our feelings, emotions, and attitudes, which in turn influence our communication behavior. In addition, certain aspects of the physical environment have a direct impact on the predictions we make about others' behavior and the way we interpret incoming stimuli. For example, a North American exchange student (a stranger) visiting a Colombian family in the living room of their home probably would predict informal behavior is called for in that setting and would act accordingly. Such a prediction, however, would not be accurate since the living room in a Colombian home is set aside for formal behavior. In order to make accurate predictions and correctly interpret incoming stimuli, we must know how the person with whom we are communicating defines the setting in which our communication is taking place. This is necessary when we are communicating with strangers on our "home turf," as well as when we are strangers on others' "home turf."

Our perceptions of the environment also have a direct impact on how we interpret incoming stimuli and make predictions about others' behavior. For example, people in some cultures perceive physical barriers (e.g., closed doors, fences) as regulators of their privacy, while people in other cultures do not perceive physical barriers as a mechanism of privacy regulation. Rather, they perceive privacy as being regulated by psychological barriers (e.g., pretending the other person is not there). Misunderstandings can occur whenever people from one type of culture find themselves to be strangers in the other type of culture. As strangers, they will be unable to find the privacy they want or desire because people of the host culture do not recognize the same barriers. Similarly, the hosts will, in all likelihood, misinterpret the strangers' behavior.

PART THREE

CULTURAL VARIATIONS AND UNIVERSALS IN COMMUNICATION

Culture affects our communication in various ways. It provides us with patterned ways of dealing with information in our environment. It determines what we perceive, how we interpret, and how we respond to messages both verbally and nonverbally. Culture shapes and colors our image of reality and conditions the way we think.

Our communication patterns are often subtle, elusive, and unconscious. It is difficult for even well-informed members of a culture to explain why, in their own culture, the custom is thus-and-so rather than so-and-thus. For example, it would probably be hard for one to explain the "rule" governing the precise time in a relationship when the other person becomes a friend. One simply "feels right." Fortunately, members of the same culture share a great number of such taken-for-granted assumptions about interpersonal relationships and the corresponding "appropriate" behavior.

For strangers, however, many of the hidden assumptions and modes of behavior are not shared. As many people who visit a foreign country soon discover, communicating with the natives can often be a challenging and novel experience. In the following chapters we present some of the recognized differences in communication patterns across cultures, focusing on message decoding and encoding. We first examine message decoding, the most fundamental process of receiving and processing information from the environment. Second, we take up the cross-cultural differences in language and verbal behavior. Third, we consider observed differences in facial, body, and vocal expressions, as well as the conception of time and space in interpersonal interaction. In addition, some of the fundamental commonalities in human communication shared across cultural boundaries are discussed.

In identifying cross-cultural variations, there is always a danger of oversimplification or of assuming everyone in a culture follows the same patterns of communication. Culture is not a homogeneous entity. As elaborated in Part Two, communication patterns of individuals within a cultural system vary according to their social group membership (i.e., sociocultural influences), their unique psychological characteristics (i.e., psychocultural influences), and the influences of the physical and psychological environment in which they communicate. For example, the "typical" French person is considered to be more expressive of affection in public than the "typical" Chinese person, but more careful observation may reveal that some French people are even more reserved than some Chinese people.

In spite of the complex, heterogeneous nature of the patterns of individual behavior within a culture, there is obviously a normative pattern commonly observed in a cultural group. Such a "central tendency" of a cultural group gives it a general character and distinguishes it from other cultures. Thus our purpose of presenting cultural variations in communication patterns is not to encourage gross cultural stereotyping but to broaden your perspective on human communication by presenting some of the rich variations, as well as the profound commonalities, in human communication behavior across cultures.

7

Cultural Variations
in Message Decoding

What has been thought of as mind is actually internalized culture. The mind-culture process which has evolved over the past four or more million years is primarily concerned with "organization" and, furthermore, the organization of "information" as it is channeled (and altered by the senses) to the brain.

Edward T. Hall

Humans are active organisms. In making sense of our environment, we create as much as we define. A large class of social objects, such as our concepts of love, friendship, beauty, and freedom, "exist" only as created and collectively understood meanings. The perception of our environment as offering opportunities, as threatening, or as irrelevant and the imputation to it of qualities more generally are somewhat arbitrary from the standpoint of their "objective" reality. In many cases such meanings cannot be derived simply from knowledge of such objective qualities. Through the process of decoding, we appraise the things and people around us and strive to assess what meanings they may have for the fulfillment of our needs. Since other people and objects are perceived and interpreted in terms of their meanings for us, it follows that our definitions and classifications reflect only in part the "real" nature of things.

Cross-cultural research has revealed much concerning the ways people in various cultures decode messages from their physical and psychological environments. The term *subjective culture* has been used often as a theoretical construct in comparing various cultures. This concept focuses on those aspects of culture manifested in the commonalities of perceptual-cognitive patterns in individuals within a given cultural group. It was introduced by Osgood (1964; 1965), who explored the notion of a universal framework for some affective and connotative aspects of language. Triandis (1972) further extended the concept to include values, beliefs, and attitudes in an attempt to construct a model to guide cross-cultural research on how people in different cultures perceive and interpret their social reality.

In this chapter we describe some of the variations in subjective cultures. We are interested particularly in cognitive differences across cultures in decoding communication messages. We first discuss the patterns of receiving and organizing information from the environment, which we refer to as perception. Next, we explore cultural variations in mental processing (interpreting, evaluating, abstracting, etc.) of the perceived information (i.e., thinking). Finally, we examine some of the characteristics of interpersonal orientation directly influencing the way people in various cultures perceive and think, as well as express themselves verbally and nonverbally.

PERCEPTION   *How we perceive ⟶ depends — hi/lo cotxt cultures*

Context ⟶

In understanding perceptual variations across cultures, the concept of *contexting*, introduced by Hall (1976), provides a useful point of view. As indicated in Chapter 1, Hall states that culture provides a selective screen between individuals and the outside world and different cultures "program" their members to pay attention to different aspects of the environment with a greater or lesser attachment of significance. Based on this observation, Hall uses the term contexting to describe the perceptual process of recognizing, giving significance to, and incorporating contextual cues in interpreting the total meaning of any stimulus in a particular communication transaction. Here contextual cues refer to all the messages implicit in a communication transaction, including the nature of the interpersonal relationship between the communicators, the nonverbal expressions of the communicators, the physical setting, and the social circumstances. Verbal messages are viewed as explicitly coded messages that *stand out against* the background of various contextual cues. For example, the act of uttering the verbal message "how wonderful!" can convey different meanings depending on the contextual cues accompanying it. The circumstances, facial expression, and vocal tone that are simultaneously emanating implicit messages help us to interpret the overall meaning of a particular communication.

Hall applies this concept of contexting to the cross-cultural comparison of communication patterns. Based on the contexting patterns of individuals, Hall distinguishes cultures as either high-context cultures or low-context cultures. Of course, such dichotomous terms as high-context and low-context should not be interpreted literally. Rather, they should be seen as extreme ends of the same continuum, on which cultures can be placed according to the relative degree of implicitness or explicitness in perceptual and message patterns. Thus cultures that tend to place greater emphasis on sensitivity to and the significance of subtle contextual cues can be characterized as high-context cultures. On the other hand, low-context cultures tend to emphasize spoken or written verbal messages that are explicitly coded. Generally speaking, many of the Western cultures that are technologically advanced tend to be low-context cultures. Among low-context cultures, according to Hall, are the cultures of the United States, Canada, England, Switzerland, Germany, and the Scandinavian nations. Other European cultures (such as French, Italian, and Spanish) and many non-European cultures (such as Asian, African, native American, and South American) are characterized as high-context cultures. One can further observe that as a high-context culture such as Japan undergoes a rapid technological advancement, its social dynamics also go through changes toward less implicit, lower-context communication patterns.

A number of other cross-cultural studies have provided supportive evidence to Hall's observation of high-context and low-context cultures. Ouchi (1981), for example, compares Japanese and North American business organizational cultures and characterizes the basic mechanisms of management control in a Japanese company as much more "subtle, implicit, and internal," so they often appear to be nonexistent to strangers from a low-context culture. Such a conclusion would be a mistake since the Japanese management mechanisms are clearly recognizable among the Japanese employees; these mechanisms are highly disciplined, thorough, demanding, and yet very flexible. Also, Adelman and Lustig (1981), in their study of the perceptions of the communication problems between Saudi Arabian and North American business personnel, observe Saudi Arabians tend to fault North Americans for their inattention to implicit social rituals. For the North Americans, the Saudi Arabians lack the explicitness and objectivity felt to be necessary in business transactions. The North American business personnel working in these two high-context cultures, Japanese and Saudi Arabian, react to the local modes of communication based on the conditioning of their low-context culture. They tend to place less significance on subtle contextual cues in business transactions, while to their Japanese and Saudi Arabian counterparts the contextual messages are an integral part of the total business transaction process.

THINKING

Cross-cultural variations in message decoding also are found in patterns of "thinking," in the sense of sustained mental processes. Once we perceive information from the environment, we "process" it; that is, we engage in such mental activities as abstracting, analyzing, evaluating, and synthesizing, among others. In other words, we make "sense" out of the perceived information through reasoning.

Just as individuals in divergent cultures perceive the environment differently, so are they observed to differ in their thinking patterns. One of the variations most widely recognized in cognitive psychology is that between *field-dependence* and *field-independence.* This concept originally was formulated to refer to how people rely on visual or other information in space in making judgments about the orientations of themselves and of objects in space (Witkin et al., 1962). This bipolarity, of course, defines only the extremes of a continuum along which people in different cultures may be ordered and compared. The concept has since been generalized to other cognitive patterns, such as global versus analytical style. Recently it has been expanded further to include personality characteristics, such as the degree to which a person differentiates between self and nonself. Jahoda (1980) summarizes relevant research findings to describe the salient features of field-independent individuals:

> Field-independent people have a higher ability to extract a constituent part than field-dependent people who find it difficult to break up such an organized whole analytically. Similarly, in the intellectual sphere, relative field-independent people display greater skill in solving the particular type of problem which requires isolating certain elements from their context and making use of it in a different context. It was also originally suggested that field-dependent individuals were more sensitive to the prevailing social field and therefore more likely to respond to social cues or conform to social pressures. (p. 100)

Note the close linkage between the above characterization of the field-dependent and field-independent cognitive styles and the earlier description of perceptual styles in high-context and low-context cultures. The field-dependent cognitive style corresponds closely to the perceptual mode of the high-context cultures, while the field-independent cognitive style is related closely to the perceptual pattern of the low-context cultures. Both perspectives provide useful conceptual tools for understanding cross-cultural variations in information decoding patterns.

Keeping the general conceptual frameworks in mind, let us now examine some specific cross-cultural patterns of thinking. Observers of Western cultures, as indicated in our discussion of world view in Chapter 3, characterize their predominant mode of thinking as "logical," "analytic," "action mode," and "linear"—all of which fit the description of the field-independent cognitive style. Their most characteristic form is known as scientific induction, which emphasizes concentrated attention on the "raw materials" provided by the senses and applying rational principles to those raw materials to bring them into a more or less orderly and self-consistent whole. Gulick (1962), in his comparative analysis of Eastern and Western cultures, describes Western thinking in the main as "the effort to make a coherent and verifiable 'world construct,' and to impose man's will on nature and society" (p. 127). Such mental characteristics of the Western

impulse

peoples have given great impetus to the development of natural science and technology.

An associated characteristic of Western cultures, particularly that of the United States, is the tendency to see the world in terms of dichotomies (Stewart, 1972). This characteristic is illustrated by the Western tendency to think in terms of good-evil, right-wrong, true-false, and beautiful-ugly. Stewart describes this tendency to polarize as "simplifying the view of the world, predisposing to action and providing individuals with a typical method of evaluating and judging by means of a comparison" (p. 29).

USA tendency

While sharing a great deal of commonality with thinking in Western cultures in general, thinking by the people in the United States is distinguishable from that of Europeans by its heavier emphasis on empirical facts, induction, and operationalism. Stewart (1972) comments:

> For Americans, the world is composed of facts—not ideas. Their process of thinking is generally inductive, beginning with facts and then proceeding to ideas. But the movement from the concrete to the more abstract is seldom a complete success, for Americans have a recurrent need to reaffirm their theories and . . . their ideas require validation by application and by becoming institutionalized. (pp. 22–23)

The operational style of thinking tends to produce a stress on consequences and to result in a disregard for the empirical world as such. What is important is the ability of the individual to affect the empirical world. Such operationally oriented thinking in the United States has led to the prevailing cultural values of pragmatism and functionalism.

In contrast, Europeans are characterized as attaching primacy to ideas and theories. Their deductive and abstract style of thinking gives priority to the conceptual world. Although the empirical world is not necessarily ignored, it often is treated with a symbolic and demonstrational attitude. Deductive thinkers are likely to have much more confidence in their ideas and theories, so it suffices for them to show one or two connections between their concepts and the empirical world. They do not feel compelled to amass facts and statistics, as is the way in the United States, and they tend to generalize from one concept to another concept, or to facts, by means of logic. Europeans have a greater faith and trust in the powers of thought, while people in the United States place a greater significance on their methods of empirical observation and measurement (Stewart, 1972). Although the cultures of the United States and Western Europe are in some respects dissimilar, they share certain basic characteristics of field-independent, low-context cultures. Even though the relative significance placed on empirical observation and verification and on the deductive and the inductive processes of deriving knowledge differs between the two cultural groups, they both emphasize a fundamental cognitive pattern that is logical, categorical, linear, and analytic.

Westerners vs Asians

Compared to those of Western cultures, the thinking patterns of non-Western cultures are often characterized as "relational," "integrative," "holistic," and "intuitive." Asians, in general, are observed to have a central mode of thinking that is not concerned as much with logic and analysis as it is with intuitive "knowing" and meditative introspection and contemplation. Asians tend to emphasize the unity between the subjective and the objective realms of the inner and the outer conditions, and thus engage less in analyzing a topic divisively by breaking it down into smaller units as Westerners often do. What seems to be of central importance in Asian thinking is a certain repose of the personality in which it "feels" it is "grasping" the inner significance of the object of contemplation. The direct sense of rapport with the outer object—whether a person, idea, or thing—is the primary end result of Asian thinking (Gulick, 1962, p. 127).

The intuitive thinking of non-Westerners tends to deemphasize the power of analysis, classification, precision, and abstraction, and the result is perhaps not as effective in attaining accurate "facts" about the object. On the other hand, intuitive thinking allows holistic and intimate identification with all of the contextual cues in a communication transaction, thus making the perceptual patterns of non-Westerners highly contextual. Their intuitive style of thinking provides a powerful cognitive mechanism for developing a harmonious rapport with the other person and the environment. This mechanism enables the non-Westerner to be sensitive to the most subtle undercurrents of emotion and mood in a particular communication event and interpersonal relationship without having to engage in a deliberate attempt to logically analyze the situation. Such an Asian sensibility, more intuitive than analytic, may appear to many people from Western cultures to be ambiguous and illogical. For strangers from Asia, it may be almost impossible to explain some of these inner experiences to their North American friends. Such cross-cultural differences in the process of experiencing external phenomena can create much frustration and frequent misunderstanding when we communicate with strangers.

Ornstein (1972), in summarizing evidence from split brain research by Sperry and his colleagues, suggests a possible physiological explanation for the observed perceptual and cognitive variations across cultures. He believes the two cerebral hemispheres of the human brain process different kinds of information and the operating characteristics of the two likewise differ. The left hemisphere is involved predominantly with analytic, logical thinking, speech, and mathematical functions. Its mode of operation is primarily linear; it seems to process information sequentially. The right hemisphere is more holistic, direct, and relational in its mode of operation. It is responsible for orientation in space, intuition, and imagination and is able to integrate information in a nonlinear, diffused fashion. In normal people, of course, the two hemispheres operate interdependently, integrating both sides of the brain. The differential emphasis in the specialized hemispheric functions, however, appears to correspond very closely to the variations in the patterns of information processing in Western and Eastern cultures.

In recognizing the above cultural variations in thinking, one must keep in mind that these identified cultural patterns do not mean Westerners think using only logic and reason or non-Westerners think using only intuition. What we have presented so far is the *relative* emphasis that different cultures place on particular methods of thinking, rather than absolute differences in kind. While non-Westerners do think and reason, as well as use their intuitive mode of "seeing" things without logical analysis, the significance of knowledge through intuition is accepted and valued more extensively in the East than in the West. Similarly, Western thinking involves intuitive processes, but Westerners tend to deemphasize the importance of such awareness through intuition and to value instead the outcome of logical, analytic thinking processes.

INTERPERSONAL ORIENTATION

As well as showing observed differences in patterns of perception and thinking, individuals in different cultures vary in their conception of self, of others, and of human relationships in various social contexts. All interpersonal communication is based on a relationship of some sort, ranging from strangers, to casual acquaintances, to intimate friends, to family relationships. A culture conditions its members to orient themselves toward specific interpersonal relationships in certain patterned ways. In this section we examine some of the culturally determined variations in individuals' orientations in their social relationships.

Relationship of the Individual to the Group

In all societies individuals belong to a number of significant groups, such as family, co-workers, and friends. These groups provide individuals with emotional support and a sense of security. At the same time they espouse in their members a respect for authority, acceptance of standards, a tendency to behave in accord with established norms, and a desire to cooperate to achieve group goals. It also has been observed that some degree of tension between the competing values of conformity and autonomy must therefore exist in every society (Segall, 1979, p. 140).

Although many group functions are universal, the extent to which an individual is dependent on the group and the equilibrium point of optimal balance between dependency and autonomy of individual members in a primary group vary across cultures and subcultures. This point was made in Chapter 3 when we examined Kluckhohn and Strodtbeck's (1960) relational value orientation and Parsons's (1951) self-collective pattern variable. To further illustrate, Berry

(1967) reports that the Eskimos, whose food-getting practices should result in training for independence, were much less conformist than the agricultural African group the Temne, whose subsistence activities demand cooperation and whose socialization practices, therefore, should stress conformity. On a continuum of the dependency (or conformity) of the individual on the group, the position of the culture of the United States is represented by the attitude that the individual is more important than the group. Francis Hsu (1981), a noted anthropologist, describes individualism as a central theme of the North American personality. In comparing the cultures of the United States and China, Hsu believes individualism is a master key to the North American character and the rest of the Western world and distinguishes the Western world from the non-Western.

Generally speaking, people in the United States stress the individual as a primary point of reference. This tendency begins at a very early age, when children are encouraged to be autonomous. The self-directedness of the child is seldom questioned. It is accepted implicitly that "each child or person should be encouraged to decide for himself, developing his own opinions, solve his own problems, have his own things, and learn to view and deal with the world from the point of view of the self" (Stewart, 1972, p. 70). Accordingly, one's social conduct is viewed as a reflection of one's own character, i.e., the internal system of moral and ethical systems. Any serious misconduct by an individual brings social disgrace to that individual and only that individual, and little to the family or other primary groups. Mir-Djalali (1980) provides a supportive finding from his comparative study of United States and Iranian samples: Iranians tend to perceive the word "me" with a heavy emphasis on "human beings" and future-oriented concerns, such as ambition and aim, while the North American responses emphasize the concept of self as "individual." Similarly, Yousef (1974) finds a difference in the basic attitudes toward life in the United States and Arab societies. North Americans value individual centeredness and self-reliance, and the Arabic attitude is one of mutual dependence.

Many non-Western cultures commonly are characterized by their relatively greater degree of submission of individual identity, individualism, and self-expression to the groups to which one belongs. The concept of *amae* is pointed out by Doi (1976) as being illustrative of the intimate nature of individual-group interdependence in Japan. It refers to the individual's emotional dependency on other members of primary groups, in much the same way as a child is dependent on the parents. In many non-Western cultures, members of a family or a company are expected to submerse their personal interests and desires in favor of those of the total group. The members are expected to behave in a manner that will not disgrace the honor of the family or the company. Thus, as Glidden (1972) and Yousef (1974) observe, the interplay between honor and shame dictates much of Middle Eastern interpersonal behavior. Also, Ouchi (1981), in comparing the corporate systems in Japan and the United States, emphasizes the collective sense of responsibility among Japanese employees. Benedict's (1934) description of the Japanese culture as a "shame culture," in contrast to the "sin culture" of the United States, appears to be still relevant, in spite of many apparent changes in the two societies. This means that, in Japan, parents often admonish their children by saying, "If you do that, people will laugh at you," implying, "If you are laughed at, you are bringing shame to your family." When North American parents say the same thing to their children, they mean, "It is wrong for you to do that and you will be punished for it." Japanese children who go through such a socialization process develop a strong "group-ego," which often supercedes their individualistic orientation. North American children, on the other hand, learn to develop a strong sense of self-reliance and independence.

The intense interdependency observed in many of the non-Western cultures, however, cannot be generalized to outside the primary group settings. In fact, there exists a tendency in these cultures to discriminate in-group members from out-group members, as we indicated in Chapter 4. People in non-Western cultures often behave in an aloof and indifferent manner to strangers, which may be perceived by Westerners as impoliteness (Morsbach, 1976, p. 255). Or, sometimes, we see them behave with exaggerated politeness to strangers or casual acquaintances, which may be perceived as being either "inappropriate" or "insincere" by Westerners. The well-known notion of "face-saving" among Japanese, for example, illustrates the psychological "distancing" of out-group members through being formal and polite. Whether one acts in an impolite manner or with exaggerated politeness, the underlying psychological tendency seems to be a concentrated involvement with in-group members and a relative distancing from out-group members. The interpersonal behavior in many Western cultures, particularly that of the United States, displays a less discriminating orientation with respect to in-group and out-group associations. People in Western cultures are generally more willing to develop relationships with strangers, without imposing too rigid a screening process. Such an orientation toward others characterizes the Westerners as friendly, open, informal, and outgoing and is typified in common social rituals such as cocktail parties, where individuals are introduced to one another for the first time. In such social gatherings, people are expected to find ways to reach out to others and to begin to develop relationships with them, if mutually agreeable. For a stranger from a non-Western culture, this Western style of social interaction can be perceived as "awkward," "unnatural," "superficial," and difficult to participate in actively. On the other hand, a stranger from the United States in an Eastern country may find the reserve and social rigidity of non-Westerners uncomfortable and difficult to penetrate.

It appears then there is a close relationship between culturally patterned in-group and out-group relationships. For Westerners, the relatively less intense interpersonal involvement and interdependency among members of primary groups appear to allow them to be more open toward out-group members. For non-Westerners, the relatively discriminatory and concentrated involvement within primary groups tends to make them distant toward out-group members.

Interpersonal Relationships

In any interpersonal relationship there are certain expectations individuals develop regarding each other's attitudes and behaviors and toward the relationship itself. Such interpersonal expectations are shaped substantially by cultural rules, norms, and values, as we pointed out in Chapter 4.

In the United States relationships are developed and maintained primarily according to activities (Stewart, 1972, p. 54). Time spent with a friend (meaning anyone, from a passing acquaintance to a lifelong intimate) centers around activity, a thing, an event, or a shared history. Thus North Americans have friendships that originate around work, children's schools, political activities, charities, leisure activities, and various occasions for sharing food and drink. This activity-oriented nature of friendship reflects one of the central Western values— the importance of each individual and the maximization of the fulfillment of individual needs. For North Americans a relationship is considered healthy to the extent it serves the expected function for each of the involved parties. The activity-oriented and functional approach, coupled with a greater degree of social mobility, tends to contribute to the relatively unstable and impermanent nature of interpersonal relationships in the United States and other technologically advanced Western societies. As people move from one residence or job to another, few old friends are retained in a lasting relationship. Instead, people tend to look forward to establishing a new circle of friends with whom they share mutually helpful and satisfying social functions and activities.

Compare such a functional, impermanent orientation toward interpersonal relationships to the more stable and lasting one found in many non-Western cultures. For people in a relatively homogeneous and less technological environment, relationships are often "given" to them according to their birth, schooling, work, and/or residence. Intimate relationships tend to develop as a consequence of prolonged affiliation rather than of actively seeking them out. The primary basis for many interpersonal relationships in non-Western cultures lies not so much in specific functions that individuals do for and with each other as in mutual liking and affection for each other's disposition and temperament and a more generalized acceptance of the whole person. Once a relationship has developed into an intimate one, it often is expected to last throughout life.

A related characteristic of the relatively stable and permanent interpersonal relationship is the strong psychological involvement and loyalty toward each other. In non-Western cultures close friends and family members are closely intertwined in their sharing of their private lives. Such intense commitment between intimates is the source of an emotional stability and security and often transcends individual needs and desires. In financial matters the distinction of material things as "yours" and "mine" is often unclear or suppressed among intimates. The common Western practice of "Dutch treat" by close friends is not as prevalent in many non-Western cultures and is encountered by non-Westerners with much discomfort and feeling of "unnaturalness." Splitting the bill according to the respective meals when two friends eat in a restaurant is considered rather impersonal and businesslike. Even on making decisions about personal affairs, such as choosing a career or a marriage partner, the opinions of family members, especially parents, exert a stronger influence in the group-oriented cultures. It is not too unusual, for instance, for a son to forsake his choice of a spouse because of the opposition of his parents, and even the opinions of his intimate friends exert a substantial influence on his choice of a mate. Further, the non-Westerners' loyalty in intimate relationships sometimes leads them to "bend the system," willingly or unwillingly, making them more likely to engage in such practices as nepotism or favoritism. It should be noted, however, that these practices may not be negatively evaluated as they are in the West.

In line with the observed intimacy, commitment, and latitude for each other's interests among non-Western intimates, the breakup of such a relationship commonly is accompanied by a great sense of tragedy. Once the emotionally based relationship reaches a point of "no return," it is difficult for the involved parties to talk things over rationally and to attempt to mend the "broken" relationship. In the United States, on the other hand, it is not uncommon to find intimate friends or married couples who remain friends even after they decide to terminate their current arrangement. Such a redefining of the nature of an existing relationship can be seen as an expression of the functional orientation many North Americans have toward interpersonal relationships. The specialized nature of a relationship makes it possible for the involved parties to terminate a relationship with relative ease and, if necessary and mutually agreeable, to redefine the function of the relationship to something more feasible. In this cultural context, the functions themselves, rather than *who* performs the functions, often take priority. If two people in a relationship cannot agree on their mutual functions, then the most logical thing for them to do is to redefine the functions or to find someone else who can more readily perform them. Comparatively, such redefining of an intimate relationship is rarely practiced in cultures where intimates expect and demand full and lasting commitment. These same patterns exist with respect to the resolution of conflict, as we indicated in Chapter 3.

Hall (1976) interprets these contrasting approaches to interpersonal relationships as characteristic of high-context and low-context cultures. The emotionally based, person-oriented approach is viewed as characteristic of high-context cultures, while the functionally based, specialized approach is seen as characteristic of low-context cultures. Hall sees interpersonal bonds in a low-context culture as fragile and notes that people in such a culture move away or withdraw with relative ease if a relationship is not developing satisfactorily. On the other hand, according to Hall, the bonds between people in a high-context culture are stronger, and thus there is a tendency to allow for considerable "bending" of individual interests for the sake of the relationship.

The specialized approach to interpersonal relationships can be extended to the prevailing reliance of people in the United States and other Western cultures on specialists and experts, who are available for almost all functions that need to be performed. This pattern seems to reflect the logical, rational thinking of Westerners, who desire the "best" solution to a given problem from an expert who is qualified in that particular area. Thus, if someone is experiencing a serious emotional distress, the person is encouraged to see a professional psychologist or counselor in order to deal with the problem more rationally. In contrast, help for many of the social and emotional problems in high-context cultures is sought from members of one's family and from close friends.

Some variations in interpersonal relationship patterns must be noted among Western cultures. Whereas North Americans tend to limit friendship to an area of common interest, Russians and other Eastern and Southern Europeans tend to be more person-oriented, embracing the whole person, as indicated in Chapter 4. In contrast to the North American, the Russian expects to form a deep bond of friendship with another person, assumes the obligation of almost constant companionship, and avoids any reticence or secretiveness toward friends (Stewart, 1972, pp. 54–55). The French, on the other hand, according to Stewart, exhibit contradictions stemming from simultaneous demands for privacy, independence, and long, close friendships. Combining features of both the North American and Russian styles, the French styles of friendship are specialized but are also organized in patterns of long duration, often with an expectation that family friendships will extend over more than one generation. A similar observation is made by Hall (1976), who examined the French business practice of being generally much more involved with their employees, customers, and clients than are their American counterparts. (For a more detailed discussion of cross-cultural differences in interpersonal relationships, see Chapter 4.)

Interpersonal Status

Another aspect of interpersonal orientation influencing communication processes is the culturally defined nature and the interpersonal functions of social status (Parsons's pattern variable of achievement versus ascription). In the United States status generally is achieved. It depends very much on what we do and how other people respond to what we accomplish, and very little on what we are as persons. It is not too difficult in the United States to find successful self-made individuals who have gained higher status fairly rapidly. In many traditional non-Western cultures, status is often ascribed; it depends on the family into which one is born and is not likely to change drastically during one's lifetime. Consequently, there is less need for behavior designed to change one's

status. Foa (1967) reports empirical evidence of the ascriptive, relatively permanent nature of social status among Middle Easterners. Similar results are reported
by D. Levine (1965) and Korten (1972) in their studies of Ethiopian culture.
Both Levine and Korten stress the extreme degree to which one's rank in Ethiopian society is determined by the rank of one's parents rather than by one's
personal achievements. Korten also documents the Ethiopians' "obsessive fear"
of incurring the disfavor of another person and the potentially disastrous effects
of doing so. Other observations of the qualities of social status are reported in
studies of Japanese and other Asian cultures. Bennett and McKnight (1966),
for example, note that in Japan a superior, such as one's professor, retains strong
"symbolic hierarchical precedence throughout the life of both parties, even
when the student has become a professional equal in productivity, rank, and
pay" (p. 600).

Comparatively, Western cultures, particularly the United States, tend to
foster an initial egalitarian response toward others; two persons are presumed
to be equal unless proven otherwise. Interpersonal relations are typically hori-
zontal, conducted between presumed equals. This egalitarian principle of North
American interpersonal behavior leads to what Asians and other non-Westerners
consider to be fluidity and unpredictability in interactions and a highly variable,
or at least less apparent, concern for status (Bennett and McKnight, 1966,
p. 602).

The relative lack of a rigid status distinction in the United States and other
Western cultures also is observed in the informality and directness with which
people in those cultures tend to treat others. The North American refers to
everyone in essentially the same way; the preferred mode is equality. International students in the United States (strangers) find it more difficult than their
North American classmates do to call their professors by their first names. On
the other hand, North Americans working overseas (strangers) frequently find it
difficult to adapt to the flowery language, complex methods of address, and
ritualistic manners reflecting the hierarchical social structure and interpersonal
orientation of the local people. Whereas the average North American considers
formality, style, and protocol as unnatural and unnecessary in many interpersonal encounters, in some cultures these cues provide a dependable basis for
predicting others' behavior.

Some of the variations in interpersonal orientation discussed so far are not
limited to cross-cultural comparisons but can be discerned among subcultural
groups within a culture. A most noticeable difference in interpersonal orientation exists between urban and rural communities. Generally speaking, a less
technological and less complex rural community provides a subcultural environment in which interpersonal relationships are more stable, more involved, and
less specialized. In cohesive rural areas, individuals tend to rely more on interpersonal sources for information and advice than on mass media or specialists.
Research findings provide strong evidence that interpersonal relationships in

rural areas tend to be more "global" and less function-specific. The "opinion leaders" in urban centers, for example, are noted more for the specialized nature of their influence on others than are their rural counterparts (Rogers and Shoemaker, 1971). Of course, there is a gradual diminishing of urban-rural distinctions in cultural and communication patterns as both areas increasingly are exposed to a similar information environment as a result of the pervasive networking of the mass media and transportation systems. Haselden (1968) goes so far as to say, "In the cultural sense there is no longer a rural America, no longer pockets where you find strange customs and people unacquainted with what occurs in the rest of the world" (p. 66). This obviously is not totally true, since groups like the Hutterites still exist in the United States today. This observation, however, points to a likely direction of change in the United States, as well as in many other countries of the world.

SUMMARY

In this chapter, we presented some of the basic cross-cultural differences in patterns of message decoding in interpersonal communication. Emphasizing the importance of recognizing individual differences within a cultural group, we described variations in subjective culture, the fundamental way people in different cultures perceive and cognitively experience their physical and social environments. We also discussed variations in orientation toward primary groups, normative characteristics of interpersonal relationships in general, and the ways in which social status plays a role in interpersonal communication processes.

The main conceptual framework instrumental in comparing perceptual and thinking patterns of various cultures is Hall's construct of contexting and the identification of cultures on the bipolar continuum of high-context to low-context. We compared cultures according to the degree of field-dependence or field-independence in their cognitive patterns of information processing. A close correspondence exists between Hall's anthropological perspective and that of cognitive psychology. Both perspectives, when applied to the characterization of different cultures, describe essentially the same variation in message-decoding patterns. Individuals in high-context cultures tend to rely more heavily on subtle, implicit contextual cues, such as the social and relational context, knowledge about the other person, situational characteristics, and nonverbal cues. Some characteristics are identified with field-dependent individuals whose perception and cognitive processes are heavily embedded in the social and physical field.

Other associated cognitive characteristics in high-context and low-context cultures also were examined. Compared to low-context cultures, high-context cultures were described as more readily accepting and valuing intuitive, holistic, direct modes of thinking. We also discussed how the observed perceptual and cognitive differences between high-context and low-context cultures closely correspond to variations in the patterns of individual-group interdependence, the basic nature of interpersonal relationships, and the significance of social status in interpersonal communication. Individuals in high-context cultures tend to have a stronger group orientation, more explicit in-group and out-group distinctions, and more intense involvement with intimates than do people in low-context cultures, who have a stronger individualistic orientation.

It often requires a long and difficult process of trial and error before some-one from a low-context culture develops an accurate understanding of the perceptual and cognitive patterns of a stranger from a high-context culture. Because our decoding process occurs mostly beyond our conscious control, we cannot easily recognize the specific discrepancies between our decoding patterns and those of the stranger. Recognizing the variations discussed in this chapter can help us to better understand the different message-decoding patterns used by strangers and thereby increase our ability to interpret and predict their behavior correctly.

8

Cultural Variations
in Verbal Behavior

Language

> In the beginning was the Word,
> And the Word was with God,
> And the Word was God.
>
> **Genesis**

The Master said, I would much rather not have to talk. Tsu-kung said, If our Master did not talk, what should we little ones have to hand down about him? The Master said, Heaven does not speak; yet the four seasons run their course thereby. The hundred creatures, each after its kind, are born thereby. Heaven does no speaking!

The Analects of Confucius

Every culture has a system of language with which people are able to communicate with one another. Language is culturally induced, and thus it reflects the values of culture. When a baby enters the world, he or she begins to perceive that people in the environment behave in rather stable ways toward objects and toward each other. The baby also begins to see that adults employ special linguistic patterns. Through the gradual development of knowledge and the use of language, the child eventually learns to behave in the manner set forth by his or her elders and hence comes to understand and participate in that culture. The particular code the child learns, in turn, exerts a powerful influence on his or her interaction with the environment. By specifying or highlighting what in the environment is relevant or irrelevant, the code influences the nature of the child's experience.

THEORETICAL PERSPECTIVE

In communicating with strangers from another linguistic or cultural group, the degree of shared meaning in experiencing the reality is likely to be minimal. This is particularly the case when the differences between two linguistic systems are considerable. For example, an English-speaking person will have fewer common-alities with a Chinese-speaking stranger than with a German-speaking stranger.

The relationship between language and culture was emphasized first by Boas (1911). He did this in a simple and obvious way by analyzing the lexicons of two languages, revealing the distinctions made by people of different cultures. A common example is the different degree of refinement in the vocabulary to describe snow. To most North Americans, snow is just one part of the weather, and their vocabulary is basically limited to two terms: snow and slush. In the Eskimo language, there are more than 20 terms, each of which describes snow in a different state or condition. This multiplicity of terms clearly reveals a dependence on an accurate vocabulary to describe what is not just a part of the weather but a major environmental feature. Since Boas's time, anthropologists have developed extensive knowledge and insights into this important relationship between language and culture.

The Sapir-Whorf Hypothesis   — *Rel*ᵃ*ship betⁿ Language & culture*

One of the most significant contributions to our understanding of the relationship between language and culture comes from Benjamin Lee Whorf's book, *Language, Thought and Reality* (1956). Drawing on his teacher Edward Sapir's (1970) ideas, Whorf analyzes the language of the Hopi Indians of Arizona and theorizes that language is not merely a reproducing instrument for expressing ideas—rather, it is itself the shaper of ideas. Instead of focusing on vocabulary, Whorf concentrates on the structural differences between the Hopi language and European languages. In his analysis of plurality, for instance, Whorf notes that English uses a plural form for both *cyclic nouns* (nouns that refer to days, years, or other units of time) and *aggregate nouns* (nouns that have a physical referent, such as apples). The Hopi, on the other hand, do not use cyclic nouns in the same way they use aggregate nouns. In the Hopi language, cycles do not have plurals; they have duration. Thus the Hopi equivalent for the English "he stayed ten days" is "he stayed until the eleventh day." Further, the Hopi language does not possess tenses, which in most European languages place time in a sequence of distinct units of past, present, and future. A speaker of English expresses an event happening in the present in one of two constructions, for example, "he runs" or "he is running," but the speaker of the Hopi language can select from a much wider variety of present tenses, which depend on the speaker's knowledge or lack of knowledge concerning the validity of the statement being made, for example, "I know that he is running at this very moment," "I know that he is running at this moment even though I cannot see him," "I am told that he is running," and so on (Farb, 1979, p. 445).

For examples of this kind, Whorf (1956) theorizes a relationship between culture and language and the associated differences in the ways speakers of different languages view the world. He believes every language plays a prominent role in actually molding the perceptual world of the people who use it.

> We dissect nature along lines laid down by our native languages. The categories and types that we isolate from the world of phenomena we do not find there. On the contrary, the world is presented in a kaleidoscopic flux of impressions which has to be organized by our minds—and this means largely by the linguistic systems in our mind. (Whorf, 1952, p. 5)

This view of the relationship between language and culture is commonly known as the Sapir-Whorf hypothesis. It is accepted enthusiastically by some scholars and attacked by others. The weakness of the Sapir-Whorf hypothesis lies in the impossibility of generalizing about entire cultures and then attributing these generalizations to the languages spoken in them. For instance, Farb (1979) argues that because of the absence of clocks, calendars, and written histories the Hopis obviously have a different view of time than do speakers of European languages, but such an observation is not the same as proving that these cultural differences are caused by the differences between the Hopi language and European languages. *conclusions*

Neither Sapir nor Whorf, however, attempts to draw inferences as to the thought world of a people from the simple fact of the presence or absence of specific grammatical categories in a given language. Sapir and Whorf view the cultural significance of linguistic form as lying on a much more submerged, profound level than the overt one of a definite cultural pattern. The concepts of time and matter Whorf (1956) reports for the Hopi "do not depend so much upon any one system (e.g., tense or nouns) within the grammar as upon the ways of analyzing and reporting experiences which have become fixed in the language as integrated 'fashions of speaking' and which cut across the typical grammatical classifications" (p. 44). Thus the true value of the Sapir-Whorf hypothesis is not in providing a definitive and deterministic relationship between specific linguistic categories and the thought patterns of the people in a cultural system but in articulating the profound alliance of language, mind, and the total culture of the speech community. Few students of language, cognition, culture, or communication today doubt such an interpretation of this hypothesis.

The illustrations of cross-cultural variations in language and verbal behavior in the remainder of this chapter further illustrate the basic premise of the Sapir-Whorf hypothesis.

Restricted and Elaborated Codes *of speeches   c/p   Hi context / Lo context.*

The Sapir-Whorf hypothesis deals with language in the sense defined, and Bernstein (1966) provides a theoretical perspective that helps us to understand the speech patterns (or verbal behaviors) of individuals in different cultures. Bernstein hypothesizes that our speech patterns are necessarily conditioned by our social context. The social context is not only the specific interpersonal relational context in which a dyadic speech interaction occurs but also the broader social structure, such as society and the cultural environment. Bernstein further observes that speech emerges in one of two types of codes, restricted and elaborated, as indicated in Chapter 1. The restricted code involves message transmission through verbal (word transmission) and nonverbal (intonation, facial features, gestures) channels. Restricted codes rely heavily on the hidden, implicit cues of the social context (such as interpersonal relationship, physical and psychological environment, and other contextual cues) and thus the vocabulary and structure of the verbalized messages are drawn from a narrow range. Bernstein explains:

> The speech is played out against a backdrop of assumptions common to the speakers, against a set of closely shared interests and identifications, against a system of shared expectations; in short, it presupposes a local cultural identity which reduces the need for the speakers to elaborate their intent verbally and to make it explicit. (pp. 433–434)

Restricted codes, then, resemble jargon or "shorthand" speech in which the speaker is almost telegraphic. For example, when you are with a close friend, you often find yourself making only a brief reference to something; yet each of you is reminded by such a reference of a wealth of experiences or concepts. The question "Bill, how was it?" can be responded to spontaneously by Bill without his having to ask what was meant by "it." An outsider would have difficulty understanding the question because of the lack of shared experiences. Jargon used by a given group also represents a type of restricted code. Code words used by doctors, engineers, prisoners, or street gangs, or between family members and close friends are highly implicit in meaning and are known primarily to the members of such groups.

In contrast, speakers using elaborated codes employ verbal amplification to communicate, placing relatively little reliance on nonverbal and other contextual cues. Whereas new information emerges primarily through nonverbal channels with restricted codes, the verbal channel is the dominant source of information with elaborated codes. Bernstein (1966) further explains elaborated codes by contrasting them to restricted codes:

> Speakers using a restricted code are dependent upon these shared assumptions. The mutually held range of identifications defines the area of common intent and also the range of the code. The dependency underpinning the social relation generating an elaborated code is not of this order. With an elaborated code the listener is dependent upon the verbal elaboration of meaning. (p. 437)

When applied to cross-cultural comparisons, Bernstein's conceptualization of restricted and elaborated codes closely corresponds to Hall's (1976) notion of communication patterns in high-context and low-context cultures. As mentioned earlier, implicit messages (contextual cues) are emphasized in high-context cultures, and explicit verbal messages are of central importance in low-context cultures. The heavy reliance of users of restricted codes on nonverbal and other contextual cues describes the common communication patterns of high-context cultures; the primary reliance on elaborated, explicit verbal messages describes the communication patterns of low-context cultures.

In illustrating this point, Hall characterizes the written Chinese language as a highly restricted language. To be literate in Chinese, one must understand the implicit meaning and significance of the characters and Chinese history. Also, one must know the spoken pronunciation system in which there are four tones and a change of tone means a change of meaning. Understanding a restricted, high-context linguistic system such as Chinese requires not only a functional knowledge in the culture and history but also a sensitivity to the specific social context in which a particular communication transaction occurs. For instance, many Asian languages, including Chinese, Japanese, and Korean, are sensitive to the social status of the addressee. These languages implicitly or explicitly indicate the other person's social position relative to the speaker. This is usually done by using either "honorific" prefixes or suffixes or by using certain words having respectful or derogatory implications. Certain nouns, pronouns, and verbs can be used only when speaking to or of a superior; a second group of words having the same basal meanings can be used only when speaking to or of an equal; a third group can be used only when speaking to or of an inferior. Yoshikawa (1978), a Japanese-American scholar, reports on his personal experiences:

> Whenever I address my Japanese superiors or elders, I call them by their last names no matter how close we may be. I still feel uncomfortable calling them by their first names even if I am communicating with them in English. In the case of American superiors, I feel quite at home calling them by their first names if our relationship is close enough. (p. 223)

This verbal pattern reflecting a sensitivity to hierarchical context is absent from most contemporary European languages, with the exception of the formal and informal forms of *you*, such as *Du* (casual) and *Sie* (formal) in German and *tú* (casual) and *usted* (formal) in Spanish.

VARIATIONS IN VERBAL MESSAGES

Given the general conceptualizations by Sapir and Whorf, Bernstein, and Hall of the relationship between culture and verbal messages, let us now examine specific cross-cultural variations in the use of verbal messages. How might individuals in high-context, restricted-code cultures perceive the meaning and function of verbal messages in the total context of communication differently from the way people in low-context, elaborated-code cultures perceive them? How might cultures differ in stressing the importance of verbal precision and explicitness? How might cultures vary in their perception and use of silence? What communicative functions can silence play in cultures? Understanding of these and other related issues is vital to increasing our understanding of the communication patterns of strangers, as well as of our own patterns of communication.

Cultural Attitudes Toward Verbal Messages

Since all cultures have a system of language, the importance of verbal messages in interpersonal communication appears to be universally acknowledged. Cultures do differ, however, in specific ways of observing the importance of words. In the West the long tradition of rhetoric as a subject matter and an academic discipline since the time of Plato and Aristotle explicitly demonstrates the crucial importance given to verbal messages. This rhetorical tradition reflects in a profound way the Western cultural pattern of logical, rational, and analytic thinking. In the West speech is considered to be an object of inquiry, more or less independent of its communicative context, and, for the purpose of systematic analysis, it can be taken out of its social context. The speaker and the listener are viewed as separate entities who are in a relationship defined primarily through the verbal messages. This is not to say the traditional Western view of speech places no emphasis on the nonverbal and relational aspects of the communication process; rather, the intent is to stress that the central concern of the Western rhetorical tradition is the effective delivery of verbal messages. A primary function of speech in this tradition is to express one's ideas and thoughts as clearly, logically, and persuasively as possible, so the speaker can be fully recognized for his or her individuality in influencing others.

In Asian and other high-context cultures, a systematic study of speech as persuasion has not been developed as fully into a distinct academic discipline as it has in the West. Oliver (1971), in his comparative analysis of the rhetorical traditions of Eastern and Western cultures, observes that in Asian cultures rhetoric has been "too important to be severed from its religio-philosophical context" (p. 11). The Asian attitude toward speech and rhetoric is characteristically a holistic one—the words are only part of, and are inseparable from, the total communication context, which includes the personal characters of the parties involved and the nature of the interpersonal relationships between them. This does not mean words are considered to be less important in Eastern cultures than they are in Western cultures. Rather, verbal messages are considered an important and integral part of the communication process in Asian cultures, inseparably interconnected with such concepts as ethics, psychology, politics, and social relations. In this holistic approach to speech and communication, verbal messages primarily serve the function of enhancing social integration and harmony rather than promoting the speaker's individuality or self-motivated purposes. Dialogue aimed at social harmony, rather than at the well-being of a specific speaker, naturally tends to lack arguments and persuasive fervor. Oliver (1971) observes: "Perhaps most basic of all is the cardinal devotion of the Asian mind to the related concepts of unity and harmony" (p. 10).

Thus, rather than encouraging the expression of individuality through the articulation of words, the tradition of Eastern cultures stresses the value of strict adherence to culturally defined social expectations and rules. The primary emphasis is placed not on the technique of constructing and delivering verbal messages for maximum persuasiveness but on conformity to the already established social relationships defined by the position of the individual speaker in the society. In such a rhetorical context, one is expected to possess a moral and intellectual integrity and a keen sensitivity to subtle and implicit contextual cues surrounding the total communication process. Without the contextual base, the speaker's verbal articulation and delivery are perceived as less meaningful, if not superficial or even deceitful.

A related attitude in Asian cultures is a strong recognition or acceptance of the limitations and biases inherent in the language used to express ideas, thoughts, and feelings. Unlike Western cultures, which traditionally have placed great faith in the power of words, the psychocultural orientation of Asian cultures can be characterized as bordering on a "mistrust" of words. Words are considered useful tools of human expression only to the extent that the user recognizes their limitations and biases. In Buddhism, for example, language is considered deceptive and misleading with regard to the matter of understanding the truth. Similarly, Confucianism cautions that one should not speak carelessly and speech should be guided by the time and place: "The Master said, If a gentleman is frivolous, he will lose the respect of his inferiors and lack firm ground upon which to build up his education" (Waley, 1938, p. 85). Even today, these religious teachings are deeply rooted in the minds of Asians. Commenting on Japanese communication patterns, Yoshikawa (1978) observes:

> What is often verbally expressed and what is actually intended are two different things. What is verbally expressed is probably important enough to maintain friendship, and it is generally called "Tatame" which means simply "in principle" but what is not verbalized counts most—"Honne" which means "true mind." Although it is not expressed verbally, you are supposed to know it by "kan"—"intuition." (p. 228)

Asians' intimate awareness of the limitations of language makes them place a great deal of importance on rigid and elaborate mannerisms and etiquette. Westerners learn such things unconsciously, but Asians make them a subject of conscious interest and attention. These nonverbal rituals of communication in non-Western cultures are highly context-bound. The mannerisms used in showing disagreement or respect vary significantly from one situational and relational context to another. For example, a non-Westerner's display of disagreement with a superior is typically much more subdued, subtle, and indirect than that with a close friend—the distinction is more clear than it is in Western cultures.

Modes of Verbal Behavior

The general cultural orientations toward verbal messages discussed so far are helpful in understanding more specific patterns of verbal behavior. The cautious attitude toward words in Asian cultures, for example, is manifested in Asians' fondness for moderate or suppressed expression of negative and confrontational verbal messages, whenever possible. In general, Asians tend to be concerned more with the overall emotional quality of the interaction than with the meaning of particular words or sentences. Courtesy often takes precedence over truthfulness, which is consistent with the cultural emphasis on the maintenance of social harmony as the primary function of speech. This leads Asians to give an agreeable and pleasant answer to a question when a literal, factual answer might be unpleasant or embarrassing (Hall and Whyte, 1979). Smutkupt and Barna (1976) also report that in Thai culture doubts are rarely verbalized, especially when one is communicating with elders and persons of higher status.

For certain Asian languages (such as Chinese, Japanese, and Korean), the language structures themselves promote ambiguity. For example, in the Japanese language, verbs come at the end of sentences, and, therefore, one is not able to understand what is being said until the whole sentence has been uttered. In addition, the Japanese language is quite loose in logical connection. As Morsbach (1976) describes it, one can talk for hours without clearly expressing one's opinion to another. Even in ordinary conversation, a Japanese person may say *hai* ("yes") without necessarily implying agreement. Frequently, *hai* is intended by the speaker, and is expected by the listener, to mean "I understand what you are saying."

The tendency among Asians to use subdued and ambiguous verbal expressions is not limited to communication situations in which one would express disagreement, embarrassment, doubt, or anger. Even when expressing strong personal affection, a style of hesitancy and indirectness is commonly preferred. Asians can even be suspicious of the genuineness of direct verbal expressions of love and respect. Excessive verbal praise or compliments sometimes are received with feelings of embarrassment. Even silence is preferred to improper words. Oliver (1971) considers silence to be a major focal point of Asian rhetoric: "In the ancient Orient . . . silence was valued rather than feared. . . . silence in Asia has commonly been entirely acceptable" (p. 264). Morsbach (1976) also points to the importance of silence among the Japanese, along with other related speech patterns such as hesitancy, unfinished sentences, and incomplete expression of thoughts. Similarly, Smutkupt and Barna (1976) observe the significance of silence in Thailand as a sign of respect, agreement, or disagreement and as a beautiful form of "speech."

This is not to suggest silence is unimportant in interpersonal communication among Westerners or that Asians always value silence more than verbalization. We are simply pointing out *relative* differences between Western and Eastern cultures in interpreting the meaning and significance of silence in the interpersonal context. Universally, silence performs vital functions in expressing sincerity, seriousness, power, respect, anger, hesitancy, etc.—clearly sending positive and negative messages without verbalization. The cross-cultural difference, however, is in the degree of recognition and conscious use of silence as an important mode of communicating.

The cross-cultural variation in the silent mode of communication is related to the different use of a third-party person in social intercourse. Stewart (1972) cites an example in Thai culture where business between two people may be conducted indirectly by means of an emissary and not directly by a face-to-face confrontation of the principals involved. This indirectness extends to other aspects of social interaction, even those that strangers may consider rather personal, intimate, and sensitive, such as choosing a mate or attempting to resolve conflicts between spouses. The use of an intermediary allows both sides to accommodate one another or to withdraw without losing face. Stewart (1972) illustrates one implication of these different orientations (Asian indirectness and North American preference for direct confrontation) in discussing the use of interpreters: The North American sees the interpreter "as a window pane that transmits the message from one language to the other; but in cultures where a third-person role is customary, the interpreter's role may become a much more active one, to the consternation of the American who is likely to interpret it as inefficiency or perhaps disloyalty" (p. 53).

The ambiguity and inexactitude common in Asian verbal communication behavior are exhibited in other high-context cultures, such as Middle Eastern societies. The Arab's mode of verbal ambiguity, however, often is the opposite of the Asian's—i.e., overexpression. Suleiman (1973), in his analysis of Arab and Western cultures, focusing on their linguistic patterns, characterizes the Arabic language as generally vague and conducive of "exaggeration." Thus a writer or speaker does not find it obligatory to be specific, as long as the reader or listener can infer the meaning.

> The Arabic language abounds with forms of assertion, and of exaggeration. There are the common ending words that are meant to be emphasized. There is also the doubling of the sounds of some consonants to create the desirable stronger effect. . . . and there are such forms of assertion as the repetition of pronouns and certain other words to get across their meanings and significance. Besides these grammatical types of over-assertion are the numerous stylistic and rhetorical devices to achieve even further exaggeration. Fantastic metaphors and similes are used in abundance, and long arrays of adjectives to modify the same word are quite frequent. (Shouby, 1951, quoted by Suleiman, 1973, p. 291)

In comparison with Asian and Middle Eastern modes of verbal expression, those of people in the United States are more direct, explicit, and exact; silence is consciously avoided in interpersonal communication. Good and competent communicators are expected to say what they mean and to mean what they say.

If North Americans discover that someone spoke dubiously or evasively with respect to important matters, they are inclined to regard the person thereafter as unreliable, if not dishonest. Most of the European low-context cultures such as the French, the German, and the English show a similar cultural tradition. These cultures give a high degree of social approval to individuals whose verbal behaviors in expressing ideas and feelings are precise, explicit, straightforward, and direct.

Thus it is apparent that our communication with strangers who use a different language and system of verbal behavior can easily lead to misunderstandings or inaccurate predictions if we assume their system is the same as ours. Consider the following description of North Americans' verbal behaviors by a Chinese student, Cheng (1974):

> The American feels obligated to make some verbal comment to react to each situation. For example, when eating, one should say, "Oh, this is delicious," or "My compliments to the chef," or "Where did you get this marvelous recipe?" . . . The Asian is unaccustomed to this kind of expression. His first reaction to it is that the American is a "big mouth" and the latter's friendship and interpersonal relationships are all equally superficial. (p. 11)

SUBCULTURAL VARIATIONS

Variations in language and verbal behavior may also be found when we encounter strangers who are members of certain unfamiliar subcultural groups within our society. Most commonly, we observe subcultural variations in language and verbal behavior among different regions, geographical areas, ethnic and racial groups, and social classes.

Acrolect, Mesilect, and Basilect

The speech variation within the United States and other English-speaking societies is conceptualized in sociolinguistic studies as including three classes: *Acrolect, Mesilect,* and *Basilect* (Nist, 1976). Briefly, the Acrolect refers to the most prestigious form of speech variety within the language, that used primarily by well-educated, culturally advantaged, socially adroit, and highly competent individuals. It is recognized as the "standard" version of its speech variety, regionalism, or geographical dialect. The Acrolectic individual is characterized as having a very extensive vocabulary that is fully responsive to the discourse demands placed on it by all social functions (colloquial, commercial, technical, literary, etc.) and contexts (intimate, familiar/casual, consultative, etc.).

The Basilect is placed at the opposite end of the social class continuum. It generally is recognized as being the substandard form of any speech variation in English-speaking societies. The Basilect, according to Nist (1976), is used primarily by those who have no more than a grade school education, are socially disadvantaged and are noticeably lacking in both speech competence and skills. Basilect users suffer from a very restricted vocabulary, bordering on illiteracy.

Between the Acrolect and the Basilect is the Mesilect, the most pervasive version of any speech variation within a given language. Speakers of Mesilect English in the United States tend to have no more than a high school education, to be neither socially advantaged nor skilled, and to be only fairly competent in communicative performance. Mesilect users have a rather restricted vocabulary that is only partially responsive to the discourse demands placed on it by the functions and contexts of social interaction. The Mesilect is not recognized as the standard or prestigious version of its speech variety, but rather as the most representative and common manifestation of it. Nist further identifies North American speakers of the Mesilect as those who come from families fostering interpersonal methods of learning (with emphasis on role obligation and differentiation), preferring closed systems of communication to open ones, and commonly using restricted codes instead of elaborated codes. On the other hand, speakers of Acrolect tend to come from families fostering intrapersonal methods of learning, open systems of communication, and elaborated codes.

A close association is apparent between the speech modes of the high-context cultures as described by Hall and those of the Acrolect, Mesilect, and Basilect subcultures in English-speaking societies as described by Nist. The communication patterns of high-context cultures evidence similarity to those of the Mesilect and Basilect subcultures of English-speaking societies; they show little similarity to those of the Acrolect subculture.

Language and Group Identity

The subcultural variations within a broader cultural system, as indicated in Chapters 4 and 5, often are accompanied by attitudinal orientations, such as stereotypes and prejudices, held by individuals toward language and speech patterns of their own and toward outside variations. A common language, as such, serves the function of being a powerful symbol of group identity. It can be the focus of loyalties expressing a simple sense of property and also a realization that when language barriers are minimized other forms of cultural separateness often diminish with them (Bourhis et al., 1979). The United States is plurilingual because of the addition of many immigrant groups, and use of "standard" English often has been a means and a measure of acculturation into the "mainstream." Plurilingualism may decline as generations pass, or it may remain an integral part of the society, reflecting and symbolizing persistent social divisions. Many regional, ethnic, racial, and social class speech varieties tend to persist for centuries, surviving strong pressures to succumb in favor of the standard dialects (Ryan, 1979).

In attempting to provide a systematic explanation for the persistence of linguistic diversity, Tajfel (1974; 1978) suggests that when members of one group interact with strangers of another, they compare themselves on a number of value dimensions with the strangers. He claims these intergroup social comparisons lead group members to search for characteristics of their own group that will enable them to differentiate themselves favorably from the out-group (as discussed in detail in Chapter 4). Such positive in-group distinctiveness not only allows individuals personal satisfaction in their own group membership but also affords them a positive social identity. Applying this psychological process to speech behavior, Giles (1973) describes the tendency to accentuate linguistic difference as *speech divergence.* On the other hand, some individuals in interaction with others shift their speech in their desire for their listeners' social approval. One tactic, consciously or unconsciously conceived, is for them to modify their speech in the direction of the listeners' speech patterns, a process Giles terms *speech convergence.*

A source of these psychological dynamics of speech convergence and divergence among members of minority speech communities is identified by Giles, Bourhis, and Taylor (1977) as the perceived "psychological threat." Giles, Bourhis, and Taylor suggest that when members of a subordinate group accept their inferior status, they attempt to converge into the dominant group socially and psychologically by means of speech convergence. If, on the other hand, they consider their inferior status to be illegitimate and the intergroup situation to be unstable, they seek "psychological distinctiveness" by redefining their group attributes in a socially and psychologically more favorable direction. They also might do this linguistically and hence, in interaction with a member of the out-group, accentuate their own in-group characteristics by means of speech divergence using their own dialect, accent, jargon, or other form of speech variation.

SUMMARY

In this chapter, we considered some of the cultural, sociological, and psychological dimensions of language and verbal behavior. The theoretical perspective provided by Sapir and Whorf warns us not to consider language to be merely a medium through which we express our thoughts and feelings. Language is much more than that. As we acquire language, we acquire culture, which, in turn, conditions our perception, thinking, and behavior. Once we realize this important contingency of the human condition, we also realize that the distinctions we make concerning language, culture, and mind are less than clear in reality, since all three simultaneously and interactively dictate the nature and the meaning of our experiences.

Following Bernstein's conceptualization of language and social context, various languages can be placed on a continuum of restricted and elaborated codes. This continuum of linguistic variations closely coincides with Hall's continuum of high-context to low-context cultural variations. While restricted codes are a predominant mode of linguistic and verbal behavior in high-context cultures, elaborated codes are relied on heavily for thinking processes and social interaction in low-context cultures. The conceptual framework of restricted and elaborated codes applies domestically to the speech variations of the three social classes: the Acrolect, the Mesilect, and the Basilect.

In addition, we noted how language ties us emotionally to the speech community to which we belong. Through group identification with our language, we develop both a sense of identification with our own speech community and a feeling of distinctiveness from other speech communities. A foreign diplomat visiting the United States (a stranger) may choose to speak at a press conference in his or her own language rather than in English. This deliberate choice of speech mode commonly is respected as a symbolic assertion of the national sovereignty represented by the diplomat. On the other hand, the heartwarming speech given by Pope John Paul II while visiting the United States recently constituted a friendly and respectful gesture to the American public in that he addressed his audience in English.

When a stranger moves from one culture to another for an extended period of time, the first and foremost task is to acquire the host language. The acquisition of the host language is necessary not only to communicate and to meet daily challenges but also to become acculturated into the new ways of living and to begin to develop a new group identity. As Lambert (1963) states, "an individual successfully acquiring a second language gradually adopts various aspects of behavior which characterize members of another linguistic-cultural group" (p. 114).

Understanding cultural and subcultural variations in the social meaning of verbal behavior as outlined in this chapter is a crucial step toward a greater understanding of ourselves and the strangers we meet. Based on such understanding, we may try to develop empathy and patience for strangers whose primary language and modes of verbal behavior are different from our own, thereby increasing our ability to understand and predict their behavior.

9
Cultural Variations in Nonverbal Behavior

— gestures
body, postures

The more I see the world of our day in greater detail, the more I consider the prodigious variety to be met with, the more I am tempted to believe that what we call necessary institutions are no more than institutions to which we have grown accustomed, and that the field of possibilities is much more extensive than men are ready to imagine.

Alexis de Tocqueville

Verbal vs Non-V

Just as verbal behaviors are conditioned by the overall cultural milieu, nonverbal behaviors reflect many of the cultural patterns we acquire throughout the socialization process. The way in which we move about in space and time when communicating with others is based primarily on our physical and emotional responses to environmental stimuli. While our verbal behaviors are mostly explicit and are processed through our cognition, our nonverbal behaviors are spontaneous, ambiguous, often fleeting, and often beyond our conscious awareness and control.

Thus, when we attempt to communicate with strangers, our understanding of the interaction is limited by the strangers' unfamiliar nonverbal behaviors as well as their unfamiliar perceptual and cognitive patterns and verbal messages. From greeting and gesturing to expressions of feelings and body postures, we may find ourselves to be at odds with strangers. Because nonverbal behaviors are rarely conscious phenomena, it may be difficult for us to know exactly why we are feeling uncomfortable.

Hall (1966) refers to the largely unconscious phenomenon of nonverbal communication as the "hidden dimension" of culture. It is considered hidden because, unlike verbal messages, nonverbal messages are embedded in the contextual field of communication. In addition to the situational and relational cues

149

of a particular communication transaction, nonverbal messages provide us with important contextual cues. Together with verbal and other contextual cues, nonverbal messages help us interpret the total meaning of a communication experience.

The purpose of this chapter is to increase our awareness of and sensitivity to the impact of this implicit, nonverbal dimension of our communication with strangers. We examine some of the variations in the nonverbal communication patterns of different cultures. First, we discuss general aspects of some nonverbal phenomena, such as people's spatial and temporal orientation and interpersonal interaction patterns. Then we present some of the more specific patterns, such as body movements, gestures, facial expressions, and vocal cues, that are idiosyncratic to specific cultures.

SPATIAL BEHAVIOR

, rel to space

People from dissimilar cultures not only use space differently, they actually experience it differently. In fact, Hall (1966) suggests these differences between cultures have their basis in the selective programming of the sensory capacities of the individuals in each culture. According to Hall, culture determines the structure of a people's perceptual world, leading to differential definitions of spaciousness, crowdedness, privacy, and appropriate or inappropriate distance between communicators.

An extensive body of research exists on the way people in various cultures relate to their physical space—how they perceive, organize, and behave in their spatial environment. Hall's work (1959; 1966; 1976; 1983) has contributed much to this line of research, called *proxemics*. Hall (1966) suggests, for example, human proxemic behavior can be classified into three general categories:

1. the *fixed feature,* such as spatial behavior in relation to an immovable and unchangeable environmental structure (e.g., organization of a town, architecture of a building);

2. the *semi-fixed feature,* which is conditioned by an environmental structure that is not permanently fixed (e.g., seating arrangement, furniture arrangement);

3. the *dynamic* (or informal) *feature,* which is codetermined by an individual's movement in space and by the movements of others with whom the person interacts.

These three categories, of course, are not mutually exclusive but are interrelated in any actual spatial behavior. For example, the way two college roommates live in a dormitory is influenced by the space as structured by their room and the building, as well as by the physical conditions of the university campus and the town in which the campus is located.

The Fixed or Semi-Fixed Feature

Most broadly, our spatial behavior is conditioned by the characteristics of the physical environment in which we live. Visitors from parts of the southwestern United States who are used to open space may find the residential areas in northeastern cities confining. Rural people are accustomed to large increments of space. In contrast, longtime urban residents have acquired a lifestyle more appropriate to metropolitan population density and the size of city buildings and rooms. Similarly, visitors from the United States to foreign countries often express surprise at the proximity of individual dwellings and the narrow roads. Generally speaking, people in the United States are accustomed to using more space than are people in many other countries.

Hall (1959; 1966) provides a great deal of data about cultural aspects of architectural space, i.e., the design of cities and houses. He identifies, for example, two major European patterns: the "radiating star" of France and Spain, and the "grid," which often is found in England. In the former pattern streets and subway lines meet at major intersections, thereby bringing activities together; the latter pattern tends to separate activities. Both systems give names to streets. In contrast, the traditional Japanese and other Asian cultures are inclined to attend to the space between objects. The Japanese system, for example, emphasizes the concept of center, and intersections rather than streets are named.

This contrast of edge versus inner space is visible in the design and use of private homes, as indicated in Chapter 6. Westerners in general tend to arrange furniture around the fixed outside walls of a room and to leave the center relatively bare. Also, rooms are divided for specific functions (such as food preparation, eating, entertaining, and resting). On the other hand, interior walls of traditional Asian homes are semi-fixed; center space is utilized and total rooms are multipurpose (Hall, 1966; Condon and Kurata, 1973). The space inside Arab homes is very different from what one finds in most Western and Asian homes. Arabs avoid partitions, and the form of their homes is such that it holds the family together inside a single protective shell. Hall (1966) attributes this spatial arrangement to Arabs' desire to avoid being alone.

The Dynamic Feature

The dynamic interpersonal space is controlled by the nature of the relationship between interactants. In general, we can say that the more intimate a relationship, the more people permit each other to come close. Ashcraft and Scheflen (1976) observe:

In the early stages of courtship, distance may be an issue of negotiation. But as courtship escalates, whatever the earlier distancing arrangements, the space between partners is reduced drastically. It disappears altogether in the physical union of copulation. (p. 7)

In the context of the United States, Hall (1966) proposes four spatial zones involved in social relations: *in USA*

1. *Intimate distance* (0–18 inches) usually is maintained only between intimates or close associates, and not often in public. At this distance a rich array of cues can be exchanged, including heat, smell, fine visual details, and touch.

2. *Personal distance* (1.5–4 feet) is a transitional distance where rich communication possibilities still exist.

3. *Social distance* (4–12 feet) is the distance of business and general public contact. Office desks, furniture arrangements in public settings, and chair locations in homes generally put people somewhere in this zone. One can still receive a fair number of communication cues, but they are not fine-grained.

4. *Public distance* (12–25 feet) usually is reserved for formal occasions, public speakers, or high status figures. Here only gross cues are available and such cues as smell, heat, and fine visual and vocal details are lost.

These spatial zones, however, are not identical in all cultures. In India, for example, one can sense the lack of respect for private use of public space when, in a crowded bus, people intrude upon one's personal space without saying "excuse me." Hall (1966) observes that Arabs are often nose to nose, touching one another and breathing in one another's faces when they communicate. To the Arab good smells are considered pleasing and a way of being involved with each other. To smell one's friend is desirable, for to deny him or her your breath is to act ashamed. In Latin America the interaction distance is typically much less than it is in the United States. According to Hall, people in Latin America often cannot talk comfortably with each other unless they are very close together, at a distance that might evoke either sexual or hostile feelings in North America.

TEMPORAL BEHAVIOR

Like space, time is an important basic dimension underlying all communication processes. Time communicates as powerfully as verbal language. Our understanding and use of time falls under a class of nonverbal communication called *temporality* (or chronemic communication).

Temporality of a cultural group is the manner in which subjective and objective forms of time-experiencing interact. Bruneau (1979b) observes that the manner in which "highly variable forms of subjective time-experiencing interact with somewhat constant or consistent objective tempo of time-experiencing in given cultures helps to determine the characteristic tempo of a culture" (p. 429). In other words, when certain forms of periodic and cyclic objective time interact with personal, social, and cultural activities and events, a particular cultural tempo develops and becomes the temporal environment of a cultural group. For example, many "developing" cultures are paced by a merging of subjective time-experiencing with cyclic, periodic forms of objective time, such as the repetition of biological, natural, and celestial movements. As these cultures become "modernized," industrialized, and more complex in their institutional structures and processes, cultural time becomes heavily reliant on artificial clock time. The pacing of life according to clocks can lead to a clock-bound condition. A clock-bound cultural group seems to stress objective clock time as the true and real form of time, which is often more important than the personal and subjective forms of time-experiencing.

Hall (1976) provides a further elaboration of cultural patterning and pacing of time as _monochronic time (or M-time) and polychronic time (or P-time)_, as indicated in Chapter 6. These two types of cultural time, of course, are not meant to represent an either-or categorization of cultures; they are intended to be used for a typification of cultures in terms of the degree of monochronic and polychronic tendencies in their temporal orientation. M-time people tend to emphasize schedules, segmentation, and promptness. Most of the clock-bound cultures, including North American and Northern and Western European cultures, can be characterized as highly monochronic. M-time cultures tend to perceive time as a linear progression marching from the past into the future. They tend to treat time as a tangible, discrete entity, which can be "saved," "borrowed," "divided," "lost," and even "killed." P-time people, on the other hand, tend to treat time in a more holistic way and to place a primary value on the activities occurring in time rather than the clock time itself. P-time cultures stress involvement of people and completion of transactions rather than adherence to schedules. P-time usually is considered a "point rather than a ribbon or a road, and that point is sacred" (Hall, 1976, p. 17). Thus in many P-time systems punctuality is not as sacred as it is in M-time systems. If something important needs to be completed, the P-time person can sacrifice the next scheduled activity more readily than can the M-time person. In contrast, it is not uncommon in an M-time system to see some of the most exciting activities being stopped abruptly simply because "time is up."

Of particular importance in understanding the temporal behavior of a stranger is to be aware of the pace of life to which the stranger is accustomed. For example, the temporal environment of the large cities in the United States, such as New York City, epitomizes the clock-bound M-time system. To a stranger who comes from a less clock-bound culture, New York's temporal environment can be particularly striking. A Korean student reports his interpretation of New York's temporal characteristics as follows:

> To be a New Yorker among New Yorkers means a totally new experience from being Japanese or Chinese or Korean—a changed character. New Yorkers all seem to have some aim in every movement they make. . . . How unlike Asiatics in an Oriental village, who drift up and down aimlessly and leisurely. But these people have no time, even for gossiping, even for staring. To be thrown among New Yorkers—yes, it means to have a new interpretation of life never conceived before: the business interpretation. Even the man who only goes to a show and is making arrangements about it, has a businesslike air. His every action is decisive, orderly, and purposeful. . . . he must know exactly what he wants to do in his mind. . . . His mind is like Grand Central Station. It is definite, it is timed, it has mathematical precision on clearcut stone foundations. (Oliver, 1971, p. 4)

African cultures generally are viewed as P-time systems that are not very clock-bound. Africans do have their objective time systems, but these are based more on seasonal cycles, natural events, and biological rhythms and are therefore generally more flexible, less rigid, and less segmented (Harris and Moran, 1979). Because of this relative flexibility, Africans tend to consider people in a hurry with suspicion and distrust. Since trust is very important among them, they want to sit and talk—get to know the other person—even in business transactions. If a North American businessperson appears to them to be too task-oriented, for example, the Africans may interpret it as planned foul play, arrogance, or insincerity.

The Sioux Indians provide us with another interesting example of a differing orientation toward time. Hall (1959) gives an account of a Sioux Indian school superintendent concerning the time behavior of his culture:

> During a long and fascinating account of the many problems which his tribe was having in adjusting to our way of life, he suddenly remarked: "What would you think of a people who had no word for time? My people have no word for 'late' or for 'waiting,' for that matter. They don't know what it is to wait or to be late." (p. 25)

We can observe similar variations in temporal orientation between urban and rural areas. As mentioned earlier, such large urban areas as New York City present an extremely time-bound and monochronic temporal environment. On the other hand, most remote rural areas and small towns still maintain a less rigid, less segmented, and less hurried temporal environment.

INTERACTION PATTERNS

The spatial and temporal environment of a cultural group is related closely to the way individuals initiate and engage in interpersonal interaction. The term *adumbration* is used by Hall (1964) to describe the nonverbal processes, particularly the time and space orientations, of people in various cultures in initiating conversations.

Generally speaking, rigidity in adumbrative behaviors is related closely to the overall emphasis and significance of nonverbal communication behaviors in a cultural group. As discussed earlier, individuals in low-context cultures tend to rely less on nonverbal and other contextual cues than do people in high-context cultures. People in the United States, for example, say there is a time and place for everything; however, compared to people in other countries, they give relatively little emphasis to such distinctions. Business is almost a universal value; it can be discussed almost anywhere, except perhaps in church. On the other hand, people in high-context cultures tend to place a greater social and psychological significance on feeling "right" about the place and time of inter-action. In India one rarely is permitted to talk business when visiting a person's home. In many Asian and South American cultures it is a common practice to go to a relaxing eating or drinking place to initiate business talk. Also, the pre-liminary steps in a business negotiation may take place on the golf course.

Once an interpersonal interaction takes place, people unconsciously move together in synchrony (in whole or in part) and failing to do so is disruptive to others around them. Hall (1976; 1983) identifies such interactional movements as interpersonal *syncing*. Syncing patterns are culture-specific and expressed through language and body movements. For instance, the synchronized move-ments of two Anglo-Saxon persons are distinctly different from those of two working-class blacks or two Pueblo Indians. Each culture has its own character-istic manner of greeting, departing, talking, gesturing, laughing, and fighting.

Interpersonal syncing is a basis for an *action chain* or a "sequence of events in which usually two or more individuals participate" (Hall, 1976, p. 41). Every action has a beginning, a climax, and an end and comprises a number of inter-mediate states. If any of the basic acts are left out or are too greatly distorted, the action must be started all over again. An action chain resembles a dance that is used as a means of reaching a common goal. Greeting, parting, engaging in serious discussion, becoming engaged, and buying something in a store are all examples of action chains of varying complexity. According to Hall, the degree to which one is committed to complete an action chain varies across cultures. High-context cultures, because of the high degree of involvement between people, the highly interrelated, cohesive nature of interpersonal relationships, and the overall sensitivity to nonverbal and other contextual cues, tend toward a high commitment to complete an action chain. The strong adherence to inter-personal syncing and completion of action chains by people in high-context cultures results in great caution and often reluctance to begin something, par-ticularly in fields or relationships that are not well-known. White North Ameri-cans and other people in low-context cultures do not ordinarily feel bound to complete action chains regardless of circumstances. Relatively speaking, many white North Americans break an action readily if they do not like the way things are going or if something or someone better comes along. This can be very frustrating to a stranger from a high-context culture emphasizing completion of action chains in interpersonal relationships. Conversely, North Americans may find the adherence to action chains by people in high-context cultures too binding and burdensome.

KINESIC BEHAVIOR → *concerning the use and communicative meaning of body movements*

In addition to the general spatial and temporal orientations and the overall inter-action patterns of syncing and action chains, people in different cultures acquire patterns of movements that are communicative in their cultural context. The line of research concerning the use and communicative meaning of body move-ments is called *kinesics*. Birdwhistell (1970) is among the best-known researchers to link body movements to their cultural and linguistic contexts. He believes human body movements such as gestures, head movements, facial expressions, and leg movements are determined primarily by the conditioning of our culture and our speech behavior. For example, Birdwhistell's initial anthropological field work in 1949 among the Kutenai Indians of western Canada suggests their pat-terns of nonverbal behavior differ when they speak English and when they speak their native language. To illustrate cross-cultural variations, we will examine several areas of kinesic behavior.

Indicating Agreement and Disagreement

In many cultures, people say yes by nodding the head and no by shaking the head. This is even the case with most of the Waika Indians, Samoans, Balinese, and Papuans. The Ceylonese, however, are observed to have two ways of saying yes (Eibl-Eibesfeldt, 1979). The Ceylonese answer "yes" to a factual question (e.g., "Are you a student?") by nodding. If, however, a Ceylonese person agrees with someone's remark (e.g., "Will you go with me?"), he or she sways the head in slow sideways movements with the head tilted slightly during the movement. In Ceylon "no" is always expressed by shaking the head in the way many cul-tural groups do. Also, Eibl-Eibesfeldt reports that in Greece "yes" is expressed with a nod as in North America, but "no" is expressed by jerking the head back, thus lifting the face. Often the eyes are closed and the eyebrows lifted. When "no" is being strongly emphasized, one or both hands are lifted up to the shoul-ders, the palms facing the opponent.

Greeting

Greeting is another social ritual that involves body movements and varies across cultures. The bow, for example, is a posture about which much has been written. In many hierarchical Asian societies, appropriate bowing should correspond to the hierarchical relationship between the persons involved. When an Asian communicates with someone considered to be superior, the common method of symbolizing one's "smallness" in comparison to the "greatness" of the other is to "shrink" oneself. The inferior must begin the bow and bow deeper, while the superior determines when the bow is complete. When participants are of equal status, they both bow the same way and begin and end the bow at approximately the same time. The intricate interpersonal difference of status appears to be difficult for many Westerners to understand, but is understood well by Asians. For Westerners in individualistic and egalitarian cultures, greeting usually takes the form of a handshake and the expression of differing status is more subtle and less ritualized than it is in a more group-oriented, hierarchical society (the intricacies of handshaking were examined in Chapter 3).

La Barre (1976) reports additional examples of greeting in different cultures. According to La Barre, bowing or handshaking often is replaced by extensive physical contact in more tactile "contact cultures," such as the Arabic, Jewish, Latin American, and Southern European. In Bali two lovers may greet each other by breathing deeply in a kind of friendly sniffing. The Burmese, Mongols, and Lapps traditionally smell each other's cheeks to say hello. Copper Eskimos are reported to welcome strangers with a buffet on the head or shoulders using the fist, while northwestern Amazonians typically slap one another on the back when greeting. Polynesian men frequently greet one another by embracing and rubbing each other's back. Some Spanish-American males greet one another with a stereotyped embrace—head over the right shoulder of the partner, pats on the back, head over the left shoulder, and more pats. In the Torres Straits the old form of greeting was to bend the right hand into a hook, then mutually scratch palms by drawing right hands across them, repeating this several times. La Barre also reports that an Ainu meeting his sister grasps her hands in his for a few seconds, suddenly releases his hold, grasps her by both ears and gives the Ainu greeting cry; then they stroke one another down the face and shoulders.

Smutkupt and Barna (1976) point out a difference in sitting posture between Western cultures and Thai culture. Although almost all Westerners tend to cross their legs while sitting on a chair, many of them are not generally aware of the direction in which the top foot is pointed. According to Smutkupt and Barna, if a Westerner happens to have the top foot pointed at a Thai, the Thai may feel embarrassed, or even offended, unless he or she is aware of Western ways. The crucial significance of this behavior is Thais consider feet to be the most objectionable and lowest body component.

In more hierarchical cultures, including many Asian and African cultures, social status differences between communicators are defined more clearly, and social rituals reflect such status differences. Accordingly, the sitting position of the inferior person shows respect and humility more explicitly than it does in more egalitarian societies. For instance, a North American student may sit back in a chair in front of a professor, relaxed and comfortable; such a posture might be perceived in African and Asian cultures as lacking in respect and reverence.

Hand Gestures

Hand gestures can be classified according to any one of a number of schemes. The most widely accepted system is put forth by Ekman and Friesen (1969; 1971). They list three categories of manual behavior: emblems, illustrators, and adaptors. *Emblems* can be translated directly into a word or phrase (such as the A-OK sign in the United States or various obscene gestures); *illustrators* are speech accompaniments that do not have discrete meaning in and of themselves but serve to emphasize verbal output; *adaptors* are hand movements oriented to the self (such as scratching) or involve the use of a physical object.

The use of emblems provides the least amount of information about a person's psychological state or relationship to another person, since emblems are used consciously and are conventionalized movements signifying a concept or affect that could be conveyed through language. Emblems generally give expression to ideas or feelings that can be verbalized but would be awkward or inappropriate to express through such a channel. Obscene gestures certainly fall in this category. Many hand gestures are reminiscent of religious and superstitious practices (Bates, 1975), such as crossing the fingers to signify luck. Johnson, Ekman, and Friesen (1975) isolate more than 100 common emblems in contemporary use in the United States, such as, for example, "shame on you," and "follow me."

The role of cultural influence on the acquisition of gesticulatory habits is discussed by Efron (1941). He observes large differences in gestural style in New York City between unassimilated members of two European cultures, Southern Italian and Eastern European Jewish. Many of these cultural differences are related to the conversational control process. For example, traditional Jews characteristically converse at very close distances. This proximity is associated with a high level of gesturing, often with head movements because of the restricted opportunities for arm motion. Manual contact between conversants is common, both as an attention-eliciting device by speakers and as a means of gaining a turn to speak by listeners. The traditional Italian displays more fluid and controlled gesticulatory habits and tends to use termination of hand movement as a signal of wanting a turn to speak.

Also, according to Morsbach (1976), a North American teacher in Laos had his "OK" signal (a circle with thumb and index finger) mistaken for "zero" or "bad" by his students. This signal is interpreted as a signal of money in Japan. In Western countries it usually means "OK," "good," "delicious," etc.

Another example of cultural differences in emblems is the way people in different cultures count to five using the fingers. Most people in the United States begin with a closed fist and extend one finger per number. Members of some other cultures, including China, Japan, and Korea, begin with an open fist and fold down one finger per number, so that five is represented by a closed fist.

Expression of Emotions

The basic human emotions are biologically based responses to external stimuli and thus are experienced universally regardless of cultural differences. People everywhere experience feelings such as happiness, sadness, and anger and exhibit a great deal of similarity in their expressions of these human emotions. Charles Darwin (1892) pointed out certain similarities in the expressive behavior of humans with different cultural backgrounds and interpreted these as being due to characteristics inborn in all humans. Biologists, biologically oriented anthropologists, and psychologists repeatedly emphasize the innate, biological base and similarities of human expressive behavior. This view, however, is challenged repeatedly. La Barre (1947) is among the best-known proponents of a culturally based theory of emotional expression. Similarly, Birdwhistell (1963) advances the hypothesis that no expressive movement has a universal meaning and that all movements are a product of culture and not biologically inherited or inborn.

These two views on human emotional expression are integrated into a third perspective, a "neuro-cultural theory of facial expressions of emotion," by Ekman (1972). Even though Ekman basically supports the innate position, he believes cultural constraints play a very important role in shaping emotional expression. He advocates both an innate basis for the connection between certain emotional states and given facial muscles ("the facial affect program") and a cultural overlay of display rules that can intensify, deintensify, neutralize, or mask the facial display to comply with the normative demands of specific situations in a culture. For example, many Asians are conditioned to use the face to control or moderate their emotional expressions and often are encouraged to conceal, rather than reveal, negative feelings. This is particularly the case when they are dealing with people they feel should be addressed politely.

Discouraging negative expressions is considered by many Asians to be an expression of courtesy, self-suppression, social discipline, or a desire to inflict no needless suffering on others. The well-known "Oriental smile" is a case in point. Perplexing to a Westerner at first, it becomes quite understandable when one learns the ethical code motivating it. For instance, when someone violates an expected etiquette, Westerners typically respond by withdrawing or with a show of displeasure. On the other hand, Asians are more apt to smile, giggle, or laugh nervously. The trained observer can distinguish between the latter and the laugh prompted by something pleasant. Gulick (1962) reports his personal experiences in Japan, where his maid smiled even when she told him of the death of her mother. Even pleasant emotions sometimes are controlled by Asians. Women tend to cover the mouth when laughing, and men often show true merriment (and also true anger) only after work hours, when their culture allows them greater freedom of behavior while drinking alcohol. Even though Asians are in fact highly emotional and sensitive, they may be perceived as the opposite by Westerners due to their lack of outward expression of emotions.

Eye Behavior

Movements of the eyes have been a subject of investigation in many cross-cultural studies. According to Hall (1959), the English sometimes have difficulty in communicating with North Americans due to subtle differences in eye behavior. The English are taught to pay strict attention and to listen carefully. They do not nod or grunt to let you know they understand. Proper English listening behavior includes immobilization of the eyes at a social focal distance, so that either eye gives the appearance of looking straight at the speaker. Also, the English blink their eyes to let you know they have heard you. On the other hand, the gaze of a North American listener directed toward his or her conversational partner often wanders from one eye to the other, and even leaves the speaker's face for long periods.

Traditionally, Asian women are not expected to look straight into the eyes of men, especially of strangers. Similarly, Asian subordinates may not look straight at their superiors; such an act may be perceived as reflecting a defiant or disrespectful attitude. Johnson (1976) and Aschcraft and Scheflen (1976) observe that blacks in the United States, as well as people in Western African cultures, often are reluctant to look at another person who is in an authority role. Instead they look at imaginary spots above, below, or to the sides of the other's body. Looking into another's eyes in the black subculture of the United States may invite the escalation of a hostile encounter. Members of this subculture are quite conscious of the rules about looking into the face, and children are taught these rules at an early age. A mother may chastise her son, "Get your eyes out of my face, boy!" Johnson (1976) compares the pattern of blacks to the act of "cutting the eyes" in the dominant culture of the United States. In cutting the eyes, according to Johnson, the movement of the eyes is always toward another person, and furthermore, after the eyes are focused on the other person, they usually remain focused in a stare. In other words, the stare follows the cutting action.

In some cultures, the up-and-down movement of eyebrows is suppressed. In most Asian cultures such movement is perceived to border on indecency. In Samoa, by contrast, it is used regularly in greeting, as a general sign of approval or agreement, when speaking in confirmation, and when beginning a statement in dialogue (Eibl-Eibesfeldt, 1979). People in many Western cultures use this signal in approximately the same situations, although they perform it less readily in a greeting encounter. In addition, it is seen frequently in Western cultures during flirting, when demonstrating approval or gratitude, and during discussions, for example, when emphasizing a statement and thus calling for attention.

Vocal Cues

Mannerisms in speaking are primarily a result of individual idiosyncracies. Yet there are some indications noticeable cultural differences in the mannerisms of speaking exist. Hall (1966), for example, observes that loudness of the voice is one of the speech mechanisms varying from culture to culture. According to Hall, people in the United States often are considered to speak loudly by the English and people in other European countries. North Americans tend to in-crease the volume of speech as a function of distance or message content, using several levels such as whisper, normal voice, and loud shout. In many situations the more gregarious people do not mind if they can be overheard. The English do care, according to Hall, because in order to get along without private offices and so as not to intrude on others, they have developed skills in beaming the carefully adjusted voice toward the person to whom they are talking.

A similar pattern of playing down the voice is observed among North Ameri-cans, particularly among males in a more formal setting such as a business con-text. North American males, according to Hall and Whyte (1979), are taught to suppress feelings in public situations. They are conditioned generally to suppress expressions of emotion, and a strict self-control is considered desirable. The more important a matter, the more solemn and outwardly dispassionate they are likely to be. In the Arab world, on the other hand, people are encouraged to express their feelings without inhibition. Grown men are free to weep, shout, and gesture expressively. In discussions among equals, Arab men attain a decibel level considered aggressive, objectionable, and even obnoxious by North Ameri-cans. To Arabs, according to Hall and Whyte, loudness connotes strength and sincerity, and a soft tone implies weakness or even deviousness.

SUMMARY

In this chapter we examined some of the identifiable patterns of nonverbal behaviors in different cultures. First, we discussed cultural variations in spatial behavior, employing Hall's conceptual framework of fixed, semi-fixed, and dynamic features. Second, different temporalities of cultures were compared in terms of the varying degree of monochronic or polychronic tendencies. Even within a cultural group, temporal differences can be noted, such as between urban temporal environment and rural temporal environment.

Applying the general information about spatial and temporal behavior pat-terns to interpersonal interaction, we discussed cultural variations in what Hall calls adumbrative behaviors in initiating conversations, general interpersonal syncing, and action chains. We noted these nonverbal dimensions of interper-sonal communication are more rigidly and consciously observed in high-context cultures, reflecting those cultures' sensitivity to and reliance on implicit, con-textual cues in interpreting communicative events.

In addition, we presented some of the culture-specific characteristics of kinesic behavior and of vocal expression of emotions. We examined cultural variations in such kinesic areas as head movements, greeting movements, sitting posture, gesticulation, facial expression of emotions, and eye behavior. Cultu-ral variations in vocal expression of emotions were explored in relation to the degree to which a cultural norm encourages or suppresses vocal expressiveness in public.

As mentioned at the beginning of this chapter, nonverbal patterns of communication are often subtle, fleeting, and hard to identify concretely and specifically. Individuals and subgroups within a cultural community vary significantly as well, which renders the analysis of nonverbal behaviors difficult and some of the observed findings tentative in nature. Yet nonverbal behaviors are profoundly influential in determining the process and the outcome of a particular transaction. When communicating with strangers, we must be keenly aware of the implicit nonverbal process. While the experiencing of human emotions may be essentially universally the same, human expression of emotions varies across cultures. To be effective in communicating with strangers, we need to develop sensitivity to their nonverbal behavior as well as to their verbal behavior. If we do not develop this sensitivity, our interpretations and predictions of strangers' behavior will inevitably be inaccurate.

10
Universals of Communication

The individual is going to be universalized, the universal is going to be individualized, and thus from both directions the whole is going to be enriched.

Jan C. Smuts

The preceding three chapters dealt with some of the cultural variations in decoding and encoding patterns of communication. Awareness of differences between individuals allows us to develop a sense of unique self, and awareness of cultural differences helps us to understand the dimension of ourselves that is conditioned by our cultural environment. As Hall (1976) states, "understanding oneself and understanding others are closely related processes. To do one, you must start with the other, and vice versa" (p. 69).

Diversity of human culture is the breath of life for humanity; it provides insight into the variety and complexity of human conditions. If all cultures shared the same communication patterns, if individuals in all cultures perceived, thought, verbalized, and nonverbally expressed their feelings in an identical manner, the lack of diversity would ultimately deter human evolution. Of all animals, humans are the most creative because we remember and express the largest variety of experiences. If we compare homogenization of individual differences to cloning, what is true for individual cloning is also true for cultural cloning. Human cloning would transform humanity into an ant hill.

Paradoxically, however, what enables humans to communicate and understand one another is their commonality in decoding and encoding processes, including the use of symbols. The commonality humans possess as individuals and groups binds us together as members of the human community. Thus, when we communicate with strangers, we need not only to recognize the differences existing between strangers and ourselves but also to search for the commonalities we share with the strangers.

Many cross-cultural researchers enthusiastically assume a universality of a common core of human culture while acknowledging the enormous variation in specifics. The basic explanation for the universality seems to be in the intrinsic nature of humans as social animals and in their capacity to use symbols and to develop a speech communication community. While the detailed manifestations of such human social activities vary from culture to culture, all humans need, and have the capacity, to communicate within their social and physical environment in one form or another.

In this chapter, we discuss some of the recognized universals of human communication behavior. Incorporating the topics of the preceding three chapters, we first present commonalities across cultures in patterns of message decoding, i.e., perception and thinking and interpersonal orientation. Second, we examine universalities in language and verbal behavior and nonverbal behavior. Finally, we briefly discuss the increasing convergence of cultures and its implications for communicating with strangers.

DECODING

The fundamental process of perception and thinking—of receiving and processing information from the environment—is present in all communication activities and is the most basic of human intellectual activities. As a cultural universal, perception and thinking are inherent capacities of humans whose cognitive abilities are functioning in a normal fashion. Each culture helps to shape individual cognitive patterns according to the common experiences of that particular culture.

Regardless of their cultural backgrounds, all humans *categorize* objects and people, as indicated in Chapter 5. All humans must employ stereotypes to organize and deal with the kaleidoscopic flow of events around them. The mere attaching of a name to more than one object, such as using chair as the name for many differently shaped pieces of furniture, is to classify objects, to treat them as exemplars of a particular category. By thus recognizing a common attribute, we are using the single most important cognitive tool available to us—namely, language. All cultures employ language to classify and categorize.

Further, the human cognitive process shows a universal tendency to *compare* or *evalute* persons, objects, and ideas. As Osgood (1964) concludes, the comparative-evaluative tendency follows a pattern of placing an object with respect to bipolar attributes. Thus we compare attributes of persons and place them on such bipolar scales as masculine-feminine, tall-short, handsome-ugly, warm-cold, aggressive-timid, strong-weak, and introvert-extrovert. Such a pattern is apparent in all cultures. All languages have words signifying opposite or complementary attributes of persons, objects, and ideas. Also, our existing cultural, sociocultural, and psychocultural values provide a familiar framework of reference against which new information is compared or evaluated (Campbell and Levine, 1968). Regardless of cultural differences, all humans share a common tendency to compare and evaluate other persons' attributes and behaviors based on their own internalized value system. This universal tendency is called egocentrism on the interpersonal level and ethnocentrism on the group level.

Everyone must perform certain other conceptual operations, such as deciding how to separate persons, things, and ideas that are related. These conceptual operations are made possible by language. In all languages the tools for these operations are apparent in the grammatical structure, although the specific characteristics of the grammatical structure vary from language community to language community. For example, in Western cultures emphasis usually is placed on facts and the logical development of ideas, while in many non-Western cultures emphasis is placed on grasping concepts by holistic intuition (see Chapter 7).

The difference in thinking patterns across cultures is one of degree and emphasis. The hemispheric specialization of functions in the human brain (discussed in Chapter 7) appears to be present in all humans. The two modes of cognitive processing (linear-logical and holistic-intuitive) are used by all individuals. The observed difference between Western and Eastern cultures is in their relative public evaluation implicit throughout the enculturation process of individuals. For instance, education in the United States focuses almost exclusively on the training of the left, analytical half of the brain, while education in the Eastern cultural milieu tends to encourage development of the holistic conceptual process of the right half of the brain (Hall, 1976; Jantsch, 1980).

Thus, whether you are a North American or a Japanese, you perform both linear-logical and holistic-intuitive modes of thinking. When you are writing a scientific report, your thinking pattern is predominantly linear-logical. At times, however, you may suddenly feel intuitively that something in the report is not quite right. On these occasions you are experiencing a holistic-intuitive mode of thinking, which can be switched back to the linear-logical mode as you begin to deliberate on possible causes for the problems. The difference between North Americans and Japanese, then, lies in the relative modality of the two modes of thinking. Generally speaking, Japanese use their holistic-intuitive mode more readily than do North Americans, given that all other social and personal characteristics of the two are similar. Conversely, "typical" North Americans are likely to use a greater modality of linear-logical thinking than are "typical" Japanese.

Interpersonal Orientation

Throughout their lives people belong to small primary groups, such as family, play, interest, and association groups, in which interaction between members is face to face, intimate, and personal. Such natural groups are found in all kinds of societies at all levels of complexity. As Coon (1946) maintains, natural groups are characteristic of humans everywhere. The only difference with respect to natural groupings between traditional and modern societies, and between high-context and low-context cultures, appears to be a quantitative rather than a qualitative one. The less technological the society, the greater is the role of the primary group; the more technological the society, the more numerous and complex are its groups and the greater is the possibility the individual may freely join and leave these groups. Similarly, the people in traditional, high-context cultures tend to be more group-oriented in their interpersonal orientation and thus more rigid in adhering to interaction rituals.

Yet in all cultures there appears to be an inherent human need to belong to a group in a significant and meaningful way. Also, cross-cultural researchers find a widespread tendency for groups to reject their deviant members and for group decisions to function as a powerful source of commitment for members (Mann, 1980). Such group influence, through its implicit and explicit pressures to conform, is the very force by which an individual becomes a cultural being and acquires the many cultural characteristics of communication. The cross-cultural variations discussed in the preceding chapters, then, are variant forms of the essentially panhuman phenomenon of individual-group interaction. The specific nature of an individual-group relationship, of course, is determined by the characteristics of its particular cultural milieu.

Given the universal interdependency of individuals and groups, the factors of status (vertical hierarchy, or "pecking order") and solidarity (intimacy) strongly influence many of the interpersonal communication patterns in every culture. People modify their communication behaviors according to the nature of the interpersonal power and/or intimacy involved in a particular transaction. Again, the cross-cultural differences observed earlier, such as the degree of rigidity with which individuals adhere to status and solidarity distinctions in their communication behaviors, reflect the nature of a specific cultural context. Thus members of a high-context culture (which is often based on a clearly defined hierarchical social structure) tend to emphasize verbal and nonverbal mannerisms that reflect interpersonal status distinction. On the other hand, the expression of status is more subtle and indirect in the United States which is a low-context culture primarily based on an egalitarian social structure and having equality as one of its core cultural values.

LANGUAGE AND VERBAL BEHAVIOR

The Sapir-Whorf hypothesis (discussed in Chapter 8) stresses the dynamic interrelatedness of culture, language, and the message-decoding patterns of individuals. Categorization of sensory information occurs through the use of language; to the extent that different languages present different categorization systems, language reflects the implicit cultural milieu in which it is used. On the other hand, certain commonalities are observed across language groups. According to Chomsky (1972), all or most "natural" languages have rules, or grammars, that distinguish the right sentences from the wrong sentences based on an innate "deep structure." The superficial structures of different languages may be vastly different, but remarkable similarities appear at the level below the surface. This linguistic perspective further holds that the base structure of the human mind permits, as well as limits, all language development. If this "innate," deep-structure model of invariant language development is correct—and most linguists appear to lean in that direction—then the basis for making universalistic assertions would be on solid ground.

Greenberg's (1966) research suggests all languages share phonetic features as well as grammar and lexicon, indicating that physiological, psychological, and pancultural dimensions link human languages and, consequently, perceptual and thinking processes. Further, Berlin and Kay's study (1969), based on small samples of speakers of 20 different languages, provides evolutionary evidence that focal colors (the "best blue," etc.) are stable, while color terms and color boundaries are somewhat variable. The simpler or more traditional a culture is, the fewer names there will be in the color perception and vocabulary. The fact one or more of eleven basic focal colors is found and named in a predictable sequence as a function of graded social complexity, however, is a good example of a type of linguistic universality.

Closely linked to the human language and verbal pattern is the recognition of the limitations of verbal messages as a medium of human expression. The limited capacity of language in accurately and fully reflecting inner thoughts and feelings is recognized widely in many Asian cultures. As discussed in Chapters 7 and 8, such awareness appears to intensify the Asian emphasis on nonverbal and other contextual cues in interpreting the meaning of a communication transaction. Even in Western cultures in which primary communicative interest is given to verbal messages, frequent observations are made concerning the limitations of language. Throughout Western European history, many philosophers and scholars express this view (Pearce and Branham, 1978). Alfred Korzybski, the founding scholar of the general semantic theory of the relationship between language, reality, and human behavior, clearly points to the limitations of language. Korzybski (1933) compares language to a map representing the territory it covers but never quite being the same as the territory itself. That is, language can no more say everything about an event than a map can show everything in a territory.

The use of silence in interpersonal communication is another universal phenomenon. Although there is a noticeable difference between, say, Chinese and North American cultures in handling interpersonal silence, such silence serves a basically similar function of "hesitancy" in both groups. As Bruneau (1979a) points out, the psychological time, or "mind time," provided by the silent moments in all human communication processes enables speakers to clarify, recognize, interpret, and engage in understanding activities. In every culture people tend to feel more comfortable about each other's silences as a relationship becomes more informal and intimate. It seems that functions of silence in interpersonal communication clearly have universal bearing and that cultural variation in the attitude toward silence is a matter of degree and emphasis.

NONVERBAL BEHAVIOR

The specific and general variations in nonverbal behavior in different cultures were discussed in Chapter 9. As it does language and verbal cues, culture programs and shapes the way people move about in space and time and in relation to each other in interaction processes. Yet underlying the observed variations are the commonalities of the human condition, i.e., the experiences of emotions and the mechanisms to find a place in time and space.

Studies have shown the existence of a panhuman need for personal space. Even though some cultures (such as the German) appear to have high needs for personal space, while others (such as the Arab) appear to have low needs, individuals in all cultures claim some space around them as their personal territory. Such claims sometimes must be compromised when available space is limited. In the Arab family, for example, where one cannot easily find any physical privacy, people try to be alone by ceasing conversation (Hall, 1966). Milgram's study (1970) of urban residents in the United States speaks of the experience of living in crowded cities as an adaptation to the cognitive overload of the environment. The study shows a tendency of residents of crowded cities to use a series of regulatory mechanisms, including allocation of less time to others, curt responses, disregard of all but the most intense message inputs, and the use of physical and electronic barriers such as doormen and unlisted phone numbers.

The variations in cultural tempo and the ways people in different cultures experience time manifest the universal human tendency to organize life activities. The unique development of a cultural tempo based on subjective and objective time experiences in rural areas appears to be clearly different from that in metropolitan areas such as New York City. Hall's classification of M-time and P-time systems, discussed in Chapter 9, is useful in understanding such cultural differences. At the same time it is important to recognize the fact that the two temporal systems are not necessarily mutually exclusive. Within most cultures we find both systems operating. For example, a New Yorker may show M-time behavior in business settings and P-time behavior during more informal hours at home or with friends.

In addition to organizing their space and time, people interacting with others tend to organize their bodily movements in response to others' movements and to the language they speak. As discussed in Chapter 9, Hall (1976;

1983) observes syncing patterns in many cultures and concludes that, even though the specific patterns of syncing and the degree of rigidity in adhering to the interactional "dance" vary across cultures, all humans do engage in interpersonal synchronization of body movements. Hall (1976) cites studies of movies of newborn children by Condon and his associates, which reveal that the newborn infants initially synchronize the movements of their bodies to speech regardless of the language. North American children, for example, sync with Chinese just as well as they do with English. From this Hall infers that synchrony is perhaps the most basic element of human communication and the foundation on which all subsequent communication behavior rests.

Also, communication transactions follow an action chain with a beginning, climax, and ending, regardless of complexity and duration. From a simple greeting to terminating a relationship, certain sequences of actions and activities are commonly expected by people in a given culture. As discussed in Chapter 9, the specific content of the action chain varies across cultures, as does the degree to which individuals follow and complete the normative sequence of actions. Regardless of the surface patterns of action chains, however, people in all cultures appear to follow certain forms of them in their interpersonal interactions. Across all cultures, deviating from the expected patterns normally produces surprise or displeasure in others.

All humans display emotions, moods, and other organismic states through facial expressions, gestures, and vocal cues. The evidence strongly suggests that there are biological universals that guide perception and certain emotions and expressions in stable, predictable ways. As stated in Chapter 9, we believe human emotions and general patterns of emotional expression are biologically based, innate, and thus universally shared. At the same time we agree with Ekman (1972) and recognize the very important role cultural constraints play in shaping specific patterns of emotional expression. In other words, our culture conditions us with a set of display rules defining the normative intensity and extensiveness of our facial expression in specific social situations.

In one experiment, Ekman (1972), stress-inducing films were shown to college students in the United States and Japan. Part of the time each person watched a film alone, and part of the time the person watched the film while talking about the experience with a research assistant from the person's own culture. The results show that, when they are alone, Japanese and North Americans have virtually identical facial expressions. In the presence of another person, however, there is little correspondence between Japanese and North American facial expressions; the Japanese mask their facial expressions of unpleasant feelings more than North Americans do. This study demonstrates that the distinctive appearance of the face for each of the primary emotions is interculturally shared but people in different cultures differ in what they have been taught about managing or controlling their facial expression of emotions.

According to Osgood (1964), human emotions are shared universally in three basic dimensions: pleasantness/unpleasantness, tension/relief, and excitement/quiet. These three dimensions closely correspond to the "E-P-A" (Evaluation-Potency-Activity) system he developed in assessing the meanings of various concepts across cultures. This conceptual structure provides a basis for the universality, as well as the cross-cultural differences, in experiences and expressions of human emotions.

INTERCULTURAL CONVERGENCE

Culture is not a static entity. It is continually in the process of dynamic evolution. Numerous factors within and outside a cultural system contribute interactively to this cultural process. Today, with the rapid advancements in communications and transportation technology, people in different parts of the world are closely connected with one another. For many, "foreign cultures" have become a substantial part of their communication environment. People are more aware of, and thus have a greater need to understand, other cultures than at any other time in human history. In the close-knit intercultural reality of today's world environment, cultures can no longer be viewed in isolated compartments.

The increased amount of contact and communication across cultures has brought about a phenomenal homogenization of cultures on a global scale. Many technologically developing, non-Western, high-context cultures have converted at least in part to Western cultural patterns. Today, life patterns in large metropolitan centers on all continents bear a remarkable resemblance to one another. In many countries you have to travel a good distance from the urban centers to discern the distinct cultural patterns that are traditionally derived. The reverse intercultural convergence also has been increasing during the last few decades. Some Westerners have begun to learn about and accept the traditional Eastern world views, beliefs, and values. Capra, for example, is one of the Western thinkers who has been profoundly influenced by the Eastern system of thinking. In his book *The Tao of Physics* (1975), Capra points out the convergence of holistic Eastern understanding of reality and analytic Western physics.

> In modern physics, the question of consciousness has arisen in connection with the observation of atomic phenomena. Quantum theory has made it clear that these phenomena can only be understood as links in a chain of processes, the end of which lies in the consciousness of the human observer. . . . If physicists really want to include the nature of human consciousness in their realm of research, a study of Eastern ideas may provide them with stimulating new viewpoints. (p. 300)

Intercultural convergence also is apparent in the areas of contemporary psychology, psychotherapy, and counseling. Jung, for example, brought about a significant change in the Western understanding of human nature, incorporating the realm of unconsciousness, which had always been an important aspect of human nature in Eastern religious and philosophical traditions. Similarly, Maslow (1971) refers to a Taoistic philosophy of "noninterference" and "letting be" in discussing his theory of psychotherapy. Continued convergence of ideas and practices among cultures is anticipated if the present trend of worldwide development of interlocking communication systems continues.

SUMMARY

In this chapter we examined some of the fundamental ways in which humans across cultures commonly resemble one another in their communication processes. While there are enormous variations in the specifics of communication patterns, the intrinsic nature of humans as biological and social beings and their need and ability to use symbols to communicate with others are basic to all humans.

Given this premise, we discussed some of the recognized universals of human communication. Individuals in all cultures categorize, compare, and evaluate messages from the environment. People share the same basic need to belong to primary groups, which in turn provide them with a sense of security and well-being. The specific nature of individual-group relationships in different cultures is viewed as a surface variation of the essentially panhuman form of human social existence.

Every known culture has a linguistic system that shares similarities in its core structure with other languages but may differ in its surface structure. Regardless of variations in specific features, all languages both delimit and extend humans' capacities to communicate with one another. The language presents its users with an invisible boundary in the perceptual and conceptual domains. At the same time, it enables its users to live in a world of ideas and to enjoy such human accomplishments as art, literature, science, technology, and other manifestations of civilization.

Further, humans share experiences and expressions of various emotions, such as joy, satisfaction, fear, and sadness. We also share many similarities in expressing these feelings. We all learn to acquire certain systems of organizing and using time and space vis-à-vis other people around us.

The existing cultures of the world today, then, are not to be viewed as either different or similar—they share both differences and similarities. The variations in the specifics and details of cultures may be enormous, but the common cultural core is undeniably certain panhuman attributes. The cross-cultural commonality and convergence present us with a vital binding force, which promotes human communication and potential worldwide understanding. The cultural variations, on the other hand, challenge all of us with respect to the collective process of human evolution. Through our commonality, we remain members of the same human community; through our differences, regeneration and possibilities for creativity come into play.

Thus neither the attempt to make the world homogeneous nor the attempt to polarize cultures by overemphasizing differences is desirable. Instead, we must recognize the fundamental duality present in the nature of the cross-cultural reality and the simultaneous interplay of similarity and difference. We must strive to maintain an optimal balance between the two by recognizing and appreciating cultural uniqueness, while at the same time embracing the shared human conditions and characteristics.

Such an orientation will bring a different light to many of the potential and real problems that we may encounter in communicating with strangers. Neither an attempt to force our ways on strangers nor an attempt to yield ourselves blindly to the strangers' ways is desirable. Instead, we must work toward recognizing and accepting the dissimilarities and must search for the shared attributes between ourselves and strangers. Based on a realistic and balanced understanding of both similarities and differences, we can then seek a communication relationship that is meaningful to all parties involved.

PART FOUR

INTERACTION WITH STRANGERS

In the first two parts of this book we examined the major influences on our communication with strangers and the ways in which communication patterns vary across cultures. In Part Two we pointed out that our predictions and interpretations of strangers' behavior are influenced by the culture from which we come and, in addition, by the groups to which we belong, the role expectations we have, and our expectations regarding interpersonal relationships (the sociocultural influences). Further, our predictions and interpretations are influenced by the way we categorize objects and people and the attitudes we hold (the psychocultural influences), as well as by the environment in which we are communicating. In Part Three we examined cultural variations in message decoding, language and verbal behavior, and nonverbal behavior. From our examination of cultural variations, we discovered there are many shared aspects of communication across cultures.

The focus of Part Four, in contrast, is on selected aspects of our interaction with strangers. More specifically, the chapters in this part address such questions as the following: What happens when we come into contact with strangers who have personal, social, and cultural differences and begin to communicate with them? How do our relationships (such as friendship and marriage) develop with strangers? What are some of the significant factors we need to consider in order to understand the development of our interpersonal relationships with strangers? What factors increase our effectiveness in communicating with strangers? How do strangers who find themselves in new and unfamiliar cultural environments cope with and adapt to the many uncertainties of their new lives? What are some of the changes occurring in strangers as a consequence of their adaptive experiences in a new environment? How can we become more "intercultural" as a result of our communication with strangers?

The last question is the focus of the concluding chapter, where we discuss the developmental process through which individuals become "intercultural" in psychic and behavioral patterns as a result of their communication with strangers. Our discussion is aimed at proposing a view of human development that goes beyond the parameters of our own cultural milieu. We believe that each of our encounters with strangers has the potential to allow us to grow personally since strangers can motivate us to stretch our knowledge, imagination, and behavioral repertoire. In light of today's increasingly complex domestic and international situations, this model presents an orientation that is timely and useful in improving our effectiveness in communicating with strangers.

11

Interpersonal Relationships with Strangers

Under cherry trees
there are
no strangers

Issa

Interpersonal relationships are sources of social contact and intimacy, two integral elements of human survival in any culture. As noted in Chapter 4, we form many different types of relationships with others. For example, we develop some relationships we call acquaintances and some we call friendships. Friendships, however, should not be confused with friendly relations. As Kurth (1970) points out, friendly relations are an outgrowth of role relationships and are possibly a prelude to friendship, while friendships are intimate relationships involving two people as individuals. These two types of relationships, therefore, differ with regard to the level of intimacy present—friendships being more intimate than friendly relations.

Another way in which friendly relations and friendships differ is with respect to the temporal dimension. Friendly relations, according to Kurth (1970), involve a present orientation, which focuses on the encounter that is taking place. In a friendship participants engage in interaction regarding the past and future, as well as the present. Further, the two types of relationships differ with respect to the normative specifications guiding them. There are cultural norms specifying what constitutes friendly relations, but "the development of friendship is based upon private negotiations and is not imposed through cultural values or norms" (Bell, 1981, p. 10). Suttles (1970) takes a similar position;

he claims friendships are the least "programmed" relationships we form. We do not mean to suggest that culture plays no role in the development of friendships; rather, culture plays a much less important role in friendships than it does in friendly relations.

In defining the term friendship, Wright (1978) focuses on two aspects of the relationship: (1) the voluntary nature of the interaction, and (2) the personalistic focus of the interaction. The voluntary nature of the interaction means friendships are entered into voluntarily and friends informally agree to get together often in the absence of external constraints or pressures. Friendships, according to Wright, also involve a focus on the person; friends react to each other as "whole persons," not as occupants of roles. In other words, friendships involve a diffuse rather than a specific orientation (Parsons, 1951).

Extensive research has been conducted by scholars in sociology, psychology, and communication on many different aspects of friendship in the United States. There also exists a rich body of research by anthropologists focusing on the unique qualities of friendship in specific cultures (see, for example, Chapter 4; Burridge, 1956; Driberg, 1935; Palisi, 1966; Piker, 1968; Reina, 1959; Srivastava, 1960). To date, however, there is very little research describing friendships with strangers. Because of the paucity of research on relationships with strangers, it is impossible to systematically discuss how they begin and develop with time. We, therefore, focus here on those areas where research has been conducted. We begin by looking at initial interactions with strangers.

INITIAL INTERACTIONS

Opening encounters between people from the same culture are not random, disorganized episodes; rather, these encounters are organized forms of behavior. In a recent study of the social organization of opening encounters, Schiffrin (1977) points out: "One reason for the coherence of talk is that both speaker and hearer recognize each other as valid partners in the interaction and, beyond that, both recognize, albeit implicitly, a set of culturally, situationally, and topically relevant standards of conversational and interactional behavior" (p. 689). This recognition allows the "speaker and hearer" to coordinate their activity.

The ease with which openings take place depends, at least in part, on the degree of similarity (including cultural, racial, sexual, and attitudinal similarity) between the two participants. Traditionally, the degree of similarity between participants is examined in terms of the degree of *perceived similarity,* the degree to which people think they are similar to others.

Perceived Similarity

The majority of research on perceived similarity focuses on the similarity-attraction hypothesis. One of the earlier theorists to propose this hypothesis was Rokeach (1960), who argues that the primary factor in social distance is the degree of similarity between a respondent and a stimulus person. That is, the more similar two people are, the closer is the relationship they form. Similarly, Byrne (1971) views attraction as a linear function of the proportion of similar opinions two people hold. These hypotheses are supported not only by data from the United States but also by cross-cultural data. For example, in testing Rokeach's hypothesis, Brewer (1968) finds that similarity of beliefs accounts for social distance among East African tribes. Further, Byrne et al. (1971) examine Byrne's "attraction paradigm" in five different cultural groups and discover that although culture influences the level of attraction, similarity also has a significant impact on it.

Previous research indicates not only that similarity plays a role in initial attraction to others but also that it is a factor in close friendships. Research in the United States by Lazarsfeld and Merton (1954), for example, reveals that partners in adult friendships are similar with respect to attitudes, interests, social class, occupation, and personality traits. Cross-cultural data from Germany (Loomis, 1938; Verbrugge, 1977) and from Norway (Barnes, 1954) also uphold these findings. Recent research by Gudykunst (in press, b) suggests that perceived similarity plays a comparable role in the close friendships we form with strangers.

Rogers and Bhowmik (1971) argue: "In a free choice situation, when a source can interact with any one of a number of different receivers, there is a strong tendency for him to select a receiver who is like himself" (p. 528). They go on to suggest that communication between people who are similar (homophilous is their term) is generally more effective than communication between dissimilar people. Although this finding is accepted widely, research indicates that moderate dissimilarities between communicators who are generally similar may bring about more effective communication (Simons, Berkowitz, and Moyer, 1970). This principle is referred to as "optimal heterophily" by Rogers and Shoemaker (1971).

In discussing the role of dissimilarity, Knapp points out: "[It] is enjoyable when the interaction is brief, when the differences are few and on peripheral beliefs, and when the chance of rejection is small, that is, when the costs of pursuing dissimilar relations are negligible relative to the rewards" (cited in Crockett and Friedman, 1980, p. 91). Knapp (1978) also suggests several qualifications that must be made with respect to the general principal of similarity and attraction:

> . . . in the early stages of a relationship, similarity may be based upon a wide range of background factors and relatively superficial opinions and interests. As the relationship intensifies, certain topics, beliefs, and values may emerge as the most critical areas of similarity; those areas must be similar if the relationship is to continue. . . . Other qualifications include those people who are attracted to others dissimilar from themselves . . . there are instances in which we seek out people who are known to be different. (pp. 102–103)

In Knapp's view, then, dissimilarities may not hinder our initial interactions with strangers.

Miller, Hintz, and Couch (1975) contend there are four elements of initial interactions (openings is their term): reciprocally acknowledged attention, mutual responsiveness, congruent functional identities, and a shared focus. In applying this schema to culturally dissimilar communicators, Sarbaugh (1979) argues:

> . . . as visible heterogeneity increases, the reciprocally acknowledged attention will increase. That attention, however, may detract from the intended purpose of the transaction. Furthermore, it is expected that the communication difficulty would tend to increase as heterogeneous participants proceed to each of the other three aspects of openings. (pp. 11–12)

Even though Sarbaugh's contention is intuitively appealing, as noted above, little research to date has examined initial interactions between culturally dissimilar communicators.

One piece of research, however, that partially supports Sarbaugh's view, is Simard's (1981) study of French/English intraethnic and interethnic initial interactions in Canada. Simard's research indicates that

> . . . when focusing on a potential friend from the other group [French and English subjects] perceive it as more difficult to know how to initiate a conversation, to know what to talk about during interaction, to be interested in the other person, and to guess in which language they should talk, than when they considered a person from their own group. (p. 183)

Further, Simard's research suggests that both groups (Anglophones and Francophones in Canada) find attitude and language similarity more important than occupational and social class similarity in the development of interethnic acquaintances. Results of her research "may imply that the dissimilarity in terms of ethnic affiliation may have been compensated for by increased similarity along a number of other dimensions or that so much dissimilarity was expected that after the actual encounters the overall similarity surprised the [subjects]" (p. 187).

Research by Sunnafrank and Miller (1981) supports Simard's conclusion. These researchers examine interpersonal attraction between attitudinally similar and dissimilar communicators. They find: "Individuals paired with an attitudinally similar partner were more attracted to partner than individuals paired with an attitudinally dissimilar partner, but only when they had not engaged in initial interaction" (p. 22). In other words, people are attracted to dissimilar strangers if they have a chance to interact with them, but they are not attracted to them if interaction does not take place.

While cultural dissimilarity may complicate initial interactions, it should not preclude the development of more intimate relationships. Following Rokeach, Smith, and Evans (1960), it appears reasonable to argue cultural similarity is not a necessary prerequisite for friendship formation. In the absence of cultural similarity, however, similarity in other areas (e.g., attitudes) may be necessary for friendships to develop. The degree of similarity between communicators plays another important role in initial interactions in that it influences the reduction of uncertainty that is present (Berger and Calabrese, 1975).

Uncertainty Reduction

Berger and Calabrese's (1975) theory of initial interactions utilizes the notion of uncertainty as its central construct. "Central to the present theory is the assumption that when strangers meet, their primary concern is one of uncertainty reduction or increasing predictability about the behavior of both themselves and others in the interaction" (p. 100). The reduction of uncertainty leads to changes in the nature of the communication that takes place; for example, it brings about increases in the amount of communication and increases in the amount of interpersonal attraction. It also can be argued that if the amount of uncertainty present in initial interactions is not reduced, further communication between the people will, in all likelihood, not take place.

Uncertainty is reduced by gathering "information which is perceived as adequate for the making of decisions within the interaction" (Clatterbuck, 1979, p. 148). Gathering the information perceived as adequate allows communicators to make both retroactive (explanatory) and proactive (predictive) attributions, according to Berger and Calabrese (1975). "For the individual, reducing uncertainty and increasing attributional confidence become synonymous" (Clatterbuck, 1979, p. 148).

The knowledge necessary to reduce uncertainty is gained through several different strategies, including interrogation, self-disclosure, deception detection, environmental structuring, and deviation testing (Berger et al., 1976). There is extensive research on the use of these strategies in the United States, but very few studies investigate their use in initial interactions with culturally dissimilar communicators. One recent study by Gudykunst (1983), based on the work of Nakane (1974) and Hall (1976), however, suggests that the typical pattern of initial interactions for the United States (a low-context culture) may not be generalizable to high-context cultures. Members of high-context cultures do reduce uncertainty in initial interactions, but the nature of the information they seek appears to be different from the information sought when two people meet for the first time in the United States.

Since much of the information in high-context cultures either resides in the context or is internalized in the individual (as opposed to being mostly in the message in low-context cultures), people in high-context cultures are more cautious concerning what they talk about with strangers than are people in low-context cultures. Data from Gudykunst's (1983) study support this position. Gudykunst's research further indicates that members of high-context cultures have a greater tendency to make assumptions about others based on cultural background than do members of low-context cultures. This finding is similar to Hall's (1976) argument that people in high-context cultures are more aware of culture's screening process and, therefore, make greater distinctions between insiders and outsiders than do people in low-context cultures. The results of Gudykunst's research also suggest that people from high-context cultures ask more questions about others' background and engage in less nonverbal activity than do members of low-context cultures. These findings are consistent with Nakane's (1974) argument (discussed in Chapter 4) that it is the background information that allows people in high-context cultures to determine whether or not a person is indeed unknown.

Initial interactions with people who are familiar also may not be generalizable to initial interactions with strangers. Research by Gudykunst (in press, c) partially supports this claim. In a study comparing perceptions of initial encounters with people who are familiar and of initial encounters with strangers, Gudykunst finds that students in the United States tend to make more assumptions about others based on cultural background in initial interactions with strangers than they do in initial interactions with people who are familiar. This result is to be expected, given the major difference between the two forms of interaction being the communicators' cultural background. Gudykunst also finds students in the United States prefer to do more of the talking in initial encounters with people who are familiar, while they prefer to ask more questions in initial encounters with strangers.

Research by Shuter (1982) suggests that there also may be differences in initial interracial and intraracial encounters in the United States. Although Shuter's research does not reveal differences in black and white intraracial patterns, he does find differences by dyadic composition:

> These results suggest that initial interaction for blacks and whites may have been governed by different conversational rules. Apparently, it was appropriate for whites to ask more questions and engage in longer conversations with males than females. Appropriate communicative behavior for blacks, however, was characterized by longer conversations with females than males and women being asked more questions than men. In addition, black conversational rules for initial interaction seem to have been more gender- and race-specific than those for whites, as indicated by the different questioning patterns used by black males and black females when conversing in interracial and intraracial encounters. (p. 50)

Shuter goes on to conclude that blacks appear to use uncertainty reduction strategies other than questioning with partners of the same gender. Following Abrahams (1976), he suggests the strategy most likely to be employed is the use of "leading statements," statements about the other people that challenge them to respond.

SELF-DISCLOSURE AND SOCIAL PENETRATION

Built on earlier models of personality developed by Lewin (1948) and Rokeach (1960), Altman and Taylor's (1973) social penetration theory gives central importance to the concept of self-disclosure. Altman and Taylor argue that interpersonal exchange gradually progresses from superficial, nonintimate areas to central, intimate areas of the personalities of the partners in a relationship. Also, this process is hypothesized to involve increased amounts of interpersonal exchange (breadth of penetration), as well as increasingly intimate levels of exchange (depth of penetration).

Although the area of cultural/racial differences in self-disclosure is given only cursory attention in the existing research to date, a number of interesting patterns emerge from the data. The finding that whites tend to disclose at higher rates than blacks is reported by a number of researchers (Diamond and Hellcamp, 1969; Jourard, 1958; Littlefield, 1974; Wolken, Moriwaki, and Williams, 1973). Additionally, Littlefield (1974) finds that blacks tend to self-disclose at a higher rate than do Mexican-Americans. These differences, however, may be attributable to social class rather than to racial factors—an interpretation suggested by Jaffee and Polanski's (1962) finding that no significant differences exist between lower-class blacks and lower-class whites.

Lewin (1936; 1948), in a comparison of Germany and the United States, observes that Germans tend to disclose little about themselves to others in general, but they do form intimate relationships with a select few. People in the United States, in contrast, tend to disclose a great deal about themselves to others but not to develop very intimate relationships. Partial support for Lewin's analysis is provided by Plog (1965), who concludes that people in the United States tend to disclose more overall than Germans do, however, there is no significant difference in disclosure rates between close friends.

Several other cross-cultural studies conclude that people in the United States tend to disclose at a higher rate than do the British (Jourard, 1961; Strassberg and Anchor, 1975), the Japanese (Barnlund, 1975), or Puerto Ricans (Jourard, 1971). Melikan (1962), on the other hand, studies nine Middle-Eastern cultures and discovers no significant differences in self-disclosure rates due to culture. His conclusion is that the similarities in self-disclosure are influenced by the similar characteristics of the nine cultures.

To illustrate these cross-cultural comparisons of self-disclosure, we look at Barnlund's (1975) study of the public and private self in Japan and the United States. Barnlund begins with the assumption that the Japanese prefer an interpersonal style in which little information about the self is made accessible to others in everyday interactions (i.e., the public self is relatively small), while the majority of information one knows about oneself is kept private (i.e., the private self is relatively large). In contrast, Barnlund hypothesizes that the preferred interpersonal style in the United States is one in which large portions of information about the self are made available to others (i.e., the public self is relatively large), while little of such information is kept to oneself (i.e., the private self is relatively small).

In his research Barnlund (1975) compares six topics of self-disclosure (interests/tastes, work/studies, opinions on public issues, financial matters, personality, and physical condition) and six targets of self-disclosure (same-sex friend, opposite-sex friend, mother, father, stranger, and untrusted acquaintance) for college students from Japan and the United States. Results of this research suggest there are similarities between the two groups of students in terms of what they consider appropriate topics for self-disclosure. Specifically, tastes and opinions are seen as being most appropriate by both groups, while physical attributes and personality traits are least preferred. Further, the hierarchy of target preferences is the same in the United States and Japan: same-sex friend, opposite-sex friend, mother, father, stranger, and untrusted acquaintance. Barnlund, however, finds the level of self-disclosure to be higher for college students from the United States (112) than it is for college students from Japan (75) on a scale ranging from 0 to 200 (0 = no disclosure; 100 = disclosure in very general terms; 200 = full disclosure). This pattern is consistent across all six topics of conversation and all six target persons. Given his results, Barnlund concludes: "Interpersonal distance, as estimated by self-disclosure, was substantially greater among Japanese than Americans" (p. 79).

Recent research by Gudykunst and Nishida (1983) partially contradicts Barnlund's findings. These researchers find that when self-disclosure in close friendships is examined, there are more similarities than differences between college students from Japan and from the United States in the frequency of self-disclosure across nine topic areas. Specifically, they find similarities in terms of the following dimensions: relationships with others, parental family, physical condition, school/work, money/property, interests/hobbies, and attitudes/values. On the other hand, Gudykunst and Nishida's research reveals differences between the two groups of students on three dimensions: love/dating/sex, own marriage, and emotions/feelings. These results suggest that the frequency of self-disclosure in close friendships may be somewhat similar in Japan and the United States.

Although there is very little research on self-disclosure with strangers, research by Gudykunst (in press, b) reveals moderate to high associations between social penetration in close friendships with culturally similar partners and social penetration in close friendships with culturally dissimilar partners. These results are to be expected given Altman and Taylor's (1973) conceptualization of the social penetration process. Communication in close friendships is characterized by "freewheeling and loose" exchange and "facile switching from one mode of communication to another," according to Altman and Taylor (p. 139). They also point out that in close friendships "the dyad has moved to the point where interaction is relatively free in both peripheral and in more central areas of the personality. Cultural stereotypy is broken down in these more intimate areas and there is a willingness to move freely in and out of such exchanges" (pp. 139–140). If cultural stereotypy is indeed broken down, the culture from which a person comes should not be a major factor influencing the interaction. Close relationships between culturally similar communicators, therefore, should not be expected to differ dramatically from those between culturally dissimilar ones.

Another explanation for the results found by Gudykunst (in press, b) comes from Miller and Steinberg's (1975) "developmental" theory of interpersonal communication. Specifically, it can be inferred that when communicators making predictions move from the cultural and sociocultural levels of data to the use of psychocultural data, the culture from which people come is not a major variable affecting the predictions made about their communication behavior. Given this, it would be expected that when predictions are made mainly on the basis of psychocultural data (e.g., in close friendships), the degree of social penetration should not necessarily differ in culturally similar and dissimilar relationships. What differences do exist are best attributed to the specific characteristics of the dyad and the people involved, and not to their cultural background.

MARRIAGE WITH STRANGERS

Recent research by Lampe (1982) on interethnic dating (white/black, white/Mexican-American, black/Mexican-American) in the United States indicates that the major motivation for interethnic dating is the same as for intraethnic dating, namely, personal liking for the other person. In fact, in Lampe's study no other reason for interethnic dating comes close to personal liking in terms of the percentage of respondents giving it (personal liking is reported by 60% of the respondents; no other reason is given by more than 16% of the respondents). In contrast, Lampe's study reveals no consistent reason against interethnic dating. "The most commonly cited reason given by both males and females was a lack of desire" (p. 118); however, this response was given by less than 35% of the respondents. The most common reasons against interethnic dating given by whites in Lampe's study are "no desire," "don't know any well enough," and "no chance." The most common reasons given by blacks are "no desire," "hadn't thought of it," and "no chance." Mexican-Americans give "don't know any well enough," "no desire," and "no chance" as the most common reasons against interethnic dating.

The decision to date or become friends with a stranger is not the same as the decision to marry such a person. A marriage with a stranger requires a lifelong commitment to live with a person who is culturally different. While any marriage calls for adjustments, marriages to strangers generally demand more adjustments on the part of both partners than do marriages to people who are familiar.

People get married for a wide variety of reasons. When one chooses to marry a stranger, it is often, like the decision to date, based on the same reasons for which one would choose to marry a person who is familiar (e.g., for love or upward mobility). There are, however, other motivations coming into play in marriages to strangers that may not be factors in marriages to people who are familiar (Char, 1977). To illustrate, while chance and availability play a major role in any marriage, these reasons often take on increased importance in marriages to strangers. When strangers are living in or visiting another culture, they are in close propinquity to potential marriage partners from the host culture and far away from any from their home culture (Char, 1977). Often marriages to strangers take place simply because people from another culture are the only available partners; for example, United States military personnel living overseas may marry host-country nationals because they are the only available candidates.

Related to chance and availability are practical reasons for marrying strangers. Char (1977) cites the following as an example of a practical reason: "A poor, white German girl may consent to marry a Negro soldier stationed in post-war Germany for the material benefits he can give her, and the opportunity to escape from her unhappy home and come to America" (p. 35). By citing this example, Char does not mean to imply this is the only reason a white German woman might marry a black serviceman from the United States.

Another reason for marrying strangers is the beliefs we hold about their culture. These beliefs, of course, may be based on actual characteristics of the strangers' culture or they may be beliefs not grounded in reality. "For example, a white male might marry a Japanese woman because he feels a Japanese female can better satisfy his desire to have a wife who is willing to wait on him" (Char, 1977, p. 37). Such a belief may be based on messages given by his parents or the mass media. Parents, for example, may consciously or unconsciously suggest that members of another culture are desirable or undesirable marriage partners.

No matter what the motivation for entering into a marriage, once married the partners must learn to adjust to living with each other. The success of a marriage depends on the ability of each party to adjust to living with the other person. One of the problems in marriages between strangers is that very often the individuals are not prepared to recognize cultural differences (Tseng, 1977). When confronted with a particular situation, both partners react on the basis of their cultural background, neither recognizing that the other is reacting from a different set of cultural standards. Tseng argues:

> Any problems or differences which may exist within an intercultural marriage will not be solved easily just because cognitively the persons are aware of the reason for the differences and strategically there is a prescribed solution for it. Culture is something which is learned through experiences in early life. An individual has developed strong emotional

attachments to his culture—associated with his belief system, values, and habits—his style of life. In the process of intercultural marriage adjustment, he has to learn how to overcome, correct, and adjust his emotional reaction to the necessary change and expansion of his cultural behavior. (pp. 96–97)

What Tseng says about marriage between culturally dissimilar partners could equally well be applied to the development of friendships between strangers.

Tseng (1977) describes five general patterns of adjustment in marriages between culturally dissimilar partners: (1) one-way adjustment, (2) alternative adjustment, (3) mid-point compromise, (4) mixing, and (5) creative adjustment. The one-way pattern of adjustment takes place when one spouse totally adopts the cultural patterns of the other. Such an adjustment may be with regard to one particular aspect of a culture (e.g., religion, food, or language) or the whole constellation of cultural behaviors. According to Tseng, this pattern of adjustment is common when one culture is extremely dominant; also, it often is selected because of the practicality of everyday life.

The second pattern, alternative adjustment, occurs when both spouses insist that their cultural patterns be followed and when it is impossible for either to mix or give up cultural behavior, according to Tseng (1977). Again, this pattern may involve only one aspect of a culture or both cultures as wholes. Tseng cites an example of a couple (one Catholic, one Buddhist) who decide to have two wedding ceremonies to meet the requirements of both their cultures.

Another pattern of adjustment is mid-point compromise. As an example of this pattern, Tseng (1977) cites a couple of which the husband is from China and the wife is from the United States. The husband feels an obligation to send his family in China $100 a month, but the wife objects because she thinks they cannot spare the money (the nuclear family is most important). In order to address both of their needs, they settle on a mid-point compromise—the husband sends his family $50 a month rather than $100 as he originally planned.

The fourth pattern Tseng (1977) discusses is one in which the couple literally mixes the two cultures in their marriage. This mixing might be random and awkward, or balanced and harmonious. While such a mixing is most obvious in concrete matters (e.g., home furnishings, eating patterns, religious behavior), it may also involve concepts and ideas, according to Tseng. That is, the partners may develop their own values, norms, and rules of behavior, which are a mix of their original cultures.

The final type of adjustment, creative adjustment, takes place when a couple gives up both of the original cultures and decides to "invent" new behaviors for their marriage, according to Tseng (1977). This pattern of adjustment may be necessary because of conflict between the couple's cultures (e.g., traditional dinner eating patterns in the United States and in some Eastern cultures are not highly compatible), or it may come about because neither partner is satisfied with his or her own culture.

Marriages between culturally dissimilar partners do have unique problems of adjustment, but they should not be viewed simply as problematic. There is also a positive side to such marriages. They can be a source of personal growth for the partners, as well as a source of social change for the culture in which they take place. (This idea is discussed in more detail in Chapter 14.)

THE DEVELOPMENT OF INTERPERSONAL RELATIONSHIPS WITH STRANGERS

Although research on development of interpersonal relationships with strangers is sparse, some tentative comments can be made at this time. To begin with, in making a decision as to whether or not to engage in interaction, we must recognize that strangers may have nothing to lose. Using Knapp's (cited in Crockett and Friedman, 1980) words, "the costs of pursuing a dissimilar relation are negligible relative to the rewards [for strangers]" (p. 91). Since proximity is one of the major factors involved in interpersonal attraction (Bersheid and Walster, 1969), strangers may be attracted to us simply because we are nearer to them than members of their own culture. In contrast to the strangers, we may very well have "something to lose" when interacting with strangers. Specifically, if we interact with strangers, we may be looked down on by members of our culture. Regardless of any actual or potential sanctions, however, some of us inevitably are attracted to strangers and interact with them. Our degree of attraction depends, at least in part, on our attitudes (e.g., level of ethnocentrism, prejudice). If our attitudes are positive, or at least not totally negative, initial interaction may occur.

Our attitudes influence our responses to strangers. Hodges and Byrne (1972), for example, point out that responses to ethnically dissimilar strangers are most positive when attitudes are expressed in open-minded, rather than dogmatic (closed) terms. Research by Broome (1981) suggests that these results are generalizable to encounters with culturally dissimilar strangers. This research strongly supports "the hypothesis that responses to differences stated in an open manner will be less defensive than responses stated in a non-open manner" (p. 231).

Our initial decision to interact with strangers is influenced by our stereotypes of the strangers' culture. Stereotypes alone, however, may not account for the majority of variance in our perception of strangers. A study by Schneider and Jorden (1981) reveals that "American students' perceptions of other American students and Chinese students are based on the individual performances of the interactants rather than on entrenched cultural stereotypes alone" (pp. 185–186). Similarly, Grant and Holmes (1981) indicate that we do not ignore information that is unrelated to our ethnic stereotype of strangers. Rather, we form impressions based on both the stereotype and any other information we gather.

Once a decision is made to interact with strangers, a major concern during the initial stages of interaction is the reduction of uncertainty. Reducing uncertainty is necessary if we are to arrive at a basis for predicting the strangers' responses. As pointed out earlier in this chapter, there is cultural variation in what is labeled as uncertainty. In one culture not knowing people's social status is considered uncertainty, while in another culture not knowing people's attitudes is considered uncertainty. In other words, in initial interactions we may seek different types of information from strangers than they seek from us.

How uncertainty is reduced also differs across cultures. As indicated earlier, in high-context cultures communicators attempt to reduce uncertainty by gathering demographic information. This data (e.g., what high school or college a person went to, his or her home town, the company for which he or she works) gives people from a high-context culture sufficient information on which to make a rich array of dependable inferences about others' future behavior. On the other hand, people from low-context cultures are not able to reduce uncertainty to the same degree using such information; they need information on the others' attitudes and values, for example. It is expected, therefore, that members of low-context cultures will seek self-disclosure of attitudes, values, etc., at a much faster rate than people from high-context cultures do (this is documented partially by Barnlund's research on Japanese and Americans, discussed earlier). These differences may cause misunderstandings in the initial stages of the development of a relationship when we communicate with strangers.

Another area where our initial interactions with strangers may differ from those with people who are familiar is the area of similarity. First, it takes longer to discover areas of similarity in initial interactions with strangers than it does in encounters with people who are familiar. Second, similarity may play a different role in uncertainty reduction in different cultures. Infante (1979) points out: "Dyadic similarity may not produce uncertainty reduction at the same rate across cultures. For example, similarity may breed certainty in liking more quickly in other cultures than our own. This may be especially true for more chauvinistic cultures" (p. 4).

The development of personal relationships with strangers requires more than knowledge of their linguistic codes. It requires the knowledge of culturally appropriate roles for conducting the process of acquaintance formation. Strangers have, in all likelihood, learned different rules for the process of acquaintance formation than we have. These different rules increase the amount of uncertainty present in our initial interactions with strangers, and if Berger and Calabrese's (1975) theory can be extended, higher levels of uncertainty lead to increases in information seeking. Stated differently, we seek more information in initial interactions with strangers than we do in ones with people who are familiar.

It appears reasonable to argue that our initial interactions with strangers will move toward the development of more intimate relationships if we perceive some minimum level of similarity between ourselves and the strangers and are able to reduce some of the tremendous amount of uncertainty present in our initial interactions. On the other hand, if we do not perceive sufficient similarity, the relationship probably will take a trajectory leading to a relationship that does not change in levels of intimacy over time; for example, we may remain acquaintances for the entire length of time we know each other.

To summarize, in the meeting and initial interaction stages our relationships with strangers may be different from our relationships with people who are familiar. The differences center around how coordinated activity is established, how uncertainty is defined and reduced, and what the role of dyadic similarity is. If we perceive ourselves as similar to strangers and reduce some uncertainty in our initial interactions, the relationship can move into a trajectory toward more intimate communication. The time frame for moving from nonintimate to intimate topics may be different for our relationships with strangers and with people who are familiar, however.

If we look at the stages that relationships go through, we can gain additional insight into the development of interpersonal relationships with strangers. For example, Altman and Taylor (1973) propose a four-stage model of interpersonal relationship development: (1) orientation, (2) exploratory affective exchange, (3) full affective exchange, and (4) stable exchange. The orientation stage is characterized by responses that often are stereotypical and reflect superficial aspects of the personalities of the actors involved. The content of the interaction at this stage is limited to the "outer public areas" of the actors' personalities. The second stage, exploratory affective exchange, is typified by those relationships labeled casual acquaintances and nonintimate friends. Relationships at this stage, according to Altman and Taylor, are generally friendly and relaxed, but commitments are only temporary. The third stage, full affective exchange, is characteristic of close friendships and courtship relationships. These relationships involve "loose" and "freewheeling" verbal interaction and an increase of self-disclosure concerning the central areas of the actors' personalities. As was pointed out previously, in this stage is where cultural stereotypy is broken down. The final stage, stable exchange, is achieved in very few relationships. If it is achieved, however, Altman and Taylor argue that there are very few instances of miscommunication between the partners because they have fully described themselves to each other.

Given Altman and Taylor's (1973) model, it makes sense to argue that the initial stages of our relationships (i.e., the first two stages) with strangers are different from those of our relationships with people who are familiar. This arises because the early stages are dominated by cultural stereotypes, and, therefore, when we communicate with strangers, differences are bound to emerge. This is not to say that our relationships with strangers do not go through these stages, because they do. Rather, the argument is that they may go through them in different ways.

If cultural stereotypy is indeed broken down in the stage of full affective exchange, it can be argued that the culture from which a person comes will not be a major factor influencing such relationships. Once a relationship reaches the stage of friendship, the majority of interaction has a personalistic focus, a focus on the other person as a unique communicator (Wright, 1978). To put this in slightly different terms, the communicators in a friendship have moved from using cultural and sociocultural levels of data for making predictions to using psychocultural data (Miller and Steinberg, 1975). When the data used in making predictions is at the psychocultural level, the culture from which strangers come is not a major factor influencing our predictions.

This is not to say that our relationships with strangers and those with people who are familiar are the same. No two friendships are exactly the same; friendships are based on "private negotiations," follow idiosyncratic rules, and are all slightly different. The argument being put forth here is that since friendship is a relationship in which cultural stereotypy is broken down and there is a personalistic focus, the differences in our behavior in the two types of friendships can be attributed to personal characteristics of the person with whom we are interacting or to other factors, not to the person's cultural background.

Before concluding, we must note that relationships do not always develop along a smooth course from superficial to intimate. Altman, Vinsel, and Brown (1981) point out: "Although people may exhibit relatively stable openness (or closedness) for a time, it is likely that openness eventually gives way to closedness and that closedness is eventually followed by openness. Such cyclical variations in accessibility of people to one another are affected by factors internal and external to an individual" (p. 139). They go on to argue that different patterns of openness-closedness may be adaptive over the life span of a relationship. Lerner (1979) makes the additional point that relationships go through cycles with respect to other dimensions, including affection, trust, and sharing. How a particular relationship ultimately develops, therefore, is influenced by the degree to which the people involved have synchrony in timing and content with respect to the openness-closedness in their interaction (Altman, Vinsel, and Brown, 1981), as well as by whether or not there is synchrony with respect to their display of affection and trust (Lerner, 1979). Following Hall (1983), we can argue establishing synchrony is easier with people who are familiar than it is with strangers. It can be established with strangers, however.

SUMMARY

In this chapter we examined selected aspects of the interpersonal relationships we develop with strangers. Cultural similarity is not a requirement for the development of an interpersonal relationship. In the absence of cultural similarity, linguistic similarity and similarity along other dimensions (e.g., occupation, attitudes) may be necessary. If sufficient similarity is perceived during initial interactions, culturally dissimilar communicators may meet again, thereby making it possible for the development of a more intimate relationship.

The initial stages of our relationships with strangers may be different from those of our relationships with people who are familiar. For example, depending on the culture from which strangers come, they may reduce uncertainty differently than we do. Strangers from high-context cultures will seek demographic information, while those from low-context cultures will seek information regarding attitudes and values.

If our relationships with strangers reach the stage of friendship, then the culture from which the strangers come becomes less important. Stated differently, since friendships have a personalistic focus in which cultural stereotypes are broken down, the culture from which the stranger comes is not a major factor in predicting behavior in a close relationship. Friendships with strangers and with people who are familiar, therefore, exhibit more similarities than differences. What differences do exist are best attributed to the idiosyncratic rules and structure of particular relationships.

12

Effectiveness in Communicating with Strangers

Effective interaction means giving of yourself—trying to see the world of others and to respect their life ways. It means not forcing your ways on them. Yet at the same time, it means being true to yourself and your ways. To be really effective, interaction must be a two-way street or, of course, it is not interaction at all. That is, all interacting individuals should be doing so from the basis of awareness, understanding, and knowledge.

Clarence C. Chaffee

In Chapter 11 we examined selected aspects of communication in the development of relationships with strangers. One important aspect of communication, however, was not addressed—namely, communication effectiveness. The purpose of this chapter is to elaborate on our view of communicating with strangers by examining the dimension of effectiveness.

Before we examine the factors contributing to effectiveness in communication with strangers, we must first specify what we mean by communication effectiveness. For the purpose of our analysis, we stipulate that *communication effectiveness means minimizing misunderstanding.* Misunderstanding occurs when different meanings are attached to the same message. If it were possible for us to communicate with no misunderstanding, then our communication would be totally effective. But this is not the case. It is impossible for any two people to communicate without any misunderstanding. Because of differing experiential backgrounds, no two people will attach exactly the same meaning to a particular message. Communication effectiveness, therefore, must be considered a matter of minimizing misunderstanding. It should be noted that minimizing misunderstanding is not the same as agreement. We can attribute approximately the same meaning to a message as another person does (misunderstanding is minimized) and either agree or disagree with that person about the message. Agreement tends to lead to cooperative activities, while disagreement can lead to conflict.

The purpose of this chapter is to examine the factors contributing to effectiveness in communicating with strangers. The first section examines the general factors involved in effective communication across cultural boundaries. The second section examines one dimension of effectiveness deserving of fuller discussion—namely, ethical issues in communicating with strangers.

COMPONENTS OF COMMUNICATING WITH STRANGERS

There are several attempts to specify the factors involved in effective communication with strangers. One of the earliest specifications is by Gardner (1962). Gardner characterizes people who are effective in communicating with strangers as "universal communicators." He describes these people as possessing five characteristics: "(1) an unusual degree of integration or stability, (2) a central organization of the extrovert type, (3) a value system which includes the 'value of all men,' (4) socialized on the basis of cultural universals, and (5) a marked telepathic or intuition sensitivity" (p. 248). Similarly, Kleinjans (1972) takes the position that the effective communicator: (1) sees people first and representatives of cultures second, (2) knows people are basically good, (3) knows the value of other cultures as well as that of his or her own, (4) has control over his or her visceral reactions, (5) speaks with hopefulness and candor, and (6) has inner security and is able to feel comfortable being different from other people. Both Gardner and Kleinjans, therefore, characterize effectiveness in communicating with strangers in terms of individual traits.

Individual traits alone can be used as a good "predictor" of communication effectiveness only if they yield consistent behavior across situations and throughout our lives. This, however, is not the case. Rather, individual traits often do not lead to consistent behavior across situations or throughout our lives (Mischel, 1973). Explanations of effectiveness, therefore, cannot rely solely on individual traits; they must include other factors.

One method of conceptualizing effectiveness in communicating with strangers is to conceive of effectiveness as having three elements: cognitive, affective, and behavioral. The cognitive component involves the way in which we process information, the affective component involves the sentiment and emotion attached to the information processed, and the behavioral component involves our ability to enact the proper behaviors.

The Cognitive Component of Communication Effectiveness

As indicated above, the cognitive component of communication effectiveness involves the ways in which we process information. The most obvious cognitive factors influencing our effectiveness in communicating with strangers are our ability to speak the other language and the knowledge we have about the strangers' culture. While it is theoretically possible to communicate effectively with no prior knowledge of the culture from which the strangers come and no ability to speak their language (assuming they can speak ours to some degree), this is obviously not the ideal situation. Even if we cannot speak fluently, our efforts to speak the strangers' language probably will be appreciated and will lead to more effective communication. In addition, our knowledge of the strangers' culture and of how it is different from and similar to our own has a direct impact on our interpretations and predictions of their behavior. If we know nothing about the strangers' culture, it is highly probable we will make inaccurate predictions and interpretations of their behavior.

Another factor influencing how we process information in our communication with strangers is our *category width*. Category width, as we discussed it previously, implies people differ in the degree of discrepancy they tolerate when including something in or excluding it from a category. Detweiler (1980) hypothesizes:

> The width of one's categories would seem to be particularly crucial in an intercultural context. It is hypothesized that the narrow categorizer would categorize (i.e., give meaning to) behavior narrowly using his/her own cultural values. This individual would be unaccepting of the idea that a behavior or situation might have different meanings, as little variation would be allowable with the "normal" or desirable categories. Hence, negative inferences and inappropriate expectations would be common. Contrarily, the broad categorizer would categorize behavior in a more general way and would be more accepting of the idea that a behavior or situation might have different meanings. Although probably initially using the categories learned in his/her own culture, the wide categorizer would allow a great deal of diversity within the "normal" or desirable categories. Thus negative inferences and inappropriate expectations should be less common, and new and different information more acceptable. Since intercultural interaction is typified by cues which have different meaning, the width of one's categories should have a major impact upon the process. (p. 282)

Detweiler's research supports his hypotheses. Specifically, he finds that Peace Corps volunteers working on a remote island in the Pacific are less likely to return early if they are broad categorizers than if they are narrow categorizers.

The width of our categories is a function of the complexity of our cognitive system. The more complex our cognitive system, the more constructs we differentiate and the better we are able to integrate these constructs. "A construct is fundamentally a bipolar dimension of judgment (e.g., tall-short, friendly-unfriendly, good-bad, etc.). These constructs are systematically organized and interrelated, permitting inferences to be drawn and predictions to be made" (O'Keefe and Sypher, 1981, p. 72). Other research in the United States indicates that the more complex our cognitive structures are, the more effectively we are able to communicate (Hale, 1980). Applegate and Sypher (1983) suggest that this is also true of communication between culturally dissimilar people.

Another concept closely related to category width is the degree to which the stereotypes we hold are open to modification. Harvey, Hunt, and Schroder (1961) argue that people differ in the degree to which they are willing to modify stereotypes they hold, or in other words, the degree of "openness-closedness" of their stereotypes. In applying this concept to interactions across national boundaries, Scott (1965) argues:

> An image is "closed" to the extent that the person regards the attributes included in it as completely defining the object. . . . The more "open" the image, the more is the person willing to entertain the possibility that essential features of the object have not yet been recognized by him, and that these additional attributes would reveal new similarities and differences in relation to other objects. (p. 81)

Holding closed stereotypes is linked directly to inaccurate interpretations and predictions of strangers' behavior. Holding open stereotypes, in contrast, increases the likelihood of making more accurate interpretations and predictions of strangers' behavior. More specifically, if our stereotypes are open, we will be open to perceiving behavior not associated with the stereotype, thereby making it possible for us to interpret and predict the behavior of strangers more accurately.

One other cognitive aspect of effective interaction with culturally dissimilar communicators involves the way in which we are taught to talk about human behavior. There is a big difference between the way we talk about physical objects and the way we talk about people. For instance, have you read a chemistry book that begins: "Oxygen is great!"? No, probably not. But you may have read a book that starts off something like this: "The Japanese (or substitute Thais, Mexicans, etc.) are a friendly people." If you picked up a book with the former sentence ("Oxygen is great!") in it, you would, in all likelihood, put the book down. On the other hand, if you ran across the latter sentence ("The Japanese are a friendly people.") in a book, you might not think anything of it and just keep on reading. If you stop and think for a minute, however, you will realize that both sentences are equally useless for understanding the specific behavior under study. Neither tells us about the behavior of oxygen or the Japanese; both tell us only how the author interpreted and/or evaluated that behavior. (This example is drawn from Bostain, 1973.)

There are at least three interrelated cognitive processes involved here: description, interpretation, and evaluation (Wendt, undated). Effective communicators can distinguish among these three processes, while ineffective communicators probably do not make a distinction. By description we mean an actual report of what we have observed with the minimum of distortion and without attributing social significance to the behavior. Description includes what we see and hear and is accomplished by counting and/or recording observations.

In order to clarify these processes, we offer the following example.

Description

The teacher is sitting on the desk in torn, faded jeans.

This statement is descriptive in nature. It does not attribute social significance; it merely tells what the observer saw. If we were to attribute social significance to this statement, or make an inference about what we saw, we would be engaged in interpretation. In other words, interpretation is what we think about what we see and hear. The important thing to keep in mind is that multiple interpretations can be made for any particular description of behavior. Returning to our example, we have the following:

Description

The teacher is sitting on the desk in torn, faded jeans.

Interpretations

The teacher likes to be informal.
The teacher doesn't care about his or her appearance.
The teacher doesn't engage in behavior appropriate to his or her role.
The teacher isn't paid enough to dress in fashion.

Each of these interpretations can have several different evaluations. Evaluations are positive or negative judgments concerning the social significance we attribute to behavior. To illustrate this, we can use the first interpretation given above.

Interpretation

The teacher likes to be informal.

Evaluations

I like that; it makes it easier for student and teacher to get to know each other.
I don't like that; teachers should dress and use appropriate manners for their occupation.

Of course, several other evaluations could be made, but these two are sufficient to illustrate potential cross-cultural differences. In the United States the first evaluation might be more common because of the informality of the educational system. In many other cultures, however, the second evaluation would predominate. For example, in Japan it is expected that teachers will dress appropriately for their position, and, in addition, it is unacceptable for a teacher to sit on a desk.

If we are unable to distinguish among these three cognitive processes, it is likely we will skip the descriptive process and jump immediately to either interpretation or evaluation when confronted with different patterns of behavior. This leads to misattributions of meaning and, therefore, to ineffective communication. On the other hand, being able to distinguish among the three processes increases the likelihood that we are able to see alternative interpretations that are used by strangers, thereby increasing our effectiveness. Differentiating among the three processes also increases the likelihood of our making more accurate predictions of strangers' behavior. If we are able to describe strangers' behavior, we can make more accurate predictions because we are able to see alternative behavior patterns.

The Affective Component of Communication Effectiveness

Gudykunst, Wiseman, and Hammer (1977) argue that people who are effective in communicating with strangers do not use the perspective of their own culture when interpreting the behavior of people from other cultures. Rather, effective communicators use a *third-culture perspective,* which acts as a psychological link between their cultural perspective and that of the stranger:

> . . . we can say that people who have highly developed this perspective can be characterized as follows: (1) they are open-minded toward new ideas and experiences, (2) they are empathic toward people from other cultures, (3) they accurately perceive differences and similarities between the host culture and their own, (4) they tend to describe behavior they don't understand rather than evaluating unfamiliar behavior as bad, nonsensical, or meaningless, (5) they are relatively astute noncritical observers of their own behavior and that of others, (6) they are better able to establish meaningful relationships with people from the host culture, and (7) they are less ethnocentric (i.e., they try first to understand and then evaluate the behavior of host nationals based upon the standards of the culture they are living in). (p. 424)

Although the third-culture perspective includes behavioral, cognitive, and affective elements, Gudykunst, Wiseman, and Hammer (1977) present it as the affective core of a more general cross-cultural attitude. For the purpose of the present analysis, we elaborate only on the affective elements.

Tolerance for ambiguity implies an ability to deal successfully with situations, even when a lot of the information needed for interaction is unknown. According to Ruben and Kealey (1979):

> The ability to react to new and ambiguous situations with minimal discomfort has long been thought to be an important asset when adjusting to a new

culture. . . . Excessive discomfort resulting from being placed in a new or different environment—or from finding the familiar environment altered in some critical ways—can lead to confusion, frustration, and interpersonal hostility. Some people seem better able to adapt well in new environments and adjust quickly to the demands of a changing milieu. (p. 19)

Research by Ruben and Kealey suggests that people who have a higher tolerance for ambiguity are more effective in completing task assignments in other cultures than are people with lower tolerances. By extension, it can be argued that people who have a higher tolerance for ambiguity are more effective in communicating with strangers than are those who have a low tolerance for ambiguity.

Closely associated with the level of tolerance for ambiguity are the attitudes of prejudice and ethnocentrism. Ethnocentrism, it will be remembered, is the attitude by which we see our own group as the center of the world and evaluate the rest of the world vis-à-vis our own group. People who have a low tolerance for ambiguity tend to be ethnocentric and prejudiced. Neither a high level of ethnocentrism nor a high level of prejudice is conducive to effective communication with strangers. Both prejudice and ethnocentrism lead us to interpret cues from strangers in terms of our own cultural perspective. In other words, highly prejudiced or ethnocentric people do not recognize alternative interpretations and/or evaluations of behavior enacted by strangers. To understand the communication behavior of strangers, we must use their cultural frame of reference, not our own. Stated differently, we need to empathize rather than sympathize.

Sympathy refers to "the imaginative placing of ourselves in another person's position" (Bennett, 1979, p. 411). Sympathy, like ethnocentrism, uses our own frame of reference to interpret incoming stimuli. According to Bennett, if we apply the "Golden Rule" ("Do unto others as you would have them do unto you.") in interactions with strangers, we are being sympathetic because the referent is our own standard of appropriate behavior. On the other hand, empathy is "the imaginative intellectual and emotional participation in another person's experience" (p. 418). The referent for empathy is not our own experience, but that of the stranger. Bennett proposes an alternative to the "Golden Rule," the "Platinum Rule," which he argues involves empathy rather than sympathy: "Do unto others as they themselves would have done unto them" (p. 422). To summarize, the use of sympathy in our interactions with strangers invariably leads to misunderstanding rather than understanding. In contrast, the use of empathy increases the likelihood that understanding occurs.

Empathy is recognized as an important factor for communication effectiveness not only in the United States but also in other cultures as well. For example, in a study comparing Chinese students, Chinese-American students, and students from the United States on their perceptions of communication competence, Hwang, Chase, and Kelly (1980) find empathy to be the only factor all three groups share. They conclude:

. . . it appears that Americans, Chinese Americans, and Chinese all share a common view of some basic prerogatives of interpersonal communication effectiveness. The dimension of empathy qualifies as the most prominent of these common points of reference, suggesting once again that it may be nothing less than the sine qua non of human interaction. (p. 76)

Examples of specific characteristics associated with empathy in this study include "listening carefully to what people say," "seems to understand how other people are feeling," "is interested in what others have to say," "is sensitive to the needs of other people," and "can easily understand another's point of view" (p. 74).

The Behavioral Component of Communication Effectiveness

In an assessment of communication competence in intercultural settings, Ruben (1976) argues that several behavioral dimensions are important. The behaviors outlined by Ruben include, but are not limited to: (1) "display of respect," which involves the ability to show positive regard and express respect for another person, (2) "interaction posture," which is the "ability to respond to others in a descriptive, nonevaluating, and nonjudgmental way" (p. 340), and (3) "interaction management," which "is displayed through taking turns in discussion and initiating and terminating interaction based on a reasonably accurate assessment of the needs and desires of others" (p. 341).

Another assessment of the behavioral component of effectiveness is presented by Hammer, Gudykunst, and Wiseman (1978). These authors reviewed the literature on effectiveness to generate a list of 24 abilities associated with effective interaction with strangers. A sample of subjects who had lived in another culture for some time (i.e., more than three months) rated the importance of these abilities in their communication effectiveness in that culture. Hammer and his associates find three major behavioral dimensions: (1) the ability to deal with psychological stress, (2) the ability to effectively communicate, and (3) the ability to establish meaningful interpersonal relationships. The dimension of being able to deal with psychological stress includes the ability to deal with frustration, stress, anxiety, pressures to conform, social alienation, financial difficulties, and interpersonal conflicts. The dimension of being able to communicate effectively includes the ability to enter into meaningful dialogue with other people, to initiate interaction with strangers, to deal with communication misunderstandings, and to deal with different communication styles. The third dimension, the ability to establish meaningful interpersonal relationships, includes the ability to develop satisfying interpersonal relationships with other people, to maintain satisfying relationships with others, to understand the feelings of others, to effectively work with others, and to deal with different social customs.

Partial cross-cultural support for these findings comes from Abe and Wiseman's (1983) "replication" of the Hammer, Gudykunst, and Wiseman (1978) study with Japanese tourists in the United States. Abe and Wiseman's research reveals five dimensions to effectiveness, with all five dimensions being related closely to the three dimensions displayed in the Hammer, Gudykunst, and Wiseman study. The differences that exist in the findings can be explained easily by the length of the subjects' experiences in another culture (the original study examined long-term visitors, while Abe and Wiseman studied tourists).

ETHICAL ISSUES IN COMMUNICATING WITH STRANGERS

The examination of the ethical aspects of our interaction with strangers cannot be omitted from our analysis. Previous analyses of ethics took various forms, including examinations of ethics in foreign policy (Lefever, 1957), of ethics in the conduct of cross-cultural research (Hamnett, 1980; Tafoya, 1980), of ethics in international business (Conine, 1979; Safire, 1975), of the right to communicate (Harms and Richstad, 1977), and of the development of a code of ethics (Sitaram and Cogdell, 1976), as well as more general treatments (Asuncion-Lande, 1980; Condon and Saito, 1976). While specific aspects of ethics have been touched on, to date there has not been a complete, systematic treatment of the ethical issues involved in our communication with strangers.

Ethical Complications in Communicating with Strangers

In his discussion of ethics, Barnlund (1980) refers to the cross-cultural arena as "an ethical void":

> . . . the moral issues that attend intercultural encounters are not simply more complicated, they are of an entirely new dimension. Despite the pervasiveness of cross-cultural contact, these complications remain overlooked and unexplored in any systematic way. The ethical vacuum that confronts us reflects not merely a failure of specialists within this evolving field, nor the negligence of outside agencies to give support to such ethical study, but is due in large part to difficulties that are inherent in the cross-cultural context. (pp. 9–10)

Barnlund goes on to isolate five specific complications of making ethical judgments when we communicate with strangers.

The first complication Barnlund (1980) identifies is the lack of a "meta-ethic," which can be used by people from different cultures when ethical dilemmas arise. Since ethical principles tend to be culture-specific, Barnlund argues that when we communicate with strangers we tend to approach ethical questions in one of two ways: (1) we make ethical judgments using our own cultural standards, or (2) we use the frame of reference of the strangers' culture. Both of these methods are unsatisfactory, according to Barnlund:

Either fosters a truncated morality that is incomplete and ethnocentric, for it subordinates the ethical premises of one culture or the other. And it thereby fails to fully illuminate or to fairly adjudicate conflicts in which people of different moral orientations must accommodate their differences and create ways of collaborating on common tasks. (p. 10)

Barnlund contends that what is needed is a metaethic, one prescribing standards applicable to both cultures.

The second complication Barnlund (1980) identifies is that "moral vacuums are transient affairs; they tend to be filled at once by moralists of one persuasion or another" (p. 11). Since cultures differ with respect to their level of influence in the world and their access to communication channels (e.g., telecommunication networks), the domination of certain moral views cannot change until all cultures have equal access to television, radio, and the press. A North American company doing business in a developing country may be unduly able to influence people because of its access to mass communication channels (e.g., North American advertising in developing countries has contributed to the "revolution of rising expectations" in these countries).

Barnlund's (1980) third complication is closely related to the second; it is that there are differences in the degree to which cultures can block outside influence and, thus, make themselves inaccessible to change. As Barnlund points out, in some cultures "ethical standards are so woven into the economic and familial fabric of society that exposure to alternatives may threaten the entire system" (p. 11).

The interdependence of interpersonal interactions and international relations in our communication with strangers is the fourth complication cited by Barnlund (1980). Although informal interaction between people from different cultures may appear to have little connection with international relations, the two are very closely related in the area of ethics. According to Barnlund, many aspects of the ethics for informal interactions have political implications, which are the affair of governments. For example, North American business personnel doing business in a culture where it is expected that gratuities be paid in order to do business cannot easily separate their individual interactions with business-persons in the other culture from legal issues (e.g., compliance with the 1977 Foreign Corrupt Practices Act).

The final complication discussed by Barnlund (1980) involves the diverse conceptualizations different cultures have of the role of communication in human affairs. Western cultures, for example, value the use of communication in "rational" discourse to resolve problems. This view, however, is not shared universally. There are cultures that value intuition over reasoning and do not trust words (Barnlund, 1980). These cross-cultural differences make it more difficult to resolve ethical dilemmas when they arise in interactions between culturally dissimilar communicators.

As was pointed out above, no metaethic for communication with strangers currently exists. The development of such a metaethic is not on the horizon. The absence of such a metaethic, however, does not necessarily mean there is an ethical vacuum in our communication with strangers, as Barnlund suggests. Ethical relativity theory offers an alternative to the development of such a metaethic for guiding behavior in intercultural contexts.

Ethical Relativity Theory

Barnsley (1972) draws a distinction between the evaluative and descriptive aspects of ethical relativity:

> Descriptive relativism . . . merely asserts the factual diversity of customs, of moral beliefs and practices. . . . The thesis itself, however, is purely a factual one. It may be termed, therefore, cultural relativism. . . . Ethical relativism proper, on the other hand, is an evaluative thesis, affirming that the value of actions and the validity of moral judgments are dependent upon their sociocultural context. The two theses are logically distinct, though not unrelated. (pp. 326–327)

In other words, Barnsley takes the position that saying ethics develop out of culture and vary across cultures (cultural relativism) is different from saying that valid moral judgments can only be made within a particular cultural context (ethical relativism). Discriminating between the evaluative and descriptive types of relativism is only a beginning; there are also different types of ethical relativism that must be differentiated.

Barnsley (1972) argues that much of the confusion with respect to ethical relativity (e.g., the argument that if we accept ethical relativity, we cannot make ethical judgments across cultures) is due to a failure to distinguish between two levels of inquiry. One level, he points out, involves a normative or practical dimension (i.e., knowledge of what to do), while the second level is analytic and involves a commitment to a specific view of what morality is. The analytic forms of ethical relativism do not readily allow for ethical judgments being made across cultures, but the normative forms do.

Another distinction can be made by looking at the object of moral judgment; it is possible to evaluate either the agent or the actions. Some moral judgments focus on evaluating actions (or the principles behind the actions), while others focus on placing blame (or praise) on the actors (agents) who commit the actions. Combining these two distinctions yields four types of ethical relativism: two normative forms (evaluative relativism and relativism of rightness) and two analytic forms (epistemological and axiological relativism).

Evaluative relativism "allows a possibility of evil actions which are not blameworthy in particular societies" (Barnsley, 1972, p. 328). According to Barnsley, the problem is the application of a particular set of moral standards to agents in other cultures. As an illustration of this type of ethical relativism, consider the situation in some countries where it is not only acceptable but also necessary to pay gratuities to officials of corporations in order to do business with their organizations (this practice is illegal for U.S. citizens, according to the 1977 Foreign Corrupt Practices Act, but the legal implications will be ignored here). The evaluative relativist sees this practice as an unacceptable (i.e., evil) action wherever it occurs. Given the beliefs of people in some cultures, however, these actions are subjectively seen as being "right," and, therefore, people who practice this custom cannot be blamed for engaging in the behavior. Further, given their culture, they cannot be expected to think their beliefs are "wrong." Evaluative relativism, then, evaluates the people or agents performing the actions, not the actions.

Relativism of rightness "allows possibility of evil actions which are not wrong in certain societies" (Barnsley, 1972, p. 328). Like evaluative relativism, relativism of rightness is a form of normative relativism. The difference is in the focus on what is being evaluated; in relativism of rightness it is the actions themselves (or the principles they embody) that are being evaluated. The argument underlying this type of relativism is that there are practices that, while intrinsically "evil," are "acceptable" in certain societies. An example can clarify the distinction between this and the first type of relativism. For the sake of comparison, we will use the example of paying gratuities to do business in some countries. The relativism of rightness proponent sees the practice of paying gratuities as a "necessary evil" of doing business in the cultures that require it. While this practice may be "evil" in the United States, it is not "wrong" in some cultures. If U.S. corporations are to do business in these cultures, they must, out of necessity, engage in such "evil" actions.

The preceding two types of relativism are normative forms, which can be applied to individual cases. The two remaining types of relativism (epistemological and axiological) are analytic forms that are general theses from which specific applications must be deduced.

Epistemological relativism "denies the validity of cross-cultural moral judgments by virtue of limitations upon our possible knowledge" (Barnsley, 1972, p. 328). In other words, the argument is that people from one culture are incompetent to make moral judgments about another culture because they do not know, and cannot know, enough about that other culture to make accurate ones. Regarding our example, an epistemological relativist would argue that people in the United States do not possess the knowledge necessary to judge the practice of paying gratuities to businesses in other countries. They are, therefore, "incompetent" to make ethical judgments about this practice or those who engage in it.

Axiological relativism is value relativism proper; it "denies the cross-cultural validity of values; the intrinsically good and evil are culture specific" (Barnsley, 1972, p. 328). This position asserts that what is "good" or "evil" is always relative to the sociocultural system in which the action originated and that no moral standards can have universal validity. With respect to our example, the axiological relativist denies the legitimacy of judging the practice of paying gratuities outside the context of the particular culture in question.

It is not necessary to discover universally valid ethical principles prior to applying ethical relativity theory. An individual can apply either the evaluative relativism or relativism of rightness positions using another set of values as a guide. Berger argues recognizing cultural relativity "does not, of course, free the individual from finding his own way morally. That would be another instance of 'bad faith,' with the objective fact of relativity being taken as an alibi for the subjective necessity of finding those single decisive points at which one engages one's whole being" (cited by Barnsley, 1972, p. 355). In other words, even if we accept cultural diversity, we must still make ethical judgments in our interactions with strangers. Both evaluative relativism and relativism of rightness allow for ethical judgments being made in the context of the relativist position with ease. Thus, if while in another culture we observe a case of "bribery," we can take the position that the action is morally "wrong," but at the same time understand that those engaging in the action may not know any better or that the action is a "necessary evil" in that culture. If we delay our ethical judgments in our interactions with strangers until we have described the strangers' behavior and looked at alternative interpretations (i.e., the strangers' interpretations), we can increase our communication effectiveness.

SUMMARY

Effectiveness in communicating with strangers is not unidimensional; rather, it is multidimensional and includes cognitive, affective, and behavioral components. The cognitive component of communication effectiveness involves knowledge of the strangers' language and culture, as well as of the way information is processed cognitively. For example, open, as opposed to closed, stereotypes increase the likelihood that we will make accurate interpretations and predictions about strangers' behavior. Our attitudes (ethnocentrism and prejudice, in particular), our ability to tolerate ambiguity, and our ability to emphathize constitute the affective component of communication effectiveness. Following Hammer, Gudykunst, and Wiseman (1978), the behavioral component of communication effectiveness can be seen as being composed of three factors: (1) the ability to deal with psychological stress, (2) the ability to communicate effectively, and (3) the ability to establish interpersonal relationships.

These three components do not take into consideration one other important aspect of effectiveness in communicating with strangers, namely, the ethical issues involved. The ethical issues involved in interaction between culturally dissimilar communicators are more complicated than those involved in interaction between culturally similar communicators. In the absence of a metaethic to guide our communication with strangers, we can look to ethical relativity theory for assistance in making ethical judgments across cultures. Using the two normative forms of ethical relativism allows us to make ethical judgments in our communication with strangers in a manner that increases our ability to communicate effectively.

13

Strangers' Adaptation to New Cultures

Be bent, and you will remain straight.
Be vacant, and you will remain full.
Be worn, and you will remain new.

Lao Tzu

Life requires a series of adaptations. No two events are quite alike, and we must continually adapt ourselves to the changing environment. When we come into contact with strangers and develop an interpersonal relationship, we are, consciously or unconsciously, adapting ourselves to the strangers and the relationship.

In the preceding two chapters we discussed various aspects of developing interpersonal relationships and communicating effectively with strangers. We are now going to shift the focus of our attention to the strangers and examine how they cope with a new cultural environment and how their communication influences the overall adaptation process.

Thus this chapter is about communication processes in a special case of human adaptation—namely, that required for a stranger to cope with a new and unfamiliar culture. Usually this adaptation is associated with a change from one society, or subsection of a society, to another, as well as with changes in the social environment. It is concerned with major cultural gaps that occur either as a result of a stranger's move from one sociocultural system to another or because of substantial changes in his or her environment.

CULTURAL ADAPTATION

Situations Involving Cultural Adaptation

An extensive list of examples of situations that involve cultural adaptation is presented by Taft (1977) under five headings: sojourning, settling, subcultural mobility, segregation, and change in society. (For a complete discussion of stranger-host relationships, see Gudykunst, in press, d.) While the first two imply geographical mobility, the latter three do not. Examples of *in situ* changes requiring adaptation include such situations as change of profession, retirement, marriage, divorce, aging, transition from school to work, and starting at a university. Also included are the processes of accepting major social and technological innovations, such as computerized information-processing systems. There are also situations in which strangers are incorporated into a new social system, such as the armed services, religious orders, residential universities, prisons, concentration camps, rehabilitation centers, and mental hospitals.

Situations that result from moving to new locations include those of foreign exchange students, Peace Corps volunteers, foreign business personnel, missionaries, diplomats, technical advisors, and administrators. Further, there are immigrants and refugees who have voluntarily or involuntarily moved from one society to another with the intention of becoming full members of the new society on a permanent basis. Also, individuals moving from a small rural town to a large metropolitan area, or vice versa, are in a situation that involves some degree of cultural adaptation, although their adaptive processes as strangers in the new environment are generally considered less difficult and encompassing than those of international migrants.

International migration, whether for a long or short term, represents a classic situation where the newly arrived strangers are required to cope with substantial cultural change. Of course, situations of international migration vary in the abruptness of the transition. For example, an abrupt cultural transition was experienced by many refugees from Southeast Asia after the Vietnam War. Due to the involuntary and sudden nature of their departure from their home country, most refugees had little chance to prepare themselves psychologically for life in the host society. At least during the initial resettlement phase, many of them suffered from a deep psychological dislocation and sense of loss (Y. Kim, 1980).

Even when the transition is a voluntary one, international migrants differ in their motivation to adapt to the new environment and to make the host society their "second home." This motivation to adapt is dependent largely on the degree of permanence of the new residence. In the case of immigrants, their move from their original culture to the host society is a permanent one. Since they must make their living and attain social membership in the host society, they need to be concerned with their relationship to the new environment in the same way as the members of the native population are. On the other hand, a peripheral contact with the new culture is typical of the situation of many sojourners. Reasons for a sojourn in a new culture are often specific—to pursue a vocation, to obtain a degree, or merely to enhance one's prestige in the eyes of the folks back home. This may require less adaptation to the host cultural system. Foreign students, for example, can reduce their cultural adaptation to the bare minimum in order to fulfill their role as student and may confine their social contact to fellow students from their home country. A similar observation can be made about military personnel and their families in foreign countries. They may perceive less need to adapt to the host culture since their stay is only temporary.

Regardless of the circumstantial variations in the degree of necessary adaptation, every individual in a new culture must respond and adapt to environmental changes at least minimally. Primary attention here is given to what is perhaps the most profound situation of cultural adaptation—the adaptation of sojourners and immigrants (including refugees) who were born and raised in one culture and who have moved to another culture for an indefinite stay. By understanding the adaptive processes of international migrants, we can make inferences about the nature of other similar adaptive life situations.

Enculturation and Acculturation

Throughout the *socialization* process, we learn and acquire "all the factors and processes which make one human being fit to live in the company of others" (Kelvin, 1970, p. 270). Socialization involves conditioning and programming in the basic social processes of communication, including decoding (perceptual and cognitive) patterns and encoding (verbal and nonverbal language) training. The form of this training depends on the particular culture and is embodied in the process of *enculturation*. Berger and Luckmann (1967) point out that in socialization and enculturation the cultural forms for expressing basic social behavior are internalized from the teachings of early "significant others" and become "the world, the only existent and conceivable world" (p. 134), with a strong emotional overtone and identification. The process of socialization provides children with an understanding of their world and with the culturally patterned modes of responding to it. The familiar culture, then, is the "home world," which is associated closely with the family or other significant others. On the other hand, an unfamiliar culture is one that is out of harmony with one's basic understanding of self and reality.

When strangers who have been fully socialized into a cultural milieu move to a new and unfamiliar culture and interact with the environment for an extended period of time, the process of *resocialization* occurs. Gradually, strangers begin to detect new patterns of thinking and behavior and to structure a personally relevant adaptation to the host society. Merely handling the transactions of daily living requires the ability to detect similarities and differences within the new surroundings. Strangers thereby become acquainted with, and adopt, some of the norms and values of salient reference groups of the host society. As resocialization takes place in the course of adapting to a new culture, some unlearning of old cultural patterns occurs, at least in the sense that new responses are adopted in situations that previously would have evoked different ones. This process of unlearning of the original culture is called *deculturation.* As the dynamics of deculturation and enculturation continue, strangers gradually undergo a cultural transformation. Of course, a complete transformation in the basic values of adults is extremely rare. Brim (in Brim and Wheeler, 1966) suggests that the only changes taking place are in overt role behavior. A person can be pressed to conform to role requirements but cannot be forced to accept the underlying values. Goffman (1961) also doubts whether true resocialization occurs in practice, even in a "total institution" such as prison.

Sometimes, however, a new culture does have a substantial impact on the psychological and social behaviors of strangers. They may become resocialized to a significant degree as a result of group support, institutional legitimization of the new identity, and the presence of new "significant others" to replace those of their childhood. Even then, the transformation is accomplished only slowly and in stages. It normally brings conflict, a struggle between the desire to retain old customs and habits and to keep the cultural traditions and the identity of the group and the desire to adopt new ways more in harmony with the changed environment. This conflict between the old and the new, between *what should be* in the mind of the stranger and *what is* in the external reality of the host culture, is not peculiar to the stranger status alone. Older generations, for example, are faced with the same problem. The putting away of old things for new places older generations in a position of "involuntary immigrants from the past to the present" (Mead, 1963).

Thus, the core of cultural adaptation is *change,* in personal and social behaviors (Dyal and Dyal, 1981, p. 20). As fully functional members of a cultural system, we see change as meaning not only changing ourselves to suit the environment but also changing portions of the environment to better suit our needs. For strangers, on the other hand, the burden of change and adaptation is on them to a greater extent than it is on the host environment. The impact of a stranger's culture on the mainstream host culture is relatively insignificant compared to the substantial influence of the host culture on the stranger. Clearly, a reason for the essentially unidirectional change in strangers is the difference between the number of people sharing their original culture and the number of people sharing the host culture. To the extent the dominant power of the host society controls the daily survival and functioning of strangers, it presents a coercive pressure on them to resocialize and adapt to the new sociocultural system.

Almost all empirical studies of historical change in immigrant communities document their gradual conversion to the mainstream culture of the host society (see, for example, Barnett and Kincaid, 1983). The directionality of change in an immigrant community toward assimilation is particularly clear when we examine the adaptive change across generations. A study of the American Jewish Committee's board of governors over the past 28 years shows a significant increase in the members' merging into non-Jewish organizations and a substantial decrease in their Jewish identification (Zweigenhaft, 1979-1980). Also, Masuda (1970) demonstrates that ethnic identification of Japanese-Americans in the United States shows a gradual decrease from the first generation to the third generation. This process of adaptive transformation through resocialization commonly is called *acculturation*. Acculturation is described as the continuous process by which strangers are resocialized into a host culture, so as to be directed toward a greater compatibility with or "fitness" into the host culture, and ultimately, toward assimilation (i.e., the highest degree of acculturation theoretically possible). For most people, even for natives, complete acculturation is a lifetime goal, and individuals vary in the degree of acculturation achieved in a given period of time. Thus, acculturation of strangers should properly be thought of as falling along a continuum from minimally acculturated to highly acculturated (Padilla, 1980, p. 3).

ACCULTURATIVE COMMUNICATION PROCESS

Underlying the acculturative process is the communication process. Acculturation occurs through the identification and internalization of the significant symbols of the host society. Just as natives acquire their cultural patterns through interaction with their significant others, so do strangers acquire the host cultural patterns and develop relationships with the new cultural environment through communication.

In viewing acculturation occurring through communication, it is important to recognize that strangers' communication capacities are reflective of their acculturation. This means the acculturation process is essentially that of achieving the communicative capacities of the host culture. Through prolonged and varied experiences in communication, strangers gradually acquire the communicative mechanisms necessary for coping with the new culture. The acquired communicative competencies, in turn, function as a set of adaptive tools assisting strangers to satisfy their personal and social needs, such as the need for physical survival and for a sense of belonging and self-esteem. Through effective communication, strangers are able to gradually increase control over their own behavior and over the host environment.

Communication, by definition, involves interaction with the environment, and each person as communicator can be viewed as an open system actively seeking and desiring interaction with the environment. A person interacts with the environment through two closely interrelated processes: personal (or intra-personal) communication and social (interpersonal and mass) communication (Ruben, 1975). In the following sections, the elements of each of these two communication dimensions that are crucial to understanding cultural adaptation phenomena are identified.

Personal Communication

Personal (or intrapersonal) communication refers to the three interrelated psychological processes (cognitive, affective, and behavioral) by which people organize themselves in a sociocultural milieu. Through personal communication, we develop ways of seeing, hearing, understanding, and responding to our environment. "Personal communication is thought of as sensing, making sense, or acting toward the objects and people in one's milieu. It is the process by which the individual informationally fits himself into (adapts and adapts to) his environment" (Ruben, 1975, pp. 168-169). In the context of acculturation, personal communication can be viewed as the process of organizing adaptive experiences into a number of identifiable patterns that are consistent or compatible with the patterns of the host culture.

The cognitive process

One of the most fundamental adaptive changes in personal communication occurs in the cognitive structure through which strangers process information from the environment. As was discussed earlier, differences in the ways in which experiences are categorized and interpreted constitute some of the main differences between cultures. As Campbell (1964) points out, communication between strangers and hosts sometimes becomes possible only by the strangers' inferring how the hosts are constructing the world from their reactions to commonly perceived events. It is only by extending the domains of common perception and interpretation that strangers can begin to comprehend the categorizing system of the host culture and to gradually match their own cognitive processing to that of the others.

Because of their unfamiliarity with the cognitive system of the host culture, strangers frequently find the "mentality" of the people difficult to comprehend. Their difficulty stems from the fact that, during the initial phases of acculturation, their perception of the host environment is relatively simple. Gross stereotypes are salient in the strangers' perception of the unfamiliar cultural patterns. The "thinking-as-usual," as we may call it, often becomes unworkable in dealing with the host environment since strangers do not share the common underlying assumptions of the host population. As Schuetz (1944; 1963) describes it: "The cultural pattern of the approached group is to the stranger not a shelter but a field of adventure, not a matter of course but a questionable topic of investigation, not an instrument for disentangling problematic situations but a problematic situation itself and one hard to master" (p. 108).

Yet, to the extent that culture is a learned phenomenon, strangers are potentially capable of increasing their understanding of the host cognitive system. Cultural learning enables strangers to recognize their cognitive structures as distinct from those of the host culture and to gradually increase their ability in "perspective taking" (Fogel, 1979, p. 25) and "coorientation relation" with members of the host society (Pearce and Stamm, 1973). Empirical data from a study of Korean immigrants suggest that strangers' knowledge of the host society becomes increasingly extensive, accurate, and refined over the years and that such increased cultural learning is reflected in the development of more complex cognitive structures for perceiving the host environment (Y. Kim, 1977b). The reverse also appears to be true. Strangers who are cognitively more complex tend to have a greater capacity to acquire understanding of the host culture than do those who are less cognitively complex (Yum, 1982).

The affective process

Not only do strangers learn to acquire cognitive structures of the host culture, they also must acquire the affective patterns, such as emotional expressions, aesthetic sensibilities, attitudes, and values, that are embodied in the behavior of the people in the host culture. Social relationships involve some measure of sentiment and emotion, and in order for strangers to develop meaningful relationships with members of the host society, they must share such feelings also. Taft (1977) identifies this affective process as the "dynamic" aspects of culture:

> There are certain universal human needs and modes of functioning that must be satisfied in all cultures. In broad terms, these needs refer to the maintenance of life processes, the need to maintain a structural society to enhance as well as regulate social relationships, and to provide for the self-expressive needs of individuals. While these needs are universal, each culture prescribes different models for satisfying them. (p. 134)

Mansell (1981) emphasizes the importance of fulfilling the aesthetic needs of individuals in an alien culture:

> The concept of aesthetic awareness is linked with ineffable, intuitive feelings of appreciation and celebration. This form of awareness creates a consciousness which transforms individuals' perceptions of the world and imparts a sense of unity between self and surrounding. . . . It is in this transformative mode of experiencing that many people create access to the momentary peaks of fulfillment which make life meaningful. (p. 99)

Because needs of this sort are often difficult to gratify within an unfamiliar culture, many strangers in a new culture attempt to satisfy them by belonging to subcultures within the larger society in which they can pursue satisfaction in the familiar manner of their original culture. In doing so, they tend to withdraw from the new host culture until they have learned to make the necessary adaptation to its affective modes.

When the affective process is integrated successfully with the cognitive orientation, strangers achieve an adequate social orientation enabling them to understand how members of the host culture feel and behave. Once strangers acquire an adequate level of adaptation to the host affective orientation, they can share the humor, excitement, and joy of the natives, as well as their anger, pain, and disappointment.

The behavioral process

Ultimately, what is critical is not whether strangers have acquired the appropriate cognitive and affective orientation but whether they carry out the appropriate role performance in the host society. The appropriate role performance requires not only cognitive and affective acculturation but also the acquisition of the relevant behavioral skills for acting in certain situations. Taft (1977) categorizes these skills into two types: technical and social. *Technical skills* include language skills, job skills, academic skills, and others that are essential as a member of a society. In the United States, for example, skills such as driving, handling commercial transactions, and filing taxes are essential. *Social skills* are generally less specific and more subtle than technical skills.

Strangers who are competent in technical skills may find it difficult to identify the patterns of social behavior that are acceptable in the host society. Even the natives of a culture, who perform various social roles "naturally" and without thinking, are often unable to explain the specific social skills relevant to a particular social transaction. A foreign student, therefore, may have to formulate "action plans" before dealing with classroom processes. Similarly, a North American businessperson visiting a Japanese company also must rely on his or her own understanding of the way Japanese business is conducted in figuring out how to behave in performing his or her role of business negotiator.

Through the process of "trial and error," strangers' action plans are refined and gradually integrated into sequences that can be used in a relatively automatic form. A highly acculturated person, therefore, can perform the required social roles without having to formulate a mental plan of action in accordance with cultural rules and norms of the host society. This means the person has internalized many culturally patterned behaviors, and the performance of roles has become automatic and largely unconscious. Insofar as these automatic actions are executed successfully, they increase the probability for strangers to experience satisfying social interaction and a sense of control.

Personal communication and related phenomena

When we are fully in control of ourselves and a situation, we possess highly effective personal communication processes—cognitive, affective, and behavioral. These three personal communication processes not only are present simultaneously but also are well-coordinated and balanced. In the process of adapting to a new cultural environment, strangers are likely to be lacking in any one or more of the three processes, which results in poor internal balance and coordination. For example, some strangers may be quite knowledgeable about the host culture and yet may be lacking in ability to relate to members of the host society on the affective level. Others may be adequately skilled in performing specific jobs in the host society but may find some of the values operative in their job performance disagreeable. When such internal imbalance is severe, maladjustment may occur (Wong-Rieger, 1982).

The cognitive, affective, and behavioral processes of an individual's personal communication in relation to the host culture are linked with many of the psychological problems associated with the stranger status. The negative self-image, low self-esteem, feeling of alienation, dissatisfaction with life in general, and other related psychological problems of strangers are associated primarily with their inability to relate to the people in the host society in any one or more of the three processes of personal communication.

Social Communication

Personal communication is linked to social communication when two or more persons interact, knowingly or not. Through social communication, people learn and regulate the cognitive, affective, and behavioral processes of one another. As strangers interact with people in the host environment, they learn and acquire the acculturative capacities in their cognitive, affective, and behavioral processes. At the same time, their greater personal communication capacities facilitate their successful communication within the host society.

Social communication occurs in many forms—from simple observations of people on the street or reading about people and events in newspapers and magazines to engaging in dialogues with close friends. Social communication can be classified broadly into interpersonal communication and mass communication. Interpersonal communication occurs in the context of interpersonal relationships, which define the purpose, function, and product of an individual's communication experiences. Mass communication, on the other hand, is a more generalized form of social communication by which individuals interact with their sociocultural environment without direct involvement in interpersonal relations with specific persons. Individuals participate in mass communication processes through such media as radio, television, newspapers, magazines, movies, theater, museums, lectures, and posters, among others.

Interpersonal communication

Strangers acquire acculturative experiences from participation in interpersonal relationships with members of the host society. Further, one can infer and predict strangers' level of acculturation from the nature of their interpersonal communication networks. For example, an immigrant with a predominantly ethnic interpersonal network is less acculturated and probably less competent in the host communication system than someone whose associates are primarily members of the host society. Also, the degree of intimacy in the relationships developed with members of the host society is an important indicator of strangers' acculturative communication competency.

There is considerable evidence of a connection between interpersonal communication with members of the host society and personal adjustment of strangers. Studies of foreign students and visitors indicate a positive relationship between the number of host friends and the stranger's positive attitude toward the host society. Also, the degree of interpersonal involvement is an important indicator of strangers' cognitive acculturation. Selltiz et al. (1963), for example, show that international students in the United States who associated extensively with host nationals and those who formed close friendships in the host culture scored higher on measures of adjustment than those who had less association with host nationals or who did not have host friends. Morris (1960) also finds that students who were high on measures of social relations with host nationals scored high on an index of satisfaction with various aspects of their experience in the host country (see also Coelho, 1958; Pool, 1965).

Studies of immigrants in the United States show a similar relationship between interpersonal communication and personal communication processes of acculturation. Y. Kim (1977a; 1979c) reports a significant relationship between Korean immigrants' positive attitude and satisfaction in the North American culture and the volume and intimacy of their interpersonal relationships with North Americans. The same observation is made in her studies of Mexican (1978b) and Indochinese (1980) communities. Wen (1976) reports a similar phenomenon in a study of the effects of social isolation and mental stress on Chinese immigrants. The indicators of mental illness vary with the degree of social isolation from the host culture. Yum's (1982) study of Korean immigrants in Hawaii suggests that the immigrants' ability to acquire information necessary for their functioning in the United States is positively influenced by their "communication diversity," or the level of integration of Hawaiians in the immigrants' information sources.

While communication with members of the host society clearly facilitates the process of acculturation, the role of intraethnic communication (i.e., communication with persons from the same cultural background) is generally considered to promote ethnicity and discourage integration into the host society. Shibutani and Kwan (1965) identify an adverse effect of intraethnic communication on acculturation. They state: "To the extent that . . . a minority group participated in different sets of communication channels, they develop different perspectives and have difficulty in understanding each other" (p. 982). Broom and Kitsuse (1955) similarly argue: "A large part of the acculturation experience of the members of an ethnic group may be circumscribed by the ethnic community" (p. 45).

Although extensive and prolonged intraethnic communication may have the effect of retarding the process of acculturation, the ethnic community plays a vital role in the initial stages of acculturation. It provides strangers with necessary emotional and social support and information. Y. Kim's studies of Korean immigrants (1977b) and Indochinese refugees (1980) in the Chicago area indicate a simultaneous growth in the numbers of both ethnic acquaintances and host acquaintances during the initial years of adaptation. In both studies the volume of intraethnic communication is not significantly related to other cognitive, affective, and behavioral indicators of acculturation. What appears to be a significant adaptive change that occurs in strangers over a period of time is the increasing heterogeneity (from primarily ethnic composition to ethnic and host composition) of their interpersonal communication networks.

Mass communication

Along with the development of interpersonal communication with members of the host society, the use of the mass media of the host society is observed to be acculturative (see, for example, Hong, 1980; Kapoor and Williams, 1979; Kim, Lee, and Jeong, 1982; Kim, 1977a; 1979a; Pedone, 1980; Ryu, 1976). Participating in the mass communication process of the host society enables strangers to learn about the broader ranges of various elements of the host culture beyond their immediate environment. In transmitting messages that reflect aspirations, myths, work and play, and specific issues and events, the mass media explicitly and implicitly convey societal values, norms of behavior, and traditional perspectives for interpreting the environment. Exposure to mass media with an information-oriented content (such as news items, analyses of various social phenomena, and documentaries) is particularly indicative of acculturation, as compared to exposure to mass media with content that is primarily entertainment-oriented (J. Kim, 1982; Y. Kim, 1977a; 1979a).

The overall acculturative function of mass communication is considered relatively limited compared to that of interpersonal communication (Kim, 1979a). Interpersonal communication experiences provide strangers with an intense and detailed influence over their acculturative process. Communication involving an interpersonal relationship provides simultaneous feedback, directly regulating strangers' communication behaviors. Because of the intrinsic intensity of face-to-face communication, strangers may find it too stressful. This means that, during the initial phases of acculturation, mass media provide alternative, less stressful channels of communication through which strangers can absorb some elements of the host culture.

Compared to the availability of the prevailing mass media environment of the host society, the availability of ethnic media is limited in most immigrant communities. The level of interest in and the perceived utility of ethnic media among immigrants decreases clearly and consistently as they become more familiar with the host language and culture. This trend is in direct contrast to the increasing use of the host mass media by immigrants (Hong, 1980; Kim, Lee, and Jeong, 1982; Y. Kim, 1977b; 1980).

So far, the process by which strangers acculturate into a new and unfamiliar culture has been explained from a communication viewpoint. Just as a native-born person undergoes enculturation through communication, so do strangers undergo acculturation into the host culture through communication. Much of the process of acculturation serves to help strangers adapt to the predominant patterns of personal and social communication in the host society. The acquired communication competency, in turn, facilitates all other aspects of adaptation to the host environment, including economic and occupational adaptation (Hurh and Kim, 1979; Y. Kim, 1980).

FACTORS INFLUENCING THE ACCULTURATIVE COMMUNICATION PROCESS

Strangers respond differently to a new cultural environment in terms of their prior experiences, accepting what promises to be rewarding and rejecting what seems unworkable or disadvantageous. At the same time, strangers' acculturative experiences are conditioned further by the host environment. The nature of the dynamic interaction between personal factors and environmental factors shapes the patterns of subsequent adaptive changes in strangers.

Acculturative Potential

One of the most important background factors that needs to be considered in understanding strangers' cultural adaptation is the *degree of similarity or difference between the original culture and the host culture.* Strangers from the United States, for example, have a greater acculturative potential when they move to Canada than when they move to Thailand. To the extent that the original cultural patterns coincide with the host cultural patterns, less adjustment is necessary. The greater the disparity between the two, the more difficulty is involved in adaptation and the larger is the cultural gap that must be bridged. Such factors as the language used by the members of the host society, their verbal and nonverbal communication behaviors, the rules and norms of their social interactions and relationships, the economic and political structure of their society, and its specific ceremonies and rituals are all highly relevant to the size of that gap. For example, research indicates that students from Europe have an easier time developing social relationships with North Americans than do other international students studying in the United States. More specifically, Lysgaard (1955) and Sewell and Davidsen (1961) describe Scandinavian students as having little difficulty in adjusting to life in the United States, while Lambert and Bressler (1956) and Bennett, Passin, and McKnight (1958) report considerable difficulty on the part of students from India and Japan, respectively. Similar results are reported by Furnham and Bochner (1982) for international students in England.

A closely related factor that contributes to the acculturative potential of strangers is the *degree of familiarity with the host culture* prior to, or during, the initial period of adaptation in the new environment. Knowledge about the host language, norms, customs, history, art, and social, economic, and political systems adds to strangers' acculturative capacity. A key component of the many existing cross-cultural training and orientation programs for sojourners and immigrants focuses on familiarizing trainees with their host culture. Peace Corps volunteers, for example, go through a language and cultural training program before being sent to the location to which they are assigned. Also, Sewell and Davidsen (1961) find that the more guidance international students receive prior to coming to the United States, the better is their academic adjustment and the greater is their satisfaction with the sojourn.

Another important factor affecting acculturative potential is *personality characteristics.* Although everyone goes through a continual process of change, we do possess certain basic dispositions that are more or less enduring in nature. Our personality patterns make us unique among the membership of our cultural group, no matter how close the intragroup resemblance may be. Unique traits of personality tend to reveal themselves in the adaptive process in a new cultural environment, making our adaptive patterns unique. Even in instances where strong prejudice or actual enmity exists toward strangers, it is still possible for the personality of a specific stranger to overcome these barriers and to win a position of respect, good will, and even intimacy within a group.

The personality characteristics identified as important for the acculturation process in studies of immigrants include tolerance for ambiguity and risk-taking (Fiske and Maddi, 1961), internal locus of control (Johnson and Sarason, 1978), gregariousness (Bradburn, 1969), cognitive flexibility (Kim, 1977a), and hardy or resilient personality (Quisumbing, 1982). In the case of sojourners, personality characteristics such as extrovertedness, positive orientation, respect for people in general, empathy, open-mindedness, tolerance for ambiguity, and self-control are observed to be positively related to effective adjustment in the host culture. These characteristics are very similar to those associated with effective communication, as discussed in Chapter 12.

Certain *demographic characteristics* also tend to increase strangers' acculturative potential. In studies of immigrants, *age* is observed to be a critical element in subsequent adaptation in the host society. The older strangers are, the greater the difficulty they experience in adapting to a new cultural system and the slower they are in acquiring new cultural patterns (Szapocznik et al., 1975; Kim, 1977a; Rogler et al., 1980). This inverse relationship between age and acculturation can be attributed to the greater rigidity (or lesser flexibility) of the personality patterns, which we acquire as we grow older, particularly once the socialization process is completed.

Another important demographic factor is the *educational level* of strangers prior to migration. Education, regardless of its cultural context, appears to expand our mental capacity for new learning and for the challenges of life in general. In many cases, strangers' education in their home country includes training in the language of the host country, which provides an added leverage for building communication competencies after moving into the new system (Y. Kim, 1977a; 1980; Yum, 1982). A number of studies also report a significant difference between male and female immigrants in their acculturation process. Generally, male immigrants display greater acculturation than female immigrants given the same stay in the host culture (Kim, 1977a). Gender, however, is associated closely with educational level. In most of the cultures from which immigrants come to the United States, the men's educational level is higher than the women's. Also, the prevailing cultural norms of these groups tend to define women as primarily homemakers, thus limiting their participation in host interpersonal communication processes. Consideration of these associated factors leads one to conclude that the influence of gender on acculturative potential is not clearly known.

Host Environmental Conditions

The acculturation process is influenced not only by strangers' acculturative potential but also by the conditions existing or developing in the host society. The process of adaptive change in strangers is an interactive one of "push and pull" between the strangers and the environment. The acculturation experiences of two very similar persons may differ in two different environments.

One of the most crucial environmental conditions affecting acculturation is called *interaction potential,* the degree of opportunity provided by the immediate physical and social environment for strangers to communicate with members of the host society. Ordinarily, if a situation is to have any interaction potential at all, it must provide for physical proximity. Beyond this basic requirement, social contexts differ greatly in interaction potential. For example, people do not usually talk to strangers sitting next to them in the subway or on a bus. If, on the other hand, strangers are assigned to work with people on a collaborative task, they soon cease to be unknown. Such social contexts are high in interaction potential, almost demanding communication of some sort and making it easy to go beyond superficial exchange if strangers so wish.

Thus, international students who live without host roommates in buildings not predominantly occupied by host students are likely to have relatively little interaction with host nationals outside of classrooms. Ting-Toomey (1981), in her study of Chinese-American college students, reports that the students' friendship-formation pattern is significantly influenced by the availability of white Anglo-Americans within their school environment. Similarly, U.S. military personnel who live in a predominantly military town have limited access to local people in their daily activities. On the other hand, a Peace Corps volunteer whose primary responsibility is to help local residents improve their health practices has a greater interaction potential and thus develops more meaningful interpersonal relationships with the host nationals.

The interaction potential for intraethnic communication also depends on the availability of ethnic individuals in the strangers' environment. Inglis and Gudykunst (1982) examine the communication patterns of Korean immigrants in the Hartford, Connecticut, area and compare them with the findings of Kim's (1977b; 1978b) studies of the same group in the Chicago area. The comparison yields a significant difference in the Korean immigrants' interaction with other Koreans. Members of the smaller and less organized Hartford-area Korean community have far fewer Korean acquaintances than do members of the Chicago-area community, which has a more established Korean group.

Another factor influencing strangers' acculturative communication process is the unfavorable or apathetic *attitudes held by members of the host society* toward the strangers' national and/or cultural group. Strong hostility against a group minimizes the receptivity of the host society toward individual members of the group and, consequently, makes communication more difficult for them. The attitudes of the host society toward a specific group may be due to a long-standing historical animosity, as exemplified in the hostility between white and black South Africans. New developments in international relationships may abruptly change a long-standing friendly attitude between groups, as was observed in the recent development of tension and hostility between the United States and Iran. Sometimes, the attitude or sentiment of the host society toward an outside group may be influenced by its own domestic economic or political situation, such as a high unemployment rate or a prevailing conservative ideology.

Mass media play a particularly important role in determining the emotional mood of the host society toward other cultural groups. Media news coverage of various international and domestic events tends to influence public sentiment and opinion concerning various target groups. Once a societal climate is developed, some unusual situations may arise in the host society vis-à-vis specific groups of strangers, such as direct social segregation in housing, discrimination in employment, and social isolation by exclusion from intimate and sympathetic social contacts. These and other discriminatory practices in the host environment make the already difficult cultural adaptation of strangers even more trying.

Finally, the acculturation experiences of strangers are influenced significantly by the *degree of rigidity of the host society* in demanding cultural conformity. The extent to which the host society expects strangers to conform to its existing cultural norms and values varies from society to society. Strangers who enter a totalitarian society or one that follows some ideological orthodoxy may need to conform rapidly to assigned roles that cover many aspects of their daily activities. On the other hand, a relatively freer and more pluralistic social system such as the United States allows a greater latitude for or shows more tolerance toward cultural differences. A similar observation can be made about the differences in the cultural rigidity of the small rural town and of the large metropolitan area. The complex and heterogeneous social and cultural structure of the metropolitan area exhibits greater openness to and freedom for new and different elements. One cannot point to this or that particular type of relationship and behavior as forming the basis of the social and cultural system of a city since many types contribute to this end, no one of which may be excluded. On the other hand, the presence of strangers can be a matter of interest in villages, and they may be subjected to close scrutiny. If the strangers are accepted by the villagers, then the strangers are likely to find it necessary to learn the accepted patterns of the surrounding culture.

SUMMARY

All in all, the process of adapting to a new and unfamiliar culture is complex, multidimensional, and interactive. The acculturative communication process of strangers is influenced by conditions of their personal background, as well as by conditions of the host environment. Figure 13-1 graphically presents the factors affecting the acculturative communication process of strangers, as discussed thus far.

Once strangers enter a new environment, the acculturation process is set in motion, and it will continue as long as they stay in direct contact with that environment. At the heart of the interactive acculturation process lies the communication process linking strangers to the host cultural milieu. Acquisition of communicative competence by strangers is not only instrumental to all aspects of cultural adaptation but also indicative of the strangers' accomplished acculturation. In other words, the degree to which strangers adapt to the host culture depends on their personal and social communication processes. At the same time, the adaptive changes that have already taken place are reflected in the strangers' communication patterns.

Figure 13-1 Factors Influencing Strangers' Acculturative Communication Process

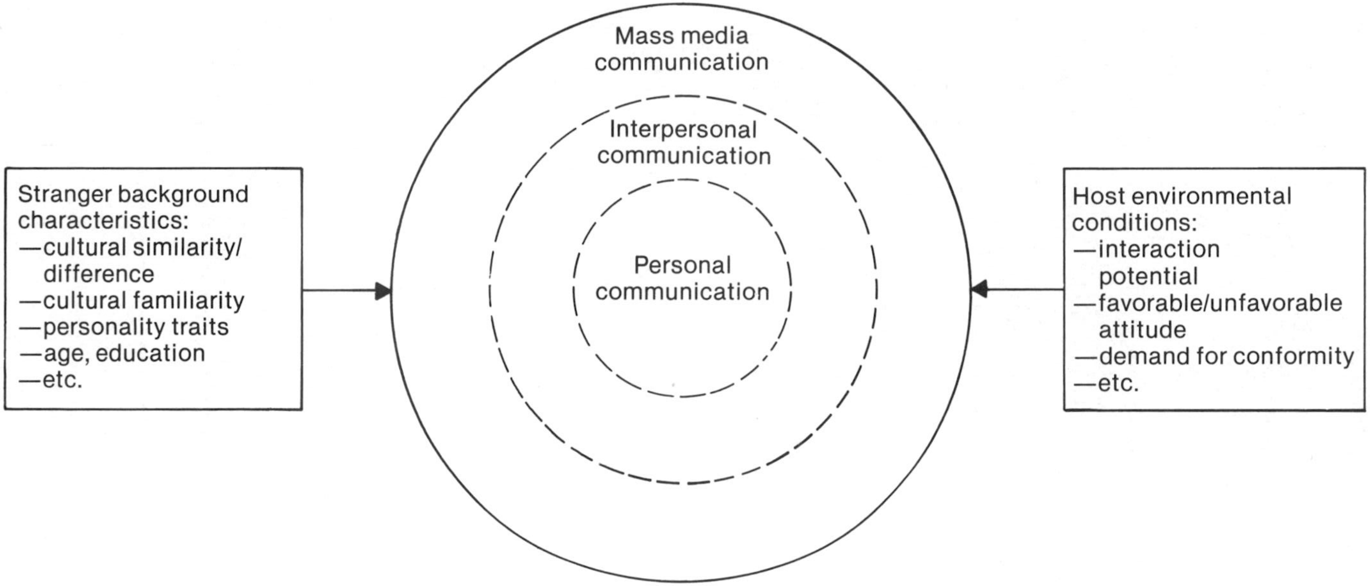

Host environmental conditions:
—interaction potential
—favorable/unfavorable attitude
—demand for conformity
—etc.

Mass media communication

Interpersonal communication

Personal communication

Stranger background characteristics:
—cultural similarity/difference
—cultural familiarity
—personality traits
—age, education
—etc.

We may also predict that those strangers who possess a cultural background similar to the host culture, those who are familiar with the host culture prior to immigration, and those who are tolerant, risk-taking, flexible, gregarious, and resilient are more likely to be successful in their acculturation process. Also, those who are better educated and younger will find it easier to adapt to a new cultural environment. If all other factors are equal, the environment providing greater access to members of the host society, showing a favorable attitude toward strangers' nationality and ethnicity, and exerting a greater pressure on the strangers to conform to existing cultural patterns is most likely to facilitate the acculturative communication process.

While the acculturative communication process provides the central dynamics in all cultural adaptation situations, every stranger's contact with the environment is a unique phenomenon. The nature of the interaction and of the relationships formed between strangers and the environment is influenced by the particular combination of factors, some of which have been presented in this chapter. For many, the acculturative communication process may not follow a smooth linear pattern of change, but a forward-moving progression is nonetheless usually observed, toward a better "fit" of the stranger to the changed environment.

14
Becoming Intercultural

*Man must now embark on the difficult journey
beyond culture, because the greatest separation
feat of all is when one manages to gradually free
oneself from the grip of unconscious culture.*

Edward T. Hall

We live in a "world of simultaneous events and overall awareness" (McLuhan, 1962, p. 40). Through mass media and other advanced information systems, we constantly are exposed to international affairs. What happens in a small nation in South America can be, directly and indirectly, a significant part of the political reality of many nations around the world. Diplomats and international business personnel work closely with strangers of other cultures and need to be keenly aware of the changing realities of the world. In urban centers many of us find ourselves working side by side with strangers from various national, racial, ethnic, and religious backgrounds.

In addition to adjusting to the technological connectedness of our international and domestic environments, all of us have to adapt to changes in many aspects of our lives—in social structure, values, politics, and, most of all, in our human relations. Even in less technological societies, change has encroached on nearly every pattern of life—on many traditional values, on the structure and functions of the family, and on the relations between generations. Every index suggests that the rate of change will increase up to the as yet untested limits of human adaptability. Our relationship to our personal and collective past is increasingly becoming one of dislocation, of that peculiar mixture of freedom and loss that inevitably accompanies massive change.

We increasingly are placed in positions in which the culture of our youth cannot be depended on to produce reliable predictions about what other people are going to do next. There is little convincing evidence that decreasing physical distance and increasing informational proximity bring improvement in the quality of human life. We continue to see international and domestic conflicts, in spite of the fact that people across cultural and subcultural boundaries perhaps know more about one another now than at any other time in history.

What we see, instead, are many different ways in which people try to cope with and adapt to the complexities of life. There are those who feel lost in the midst of all this change and who shy away from such concepts as "social consciousness" or "world consciousness." Others busily organize people to join together to fight for traditional values and to reverse the changing trends. There are also those who try desperately to keep up with the changes that occur around them, often finding only experiences of failure and despair.

What appears to be lacking in our efforts to cope with the changes and complexities of our contemporary world is a clear understanding of its fundamental dynamics and a clear sense of direction for change. We fail to recognize the pervasive "interculturalness" of our domestic and international realities, and instead we try to deal with many intercultural problems in a manner shaped by our own culture. Even though the problems we face demand an intercultural orientation and new ways of dealing with one another, we try to "force" our own cultural ways on others. Such seems to be the case with many international problems and domestic clashes of diverse interest groups, as well as with our attempts to resolve conflicts between individuals.

What we need to do in order to be more effective in our changing world is to make a conscious decision concerning our basic attitudes toward ourselves and toward our relationships to others and the world at large. This means we need to search for a new image of ourselves that will help us develop specific strategies for daily activities and problems. Reorienting ourselves and becoming less ethnocentric is, of course, a difficult challenge. For most of us, who have grown up in one cultural milieu during our formative years, it is difficult to change our cultural inertia and habits even if we would like to. "One acquires a personality and a culture in childhood, long before he is capable of comprehending either of them" (Barnlund, 1982, p. 14).

Yet it is crucial that we do our utmost to work toward becoming less ethnocentric if we are to become more functional and effective in our intercultural environment. For example, to be an effective business manager in a multinational company, one cannot be highly ethnocentric. To be an effective teacher in a multiethnic urban school, one must be able to deal with children and their parents whose cultural attributes are different from one's own. To be an effective ambassador to Brazil, one must be an effective communicator with a great deal of sensitivity, understanding, and the social skills of the local culture.

Experiences of immigrants and sojourners who successfully adapt to new

cultural environments are invaluable in providing us with insights into the fundamental changes we must undergo if we are to develop an intercultural perspective. In this chapter we continue our discussion on communication and cultural
adaptation, focusing on the psychic growth one may experience from intercultural encounters. Also, the concept of the "intercultural person," is presented
as a desirable image of human development toward which we can strive.

ENCOUNTERING DIFFERENT CULTURES

Every one of us came into this world knowing literally nothing of what we need
to know to function acceptably in human society. Through the process of enculturation, cultural patterns are etched into our nervous system and become
part of our personality and behavior. This internalized learning enables us to
interact easily with other members of our culture who share a similar image
of reality. In other words, the culture of our youth provides a common pattern
for our cognitive, affective, and behavioral structure and processes, so that persons belonging to the same culture tend to have a similar understanding of, and
similar responses to, reality. It is culture that programs us to define what is real,
what is true, what is right, what is beautiful, and what is good.

Yet we remain largely unconscious of the cultural imprinting that governs
our personality and behavior. Our cultural unconscious can be understood only
by detailed analysis. We automatically treat what is most characteristically our
own as though it were innate. We are programmed to think, feel, and behave as
though anyone whose behavior is not predictable or is peculiar in any way is
strange, improper, irresponsible, or inferior. In this sense, all of us have a natural
tendency to be ethnocentric as a result of our very inseparable relationship to
our culture.

The only time we become aware of our hidden control system is when
things do not follow the hidden program. In fact, according to Boulding (1956),
the human nervous system is structured in such a way that the patterns that
govern behavior and perception come into consciousness only when there is a
deviation from the familiar. Thus, to be functional and mature in a given culture, one must experience a multitude of challenges, and the full impact of the
process is not experienced until one has "cut the apron strings and established
oneself as independent of one's parents" (Hall, 1976, p. 225). Similarly, the
only time we become fully aware of the hidden control system of our own culture is when we separate ourselves mentally or physically from our own cultural
milieu and encounter experiences that challenge our taken-for-granted images
and assumptions.

Encounters with strangers bring surprises and stresses. Some of the surprises
may shake our self-concept and cultural identity and bring the anxiety of temporary rootlessness. Similarly, when we are strangers in other cultures, we are

confronted with situations in which our assumptions and premises are called into question, which often produces a conflict in which we must abandon our identification with our cultural patterns that symbolize personal integration. Ill-equipped to deal with such inconsistencies, some of us are, temporarily at least, in a state of mental and sometimes physical disturbance. The many examples of cross-cultural confusion experienced by international students, Peace Corps volunteers, and international business personnel suggest a wide spectrum of responses and reactions to new cultural surroundings. Similarly, a woman who returns to work after many years of being out of the work force may experience some of these transitional problems.

Reactions to such situations are known as *culture shock.* Oberg (1958) uses the term in connection with the experience of anthropologists, who must learn to manage the violation of their social reality implicit in unfamiliar social norms, values, and mores. This violation represents a challenge to their primary socialization since the accustomed validation of basic values and role concepts virtually ceases. Lundstedt (1963) describes culture shock as "a form of personality maladjustment which is a reaction to a temporary unsuccessful attempt to adjust to new surroundings and people" (p. 8).

Many writers describe the various psychological, social, and physical reactions associated with culture shock. In reviewing the literature, Taft (1977) identifies a number of common psychological reactions to cultural dislocation, for example: (1) "cultural fatigue," as manifested by irritability, insomnia, and other psychosomatic disorders, (2) a sense of loss arising from being uprooted from one's familiar surroundings, (3) rejection by the individual of members of the new environment, and (4) a feeling of impotence from being unable to competently deal with the environmental unfamiliarity. Others describe the reactions of people to stressful situations under more severe conditions, such as those of concentration camp inmates, prisoners of war, and returned prisoners of war. In each of these cases the features associated with the change are the "shock" effects involving heightened emotions and intense suffering.

At the heart of culture shock is the lack of fitness between strangers' subjective experiences and the commonly accepted modes of experience in the unfamiliar surroundings. Everyone requires the ongoing validation of their life-world, and being unable to meet this basic human need can lead to symptoms of mental, emotional, and physical disturbance (Berger and Kellner, 1970). The shifting of the self-world relationship brings about heightened levels of consciousness through an increased awareness of the split between inner, subjective experiences and external, objective circumstances. In its most basic form, existential despair is the painful discrepancy between what *is* and what *should be.* For some strangers the process of adapting to a new or changed environment may involve such an existential dilemma.

THE PROCESS OF PSYCHIC GROWTH

How can a person brought up to be a certain type of cultural being through the primary enculturation process ever overcome the existing barriers in order to cope with an unfamiliar culture? The answer seems to lie in the profound plasticity and adaptability of the human organism. From the moment of birth, we are active agents in our own development, constructing the very reality in which we live. As we change, there is a progression of stages, where each stage in the developmental sequence is a necessary result of the preceding stage and integrates previous behaviors, concepts, and actions into a present condition. We simultaneously go through qualitative changes and maintain integrity throughout the lifespan, although it is still not clearly understood how such qualitative changes occur between stages. In this framework of mental development, successive levels and forms of equilibrium are conceived as levels of adaptation, with change being caused by a mismatch or discrepancy between our internal world and the external reality (Fogel, 1979, p. 3).

This adaptive principle governing the human organism is evidenced most dramatically in individuals who have gone through such extreme life circumstances as prisons and death camps. The adjustment of many inmates to such settings reveals an almost limitless human resilience. Numerous immigrants, refugees, and missionaries also demonstrate that they are able to learn gradually to evoke appropriate situations and relations in the host society. Perhaps because of the immediate concern about maladjustment problems of immigrants and sojourners, little attention has been paid to the phenomena beyond the initial culture shock. The phenomenon of "growth" beyond this stage in successful strangers has not been adequately examined.

Strangers are capable not only of adapting to new cultures but also, more importantly, of growing and developing through the adaptive process. The psychological movements of strangers into new dimensions of perception and experience often produce forms of personality disintegration, stress, or mental illness in some extreme cases. And yet temporary disintegration is the very basis for subsequent growth in the awareness of life conditions and ways to deal with them.

Thus, in the process of adapting to a new or changed environment, strangers not only acquire the knowledge, attitudes, and behavioral capacities that are adaptive in different cultural contexts but also, if successful, grow into a new kind of person at a higher level of integration. Even extreme mental illness can be viewed as a process of a potentially positive disintegration in order to reintegrate with new material at a higher level (Dabrowski, 1968).

Hall (1976) calls this fundamental nature of psychic growth processes, "identity-separation-growth dynamisms" or "boundary-ambiguity syndromes" (p. 227). A similar view is expressed by Jourard (1974):

Growth is the dis-integration of one way of experiencing the world, followed by a reorganization of this experience, a reorganization that includes the new disclosure of the world. The disorganization, or even shattering, of one way to experience the world, is brought on by new disclosures from the changing being of the world, disclosures that were always being transmitted, but were usually ignored. (p. 456)

Empirical research provides some indirect indication that the stresses in cultural adaptation may indeed lay the groundwork for subsequent psychic growth. On the basis of their study among Canadian immigrants in Kenya, Ruben and Kealey (1979) find tentative empirical data to suggest, in some cases at least, that the stranger who is ultimately the most effective in adaptation to a new culture can be expected to undergo the most intense culture shock during transition. Other acculturation studies of immigrants and foreign students show that, once the initial phase is managed successfully, strangers go through a gradual process of adaptation to the new cultural system (see, for example, Coelho, 1958; Y. Kim, 1978; 1980).

The theory of personal constructs developed by Kelly (1955) provides a further theoretical basis for psychic growth processes. Personal constructs, Kelly argues, are the conceptual tools we use in understanding and differentiating among similar or adjacent objects in the psychological environment. The cognitive schemes we employ define our intentions and imply alternative lines of action in a given situation. The greater the number of constructs present in our cognitive system, the greater is our ability to recognize differences and articulate and respond to events.

Bieri (1955) applies the label "cognitive complexity" to describe this psychological construct. Cognitive complexity, according to Bieri, is the "degree of differentiation of the construct system" (p. 263). Subsequent research demonstrates three structural features of the complexity-simplicity continuum: (1) differentiation of the number of dimensions in one's personal constructs, (2) the relative articulation (or abstraction) of dimensions or the number of categories in a behavioral dimension that a person can discriminate (Rigney, Bieri, and Tripodi, 1964), and (3) integration of various dimensions of cognition into a meaningful whole, which is called "integrative complexity" (Schroder, Driver, and Streufert, 1967).

An important aspect of the human cognitive system relevant to our present discussion is the intrinsically social and developmental nature of its structure. As Schroder and his associates (1967) explain, the level of cognitive complexity in a given area is not necessarily static over time but develops further with new learning experiences. In other words, our cognitive structure is developed through various social experiences, creating a relatively differentiated, articulated (or abstracted), and integrated schematic structure.

This developmental principle is demonstrated in the research on strangers' adaptation to new cultures. Just as comparative analyses of children, adoles-

[margin note: personal constructs]

cents, and adults reveal an increasing cognitive complexity, research on immigrants and sojourners indicates that, in general, strangers' perception of the new culture becomes more complex and refined in time with increased interactions with the host environment. Through the cumulative experiences of adaptation in the new culture, strangers gradually attain a significant degree of cognitive capacity to differentiate between the original culture and the host culture along increasingly more dimensions and categories and to synthesize the cultures and their dimensions into an integrated whole.

What is significant about successfully adjusted immigrants and sojourners is that, as strangers in the host culture, they separate themselves mentally and physically from their original culture. As they become less like strangers and more familiar with the host society, they simultaneously go through a process of transforming their original cultural identity and of becoming intercultural. This means their disposition and behavioral patterns are reorganized on a higher level of complexity and awareness. They acquire a greater capacity to overcome cultural parochialism.

THE INTERCULTURAL PERSON—A MODEL
FOR HUMAN DEVELOPMENT

The process of personal transformation from being a stranger to becoming intercultural is potentially a process of growth—growth beyond our original cultural conditioning toward the ideal end state of the *intercultural person*. If strangers successfully overcome the multitude of challenges and frustrations that invariably accompany the process of cultural adaptation, they develop a mental and behavioral capacity more adaptable, flexible, and resilient than that of people who have limited exposure to the challenges of continuous intercultural encounters.

The concept of the intercultural person is presented here as an attempt to project an ideal image of personhood in the increasingly intercultural world of our time. The intercultural person represents one who has achieved an advanced level in the process of becoming intercultural and whose cognitive, affective, and behavioral characteristics are not limited but are open to growth beyond the psychological parameters of any one culture.

Other similar terms such as "international" person (Lutzker, 1960), "universal" person (Walsh, 1973), "multicultural" person (Adler, 1982), and "marginal" person (Lum, 1982) are used to project an essentially similar image, with varying degrees of descriptive and explanatory value. The term intercultural person is preferred since it is more inclusive than the other terms in portraying the type of person whose psychological makeup transcends any type of group identity including national, racial, ethnic, gender, professional, or other sociological typifications of people. As we stated in Chapter 1, the term culture is used broadly and flexibly here to refer to the collective life patterns shared by individuals in these and other human groups. Unlike the term multicultural person, the term intercultural person does not have the connotation that the individual necessarily "possesses" more than one culture. Unlike the term universal person, the term intercultural person does not imply an awareness and appreciation of all groups of the world. The term international person, on the other hand, focuses on the expanded psychological orientation beyond one's national boundary and does not emphasize numerous groups within a nation. The term marginal person implies a psychological sense of inferiority and alienation, which is not necessarily a life condition for an intercultural person.

The intercultural person, as a model for human development, stands for a fundamental change in the structure and process of our identity; this model is far from being frozen in a social character but is more flexible and open to variations. The intercultural person is often undergoing personal transitions and, thus, is in a state of becoming something different. This does not mean intercultural persons are culture-free or culture-less, but that they are not bound by membership to any one particular culture. Adler (1982), in his explication of "multicultural man," characterizes this unique cultural identity:

> The identity of multicultural man is based, not on "belongingness" which implies either owning or being owned by culture, but on a style of self-consciousness that is capable of negotiating ever new formations of reality. In this sense multicultural man is a radical departure from the kinds of identities found in both traditional and mass societies. He is neither totally *a part of* nor totally *apart from* his culture; he lives, instead, on the boundary. (p. 391)

The intercultural person also possesses an intellectual and emotional commitment to the fundamental unity of all human beings and, at the same time, accepts and appreciates the differences that lie between people of different cultures. Adler (1982) identifies three fundamental premises underlying the thinking and behavior of the intercultural person: (1) every culture has its own internal coherence, which provides a logic for interrelatedness among its elements; (2) all cultures are equally valid in organizing human experiences; and (3) all persons are at least partly culture-bound. Similarly, Walsh's (1973) concept of "universal man" emphasizes three aspects of a "cosmopolitan" viewpoint: (1) respect for all cultures, (2) understanding of what individuals in other cultures think, feel, and believe, and (3) appreciation for differences among cultures.

The intercultural person further embodies attributes that are preparation for serving as a facilitator and catalyst for contacts between cultures. As we come to terms with the roots of our own ethnocentrism and gain new perspectives and outlooks on the nature of culture, we achieve an objectivity that comes from not being rooted in one particular cultural group. Intercultural persons, due to their interculturalness, develop a "third-culture" perspective (Gudykunst,

Wiseman, and Hammer, 1977), which enables them to interpret and evaluate intercultural encounters more accurately and thus to act as a communication link between two cultures. Lum (1982) points out that the intercultural person is capable of uniting and reconciling cultural differences and of playing a potentially invaluable role for positive social change.

Most of all, the intercultural person acquires resources for coping with social situations and experiences an increase in the possibilities for communicating and communing with diverse groups. By definition, the intercultural person is equipped with the capacity to function in more than one culture effectively. The intercultural person possesses cultural sensitivity, which is linked closely with the ability to show cultural empathy—not only to be able to step into another person's shoes but also to "imaginatively participate in the other's world view" (Bennett, 1977, p. 49). A highly intercultural person has the skills to perform the roles required by each cultural context competently and is able to avoid conflicts that could result from inappropriate switching between cultures (Taft, 1977, p. 143). Intercultural persons develop adaptability and social communication competency along with their personal (or intrapersonal) communication competency (i.e., a psychology enabling appropriate responses to specific life situations).

At this level of human growth, differences and distinctions between human groups do not necessarily mean polarities and opposites without relationships. The intercultural person is better able to resolve and integrate seemingly contradictory characteristics of peoples and cultures and to transform them into complementary, interacting parts of an integral whole. Indeed, the process of becoming intercultural presents a potential for achieving what L. Harris (1979) refers to as the optimal level of communication competence. As one achieves a significant level of interculturalness, one may be better able to make deliberate choices of actions in specific situations rather than simply being bound by the culturally normative courses of behavior. According to Harris, an optimally competent communicator has

> . . . the skills of a satisfactorily competent individual plus a sophisticated *meta system* for critiquing his/her own managing system and interpersonal system. The existence of the meta system makes the difference between the optimal level and the other two levels of competence a qualitative one. (p. 31)

This optimal, inclusive, and transcendental perception and awareness also are seen as one of the highest aims of humans in the spiritual traditions of the East. Suzuki (1968) writes:

> The fundamental idea of Buddhism is to pass beyond the world of opposites, a world built up by intellectual distinctions and emotional defilements, and to realize the spiritual world of non-distinction, which involves achieving an absolute point of view. (p. 18)

A virtuous person in the East, therefore, is not one who undertakes the impossible task of striving for the good and eliminating the bad, but rather one who is able to maintain a dynamic balance between good and bad. This notion of dynamic balance is emphasized extensively by the Chinese sages in their symbolism of the archetypal poles of *yin* and *yang*. They call the unity lying beyond yin and yang the *tao* and see it as a process that brings about the interplay of yin and yang.

In becoming intercultural, we rise above the hidden grips of culture and discover that there are many ways to be "good," "true," and "beautiful." In this process, we acquire a greater capacity to overcome cultural parochialism and develop a wider circle of identification, approaching the limit of many cultures and ultimately of humanity itself. The process of becoming intercultural, in this view, is like climbing a high mountain. As we reach the mountaintop, we see that all paths below ultimately lead to the same summit and that each path presents a unique scenery. In a way becoming intercultural is a process of liberating ourselves from a limited perspective on life—of becoming more fully human, with a greater awareness of and sensitivity to self, others, and the relationships between them. The self-reflection of Yoshikawa (1978), who was born in Japan and acculturated in the United States, succinctly illustrates the above characteristics of an intercultural person:

> I am now able to look at both cultures with objectivity as well as subjectivity; I am able to move in both cultures, back and forth without any apparent conflict; I am able to switch the linguistic and cultural code systems almost at will, as if there are two distinct individuals in me—one Japanese and the other American. However, it is more than a mere fusion of two "cultural selves." I think that something beyond the sum of each identification took place, and that it became something akin to the concept of "synergy"—when one adds 1 and 1, one gets three, or a little more. This something extra is not culture-specific but something unique of its own, probably the emergence of a new attribute or a new self-awareness, born out of an awareness of the relative nature of values and of the universal aspect of human nature. Now I feel I have arrived at the stage where I really am not concerned whether others take me as a Japanese or an American; I can accept myself as I am. I feel I am much freer than ever before, not only in the cognitive domain (perception, thoughts, etc.), but also in the affective (feeling, attitudes, etc.) and behavioral domains. (p. 220)

FACILITATING INTERCULTURAL GROWTH

Just as democracy is an ideal end state of government, the intercultural person is an ideal toward which we can strive. The process of psychic growth from monocultural to intercultural is a process of change in which we continually are integrating new elements of life with a clear understanding of cultural conditioning. Thus, the process of becoming intercultural necessitates openness to the dynamics of change and possession of attitudes that are less criticizing, less prejudging, less selecting, and less rejecting of other peoples and cultures. We need to develop the "uncommitted potentiality for change" (Bateson, 1972, p. 497) and to doubt our own culturally colored perception by suspending our own value priorities.

People differ, of course, in the degree to which their perceptions and interests are flexible. Some react with curiosity and delight to unpredictable and uncategorizable events. Others are disturbed or uncomfortable in the presence of confusing and complex information. Some show a high level of resilience and tolerance for ambiguity, while others become extremely insecure. When confronted with the complications and confusions that surround many daily events, the former tend to avoid immediate closure and delay judgments, and the latter seek immediate closure and evaluation.

One of the crucial factors influencing the rigidity or flexibility of our psyche is age. As discussed in Chapter 13, age at the time of immigration significantly determines the subsequent rate of acculturation in the host society. Also, a recent study of children of Hispanic cultural background (Seelye and Wasilewski, 1981) suggests that well-adjusted immigrant children already manifest a type of character structure on which a different but integrated intercultural personality can be built. Some of the children in the study demonstrate a noticeable amount of "situational flexibility" and a wide enough "behavioral repertoire" to negotiate differences of opinion in the multitude of cultural contexts of their daily activities, including home, school, and street environments.

The process of becoming intercultural presents stresses and strains principally due to the environmental pressures to conform. Thus, to the extent that the concept of the intercultural person is desirable for the future of humanity, we need to design ways to minimize the social pressure by promoting the concept of interculturalness as an important human and social value. One of the most powerful means for promoting the value of interculturalness is, of course, education. The educational system has a monumental task of projecting and cultivating a new direction for human character formation, which will help members of future generations to manage themselves and their intercultural environments effectively. The educational system must face the staggering task of helping them give up outdated national, racial, ethnic, and territorial perspectives and replace these with ways of thinking that are more adaptive to the closely-knit international and domestic realities.

In response to the increasingly intercultural nature of society and to a revitalized value of cultural pluralism, the educational system of the United States has developed such specialized programs as bilingual-bicultural (or multilingual-multicultural) programs, ethnic studies, and intercultural communication studies. These programs, although useful for enlarging appreciation of diverse cultures and nations, are not aimed at cultivating fundamental character formation, psychic maturity, and a clear direction for change in human development. Lum (1982) inquires with regard to the bilingual-bicultural programs of the United States:

> Will they produce students who live in, between, and beyond cultures? That is, will they produce people who will make our pluralistic society and world survive? What will these pupils look like? How will we know we have produced children with non-separatist outlooks? (p. 384)

If appreciation for the intercultural person is a valid educational goal, and we can assume that critical unsolved global and domestic problems threaten all of us, there must be undertaken an extensive search for ways to articulate and implement intercultural human development. Further, the "selling" of the goal must go beyond the educational process directly to the political processes and the mass media. Media, in particular, can play a pivotal role in the spread of interculturalness as a human social value and thus produce a gradual change in the normative thinking of the general public.

For better or worse, humans not only have evolved but are continually evolving. We must recognize that the world evolves and that we evolve with it. The world has become, and is becoming, intercultural. We must recognize this fact and attempt to increase our fitness with our increasingly intercultural environment by becoming intercultural in our cognition, affectation, and behavior. We believe that the concept of the intercultural person presented in this chapter is a viable future image of ourselves that projects hope for the continuing growth of humanity.

SUMMARY

In this final chapter we presented a model of human growth toward becoming intercultural—a process of psychic transformation toward becoming less rigid and provincial and more open and committed to the fundamental oneness of all human beings. An intercultural person will be better able to accept and appreciate human variations, to resolve and integrate seemingly conflicting views from the basis of a third-culture perspective transcending any one particular point of view.

In presenting this model, we relied on the knowledge and insights suggested in the experiences of many individuals who have successfully gone through the process of adapting to a new and different cultural environment, such as immigrants, refugees, sojourners, and others who moved from their home culture to another culture by choice or as a result of circumstances. We learned from their experiences that the process of becoming intercultural is full of challenges as well as stresses. As strangers in a new environment, their personal and social communication modes do not fit with those of the unfamiliar environment.

They need to undertake the often painful experiences of acculturation—of unlearning the old culture and learning the new.

We also learned about the resilience and adaptability of humans, which enable strangers not only to learn to live in a new environment but also to grow and develop in new dimensions of psychic processes. The simultaneous interplay of psychic disintegration and reintegration provides the groundwork for potential growth and subsequent adaptation—strangers become less like outsiders and more integral parts of the new environment.

The insights from the experiences of strangers are invaluable to all of us. We are living in a domestic and global reality that increasingly demands a great deal of adaptability to change and accommodation of intercultural differences. In order to be effective in managing our changed and changing environment and to work toward more sensible ways of maintaining harmony in our intercultural world, we need to transform our culturally conditioned cognition and behavior into those of the intercultural person. Reaching this goal means a lifetime commitment, and visible results may be limited. Decades pass, generations come and go, but if we are to survive, we must maintain our faith in human possibilities and the oneness of the human community. Strangers who have already experienced the long and difficult journey from being unfamiliar to becoming familiar with a new culture show us that becoming intercultural is not an impossible fiction but a viable goal toward which we may strive. Individually and collectively, we may start this process of change and growth, which is an important unifying force in this diverse and yet so intricately interdependent world. Let us begin.

Bibliography

Abe, H., and Wiseman, R. A cross-cultural confirmation of the dimensions of intercultural effectiveness. *International Journal of Intercultural Relations,* 1983, 7, 53–68.

Abelson, R. Script processing in attitude formation and decision making. In J. Carroll and J. Payne (eds.), *Cognition and social behavior.* Hillsdale, N.J.: Lawrence Erlbaum Associates, 1976.

Abrahams, R. *Talking black.* Rowley, Mass.: Newbury House, 1976.

Adelman, M. B., and Lustig, W. Intercultural communication problems as perceived by Saudi Arabian and American managers. *International Journal of Intercultural Relations,* 1981, 5, 365–381.

Adler, P. S. The transitional experience: An alternative view of culture shock. *Journal of Humanistic Psychology,* 1975, 15, 13–23.

Adler, P. S. Beyond cultural identity: Reflections on cultural and multicultural man. In L. Samovar and R. Porter (eds.), *Intercultural communication: A reader,* 3rd ed. Belmont, Calif.: Wadsworth, 1982.

Adorno, T., Frankel-Brunswick, D., Levinson, D., and Sanford, N. *The authoritarian personality.* New York: Harper and Row, 1950.

Aitken, T. *The multinational man: The role of the manager abroad.* New York: Wiley, 1973.

Allen, B. P. Race and physical attractiveness as criteria for white subjects' dating choices. *Social Behavior and Personality,* 1976, 4, 289–296.

Allen, I. *The language of ethnic conflict.* New York: Columbia University Press, 1983.

Allport, G. W. *The nature of prejudice.* New York: Macmillan, 1954.

Altman, I. *The environment and social behavior.* Monterey, Calif.: Brooks/Cole, 1975.

Altman, I. Privacy regulation. *Journal of Social Issues,* 1977, 33, 66–84.

Altman, I., and Chemers, M. *Culture and environment.* Monterey, Calif.: Brooks/Cole, 1980a.

Altman, I., and Chemers, M. Cultural aspects of environment-behavior relationships. In H. Triandis and R. Brislin (eds.), *Handbook of cross-cultural psychology,* vol. 5. Boston: Allyn and Bacon, 1980b.

Altman, I., and Taylor, D. *Social penetration.* New York: Holt, Rinehart, and Winston, 1973.

Altman, I., Vinsel, A., and Brown, B. Dialectical conceptions in social psychology: An application to social penetration and privacy regulation. In L. Berkowitz (ed.), *Advances in experimental social psychology,* vol. 14. New York: Academic Press, 1981.

Amir, Y. Contact hypothesis in ethnic relations. *Psychological Bulletin,* 1969, 71, 319–342.

Amir, Y., and Garti, C. Situational and personal influence on attitude change following ethnic contact. *International Journal of Intercultural Relations,* 1977, 1, 58–75.

Applegate, J. The impact of implicit cultural communication theories on social cognitive and communication development. Paper presented at the Speech Communication Association convention, Anaheim, Calif., November, 1981.

Applegate, J., and Sypher, H. The constructivist approach. In W. Gudykunst (ed.), *Intercultural communication theory.* Beverly Hills, Calif.: Sage, 1983.

Argyle, M. *Social interactions.* Chicago: Aldine, 1969.

Argyle, M. Inter-cultural communication. In S. Bochner (ed.), *Cultures in contact.* Elmsford, N.Y.: Pergamon, 1982.

Argyle, M., Furnham, A., and Graham, J. *Social situations.* Cambridge: Cambridge University Press, 1981.

Argyle, M., Shimoda, K., and Little, B. Variance due to persons and situations in England and Japan. *British Journal of Social and Clinical Psychology,* 1978, 17, 335–337.

Aronson, E. *The social animal.* San Francisco: W. H. Freeman, 1972.

Asante, M., Newmark, E., and Blake, C. (eds.). *Handbook of intercultural communication.* Beverly Hills, Calif.: Sage, 1979.

Ashcraft, N., and Scheflen, E. *People space: The making and breaking of human boundaries.* Garden City, N.Y.: Anchor Press, 1976.

Asuncion-Lande, N. C. *Ethical perspectives and critical issues in intercultural communication.* Falls Church, Va.: Speech Communication Association, 1980.

Atkenson, P. Building communication in intercultural marriage. *Psychiatry,* 1970, 33, 396–408.

Baddassare, M., and Feller, S. Cultural variation in personal space. *Ethos,* 1975, 3, 481–503.

Barnes, J. Class and communities in a Norwegian island parish. *Human Relations,* 1954, 7, 39–58.

Barnett, G. Linguistic relativity: The role of the bilingual. In B. Ruben (ed.), *Communication yearbook 1.* New Brunswick, N.J.: Transaction, 1977.

Barnett, G., and Kincaid, D. L. A mathematical theory of cultural convergence. In W. Gudykunst (ed.), *Intercultural communication theory.* Beverly Hills, Calif.: Sage, 1983.

Barnett, V. M. *The representation of the United States abroad.* New York: Praeger, 1965.

Barnlund, D. Toward a meaning-centered philosophy of communication. *Journal of Communication,* 1962, 2, 197–211.

Barnlund, D. *Interpersonal communication.* Boston: Houghton Mifflin, 1968.

Barnlund, D. *Public and private self in Japan and the United States.* Tokyo: Simul Press, 1975.

Barnlund, D. The cross-cultural arena: An ethical void. In N. Asuncion-Lande (ed.), *Ethical perspectives and critical issues in intercultural communication.* Falls Church, Va.: Speech Communication Association, 1980.

Barnlund, D. Communication in a global village. In L. Samovar and R. Porter (eds.), *Intercultural communication: A reader.* Belmont, Calif.: Wadsworth, 1982.

Barnsley, J. *The social reality of ethics.* London: Routledge and Kegan Paul, 1972.

Batchelder, D., and Warner, E. *Beyond experience: Approach to cross-cultural education.* Brattleboro, Vt.: Experiment in International Living, 1977.

Bates, J. A. V. The communicative hand. In J. Benthall and T. Polhemus (eds.), *The body as a medium of expression.* New York: Dutton, 1975.

Bateson, G. *Steps to an ecology of mind.* New York: Ballantine Books, 1972.

Bateson, G. The pattern which connects. *Co-Evolution Quarterly,* 1978, 18, 4–15.

Batz, R., and Dold, E. Cross-cultural homestays. *International Journal of Intercultural Relations,* 1977, 1, 61–76.

Beals, R., and Humphrey, N. *No frontier to learning: The Mexican student in the United States.* Minneapolis: University of Minnesota Press, 1957.

Beardsley, R. K. Cultural anthropology. In J. Hall and R. Beardsley (eds.), *Twelve doors to Japan.* New York: McGraw-Hill, 1965.

Becker, S. L. Directions for intercultural communication research. *Central States Speech Journal,* 1969, 20.

Bell, R. *Worlds of friendship.* Beverly Hills, Calif.: Sage, 1981.

Benedict, R. *Patterns of culture.* Boston: Houghton Mifflin, 1934.

Bennett, J. Transition shock. In N. Jain (ed.), *International and intercultural communication annual,* vol. IV. Falls Church, Va.: Speech Communication Association, 1977.

Bennett, J., and McKnight, R. Social norms, national imagery and interpersonal relations. In A. Smith (ed.), *Communication and culture.* New York: Holt, Rinehart, and Winston, 1966.

Bennett, J., Passin, J., and McKnight, R. *In search of identity: Japanese overseas scholars in the United States.* Minneapolis: University of Minnesota Press, 1958.

Bennett, M. Overcoming the golden rule: Sympathy and empathy. In D. Nimmo (ed.), *Communication yearbook 3.* New Brunswick, N.J.: Transaction, 1979.

Berger, C. Beyond initial interaction. In H. Giles and R. St. Clair (eds.), *Language and social psychology.* Oxford, England: Basil Blackwell, 1979.

Berger, C., and Calabrese, R. Some explorations in initial interaction and beyond. *Human Communication Research,* 1975, 1, 99–112.

Berger, C., and Douglas, W. Thought and talk: "Excuse me, but have I been talking to myself?" In F. Dance (ed.), *Human communication theory.* New York: Harper and Row, 1982.

Berger, C., Gardner, R., Parks, M., Schulman, L., and Miller, G. Interpersonal epistemology and interpersonal communication. In G. Miller (ed.), *Explorations in interpersonal communication.* Beverly Hills, Calif.: Sage, 1976.

Berger, P., and Kellner, H. Marriage and construction of reality. In H. Dreitzel (ed.), *Recent sociology, no. 2: Patterns of communication behavior.* New York: Macmillan, 1970.

Berger, P., and Luckman, T. *The social construction of reality.* New York: Doubleday, 1967.

Berlin, B., and Kay, P. *Basic color terms: Their universality and evolution.* Berkeley: University of California Press, 1969.

Berlo, D. K. *The process of communication.* New York: Holt, Rinehart, and Winston, 1960.

Berlyne, D. Psychological aesthetics. In H. Triandis and W. Lambert (eds.), *Handbook of cross-cultural psychology,* vol. 3. Boston: Allyn and Bacon, 1980.

Bernstein, B. Elaborated and restricted codes. In A. Smith (ed.), *Communication and culture.* New York: Holt, Rinehart, and Winston, 1966.

Bernstein, B. *Class, codes and control.* Boston: Routledge and Kegan Paul, 1971.

Berreman, G. Race, caste and other invidious distinctions in social stratification. *Race,* 1972, 13, 385–414.

Berrien, F. Japanese social values and the democratic process. *Journal of Social Psychology,* 1966, 168, 129–138.

Berrien, F. A super-ego for cross-cultural research. *International Journal of Psychology,* 1970, 5, 33–39.

Berry, J. Independence and conformity in subsistence-level societies. *Journal of Personality and Social Psychology,* 1967, 7, 415–418.

Berry, J. On cross-cultural comparability. *International Journal of Psychology,* 1969, 4, 119–128.

Berry, J. Acculturation as varieties of adaptation. In A. Padilla (ed.), *Acculturation: Theory, models and some new findings.* Boulder, Colo.: Westview Press, 1980.

Bersheid, E., and Walster, E. *Interpersonal attraction.* Reading, Mass.: Addison-Wesley, 1969.

Bieri, J. Cognitive complexity-simplicity and predictive behavior. *Journal of Abnormal and Social Psychology,* 1955, 51, 263–268.

Birdwhistell, R. The kinesis level in the investigation of the emotions. In P. H. Knapp (ed.), *Expressions of the emotions in man.* New York: International University Press, 1963.

Birdwhistell, R. *Kinesics in context.* Philadelphia: University of Pennsylvania Press, 1970.

Birenbaum, A., and Sagarin, E. *Norms and human behavior.* New York: Praeger, 1976.

Blalock, H. *Toward a theory of minority-group relations.* New York: Capricorn Books, 1967.

Blalock, H., and Wilken, P. *Intergroup processes.* New York: Free Press, 1978.

Blumbaugh, J., and Pennington, D. *Crossing-difference: Interracial communication.* Columbus, Ohio: Charles E. Merrill, 1976.

Boas, F. Introduction. In *Handbook of American Indian languages,* vol. 40. Washington, D.C.: Smithsonian Institute, 1911.

Bochner, S. (ed.). *Cultures in contact.* Elmsford, N.Y.: Pergamon Press, 1982.

Bochner, S., Baker, E., and McLeod, B. Communication patterns in an international student dormitory. *Journal of Applied Social Psychology,* 1976, 6, 275–290.

Bochner, S., Lin, A., and McLeod, B. Cross-cultural contact and the development of an international perspective. *Journal of Social Psychology,* 1979, 107, 29–41.

Bogardus, E. *Social distance.* Yellow Springs, Ohio: Antioch Press, 1959.

Bosmajian, H. *The language of oppression.* Washington, D.C.: Public Affairs Press, 1974.

Bostain, J. "How to read a foreigner." Videotaped presentation. Intercultural Relations Course, Naval Amphibious School, Coronado, Calif., 1973.

Boulding, K. *The image.* Ann Arbor: University of Michigan Press, 1956.

Bourhis, R., Giles, H., Leyens, J., and Tajfel, H. Psycholinguistic distinctiveness. In H. Giles and R. St. Clair (eds.), *Language and social psychology.* Baltimore: University Park Press, 1979.

Bradburn, N. *The structure of psychological well-being.* Chicago: Aldine, 1969.

Bram, J. *Language and society.* Garden City, N.Y.: Doubleday, 1955.

Branham, R. Ineffability, creativity and communication competence. *Communication Quarterly,* 1980, 3, 11-21.

Brein, M., and David, K. Intercultural communication and the adjustment of the sojourner. *Psychological Bulletin,* 1971, 76, 215-230.

Brewer, M. Determinants of social distance among East African tribal groups. *Journal of Personality and Social Psychology,* 1968, 10, 279-289.

Brewer, M. Ingroup bias in the minimal intergroup situation. *Psychological Bulletin,* 1979, 86, 307-324.

Brewer, M., and Campbell, D. *Ethnocentrism and intergroup attitudes.* New York: Wiley, 1976.

Brim, O., and Wheeler, S. *Socialization through the life cycle.* New York: Wiley, 1966.

Brislin, R. Back-translation for cross-cultural research. *Journal of Cross-Cultural Psychology,* 1970, 1, 185-216.

Brislin, R. Interaction among members of nine ethnic groups and the belief-similarity hypothesis. *Journal of Social Psychology,* 1971, 85, 171-179.

Brislin, R. (ed.). *Culture learning.* Honolulu: University of Hawaii Press, 1977.

Brislin, R. Increasing the range of concepts in intercultural research: The example of prejudice. In W. Davey (ed.), *Intercultural theory and practice.* Washington, D.C.: Society for Intercultural Education, Training and Research, 1979.

Brislin, R. *Cross-cultural encounters.* Elmsford, N.Y.: Pergamon, 1981.

Brislin, R., Bochner, S., and Lonner, W. (eds.), *Cross-cultural perspectives on learning.* New York: Wiley, 1975.

Brislin, R., Lonner, W., and Thorndike, R. *Cross-cultural research methods.* New York: Wiley, 1973.

Broom, L., and Kitsuse, J. The validation of acculturation. *American Anthropologist,* 1955, 57, 44-48.

Broome, B. Facilitating attitudes and messages characteristic in the expression of differences in intercultural encounters. *International Journal of Intercultural Relations,* 1981, 5, 215-238.

Brown, R. *Words and things.* Glencoe, Ill.: Free Press, 1966.

Bruneau, T. Communication silences. In C. D. Mortensen (ed.), *Basic readings in communication theory.* New York: Harper and Row, 1979a.

Bruneau, T. The time dimension in intercultural communication. In D. Nimmo (ed.), *Communication yearbook 3.* New Brunswick, N.J.: Transaction, 1979b.

Bruner, J. On perceptual readiness. *Psychological Review,* 1957, 64, 123-152.

Bruner, J., Goodnow, J., and Austin, G. *A study of thinking.* New York: Wiley, 1956.

Bruner, J., and Perlmutter, H. Compatriot and foreigner. *Journal of Abnormal and Social Psychology,* 1957, 55, 253-260.

Bruner, J., Oliver, R., and Greenfield, P. *Studies in cognitive growth.* New York: Wiley, 1966.

Buchanan, W., and Cantrill, H. *How nations see each other.* Urbana: University of Illinois Press, 1953.

Budner, S. Intolerance of ambiguity as a personality variable. *Journal of Personality,* 1962, 30, 29-50.

Burk, J. The effects of ethnocentrism on intercultural communicators. In F. Casmir (ed.), *International and intercultural communication annual,* vol. III. Falls Church, Va.: Speech Communication Association, 1976.

Burridge, K. Friendship in Tangu. *Oceana,* 1956, 177-189.

Byers, P., and Byers, H. Nonverbal communication and the education of children. In C. Cozden et al. (eds.), *Functions of language in the classroom.* New York: Teachers College Press, 1972.

Byrne, D. *The attraction paradigm.* New York: Academic Press, 1971.

Byrne, D., and Wong, T. Racial prejudice, interpersonal attraction and assumed dissimilarity of attitudes. *Journal of Abnormal and Social Psychology,* 1962, 65, 246-253.

Byrne, D., et al. The ubiquitous relationship: Attitude similarity and attraction. *Human Relations,* 1971, 24, 201-207.

Campbell, D. Distinguishing differences in perception from failures in communication in cross-cultural studies. In F. Northrop and H. Livingston (eds.), *Cross-cultural understanding.* New York: Harper and Row, 1964.

Campbell, D. T., and Levine, R. A. Ethnocentrism and intergroup relations. In R. Abelson, E. Aronson, W. McGuire, T. Newcomb, M. Rosenberg, and P. Tannenbaum (eds.), *Theories of cognitive consistency: A sourcebook.* Chicago: Rand McNally, 1968.

Capra, F. *The tao of physics.* Boulder, Colo.: Shambhala, 1975.

Carr, W. Interpersonal behavior patterns in Asia. Lecture to Japan and East Asia Area Studies Course, Foreign Service Institute, Washington, D.C., May, 1973.

Casmir, F. (ed.). *International and intercultural communication.* Washington, D.C.: University Press of America, 1978.

Cathcart, D., and Cathcart, R. Japanese social experience and concept of groups. In L. Samovar and R. Porter (eds.), *Intercultural communication: A reader,* 2nd ed. Belmont, Calif.: Wadsworth, 1976.

Catton, W. R. The functions and dysfunctions of ethnocentrism. *Social Problems,* 1961, 8, 201-211.

Chaffee, C. *Problems in effective cross-cultural interaction.* Columbus, Ohio: Battelle Memorial Institute, 1971.

Char, W. Motivations for intercultural marriages. In W. Tseng, J. McDermott, and T. Maretzki (eds.), *Adjustment in intercultural marriage.* Honolulu: University of Hawaii Press, 1977.

Cheng, A. Clashes in courtship across cultures. *East-West Center Magazine,* 1974, Summer, 11-12.

Cherry, C. *World communication,* rev. ed. New York: Wiley, 1978.

Chomsky, N. *Language and mind.* New York: Harcourt Brace Jovanovich, 1972.

Chomsky, N. *Rules and representations.* New York: Columbia University Press, 1980.

Clatterbuck, G. Attributional confidence and uncertainty in initial interactions. *Human Communication Research,* 1979, 5, 147-157.

Cleveland, H., and Mangone, G. (eds.). *The art of overseasmanship.* Syracuse, N.Y.: Syracuse University Press, 1957.

Cleveland, H., Mangone, G., and Adams, J. *The overseas Americans.* New York: McGraw-Hill, 1960.

Coelho, G. *Changing images of America.* Glencoe, Ill.: Free Press, 1958.

Coelho, G. (ed.). Impacts of studying abroad. *Journal of Social Issues,* 1962, 78 (whole issue).

Cohen, E. Toward a sociology of international tourism. *Social Research,* 1972, 39, 164-182.

Cohen, E. Who is a tourist? *Sociological Review,* 1974, 22, 527-555.

Cohen, E. Expatriate communities. *Current Sociology,* 1977, 24, 5-133.

Cohen, E. A phenomenology of tourist experiences. *Sociology,* 1979, 13, 179-201.

Cohen, M. *Learning to live as neighbors.* Washington, D.C.: Association for Childhood Education International, 1972.

Cole, M., and Bruner, J. Cultural differences and influences about psychological processes. *American Psychologist,* 1971, 27, 867-876.

Cole, M., and Scribner, S. *Culture and thought.* New York: John Wiley, 1974.

Collett, P. Training Englishmen in the nonverbal behavior of Arabs. *International Journal of Psychology,* 1971, 6, 209-215.

Condon, J. *Mexicans and North Americans.* Chicago: Intercultural Press, 1980.

Condon, J., and Kurata, K. *In search of what's Japanese about Japan.* Tokyo: Simul Press, 1973.

Condon, J., and Saito, M. *Intercultural encounters with Japan.* Tokyo: Simul Press, 1974.

Condon, J., and Saito, M. *Communicating across cultures for what?* Tokyo: Simul Press, 1976.

Condon, J., and Yousef, F. *An introduction to intercultural communication.* Indianapolis, Ind.: Bobbs-Merrill, 1975.

Conine, E. Greasing foreign palms. *Hartford Courant,* July 26, 1979, p. 23.

Cook, S. Desegregation: A psychological analysis. *American Psychologist,* 1957, 12, 1–13.

Cook, S., and Selltiz, C. Some factors which influence the attitudinal outcomes of personal contacts. *International Social Science Bulletin,* 1955, 7, 51–58.

Coon, C. The universality of natural groupings in human societies. *Journal of Educational Sociology,* 1946, 20, 163–168.

Crockett, W., and Friedman, P. Theoretical explorations of the process of initial interactions. *Western Journal of Speech Communication,* 1980, 44, 86–92.

Cushman, D., and Whiting, G. An approach to communication theory: Toward a consensus on rules. *Journal of Communication,* 1972, 22, 217–233.

Dabrowski, K. Theory of positive disintegration. Audio recording. Big Sur Recordings #1120, 1968.

Dance, F., and Larson, C. *Speech communication.* New York: Holt, Rinehart, and Winston, 1972.

Daniel, J. The poor: Aliens in an affluent society. In L. Samovar and R. Porter (eds.), *Intercultural communication: A reader,* 2nd ed. Belmont, Calif.: Wadsworth, 1976.

Darrow, K., and Palmquist, B. *Trans-cultural study guide.* Stanford, Calif.: Volunteers in Asia, 1975.

Darwin, C. *Journal of researches into natural history and geology of the countries visited during the voyage of H.M.S. "Beagle" round the world, under the command of Capt. Fitzroy, R.N.* London: Ward, Lock and Bowden, 1892.

Davey, W. (ed.). *Intercultural theory and practice.* Washington, D.C.: Society for Intercultural Education, Training and Research, 1979.

David, K. Culture shock and the development of self-awareness. *Journal of Contemporary Psychotherapy,* 1971, 4, 44–48.

David, K. Intercultural adjustment and applications of reinforcement theory to problems of culture shock. *Trends,* 1972, 4, 1–64.

Davidson, A., and Thompson, E. Cross-cultural studies of attitudes and beliefs. In H. Triandis and R. Brislin (eds.), *Handbook of cross-cultural psychology,* vol. 5. Boston: Allyn and Bacon, 1980.

Deregowski, J. Perception. In H. Triandis and W. Lonner (eds.), *Handbook of cross-cultural psychology,* vol. 3. Boston: Allyn and Bacon, 1980.

Deriveria, J. *The psychological dimension of foreign policy.* Columbus, Ohio: Charles E. Merrill, 1968.

Detweiler, R. On inferring the intentions of a person from another culture. *Journal of Personality,* 1975, 43, 591–611.

Detweiler, R. Culture, category width and attributions. *Journal of Cross-Cultural Psychology,* 1978, 9, 259–284.

Detweiler, R. Intercultural interaction and the categorization process. *International Journal of Intercultural Relations,* 1980, 4, 275–293.

Deutsch, M. Field theory in social psychology. In G. Lindzey (ed.), *Handbook of social psychology,* vol. 1. Reading, Mass.: Addison-Wesley, 1954.

Deutsch, M. The interpretation of praise and criticism as a function of their social context. *Journal of Abnormal and Social Psychology,* 1961, 62, 391–400.

Deutsch, S. *International education and exchange.* Cleveland, Ohio: Case Western Reserve Press, 1970.

DeVos, G. Selective permeability and reference group sanctioning. In J. Yinger and S. Cutler (eds.), *Major social issues.* New York: Free Press, 1978.

Diamond, R., and Hellcamp, D. Race, sex, ordinal position of both and self-disclosure in high school students. *Psychological Report,* 1969, 25, 235–238.

Dittmann, A. T. The body movement–speech rhythm relationship as a cue to speech encoding. In A. E. Siegman and B. Pope (eds.), *Studies in dyadic communication.* New York: Pergamon, 1972.

Dobzhanzky, T. *Mankind evolving.* New Haven, Conn.: Yale University Press, 1962.

Dodd, C. *Perspectives on cross-cultural communication.* Dubuque, Iowa: Kendall/Hunt, 1977.

Doi, T. The Japanese patterns of communication and the concept of amae. In L. Samovar and R. Porter (eds.), *Intercultural communication: A reader,* 2nd ed. Belmont, Calif.: Wadsworth, 1976.

Doob, L. *Communication in Africa.* New Haven, Conn.: Yale University Press, 1961.

Doob, L. (ed.). *Resolving conflict in Africa.* New Haven, Conn.: Yale University Press, 1970.

Downs, J. *Cultures in crisis.* Beverly Hills, Calif.: Glencoe Press, 1971.

Downs, R., and Stea, D. (eds.). *Image and environment.* Chicago: Aldine, 1973.

Driberg, H. The "best friend" among the Dianja. *Man,* 1935, 35, 101–102.

Driver, E. Self-conceptions in India and the United States. *Sociological Quarterly,* 1973, 14, 576–588.

Dubois, C. *Foreign students and higher education in the United States.* Washington, D.C.: American Council on Education, 1956.

Dubos, R. *Celebrations of life.* New York: McGraw-Hill, 1981.

Dyal, J., and Dyal, R. Acculturation, stress and coping. *International Journal of Intercultural Relations,* 1981, 5, 301–328.

Edwards, A. *Language in culture and class.* New York: Crane, Russak and Co., 1976.

Efron, D. *Gestures and environment.* New York: King's Crown Press, 1972. (First published in 1941.)

Ehrenhaus, P. The implications of attribution theory for intercultural communication. In M. Burgoon (ed.), *Communication yearbook 6.* Beverly Hills, Calif.: Sage, 1982.

Ehrlich, H. *The social psychology of prejudice.* New York: Wiley, 1973.

Eibl-Eibesfeldt, L. Similarities and differences between cultures in expressive movements. In S. Weitz (ed.), *Nonverbal communication,* 2nd ed. New York: Oxford University Press, 1979.

Eide, I. (ed.). *Students as links between cultures.* Paris: UNESCO, 1970.

Eisenstadt, E. *The absorption of immigrants.* London: Routledge and Kegan Paul, 1954.

Ekman, P. Universals and cultural differences in facial expressions of emotion. In *Nebraska symposium on motivation.* Lincoln: Nebraska University Press, 1972.

Ekman, P. Facial expressions. In A. Siegman and S. Feldstein (eds.), *Nonverbal behavior and communication.* Hillsdale, N.J.: Lawrence Erlbaum, 1978.

Ekman, P., and Friesen, W. The repertoire of nonverbal behavior: Categories, origins, usage, and coding. *Semiotica,* 1969, 1, 49–98.

Ekman, P., and Friesen, W. Constants across cultures in the face and emotion. *Journal of Personality and Social Psychology,* 1971, 17, 124–129.

Ellingsworth, H. Conceptualizing intercultural communication. In B. Ruben (ed.), *Communication yearbook 1.* New Brunswick, N.J.: Transaction, 1977.

Emerson, R. *From empire to nation.* Cambridge, Mass.: Harvard University Press, 1960.

Engebretson, D., and Fullmer, D. Cross-cultural differences in territoriality. *Journal of Cross-Cultural Psychology,* 1970, 1, 261–269.

Farb, P. Man at the mercy of language. In D. Mortensen (ed.), *Basic readings in communication theory,* 2nd ed. New York: Harper and Row, 1979.

Feig, J. *Thais and North Americans.* Chicago: Intercultural Press, 1980.

Feig, J., and Blair, J. *There is a difference.* Washington, D.C.: Meriden International House, 1975.

Feldman, R. Response to compatriot and foreigner who seek assistance. *Journal of Personality and Social Psychology,* 1968, 10, 202–214.

Fisher, B. A. *Perspectives on human communication.* New York: Macmillan, 1978.

Fisher, G. *Public diplomacy and the behavioral sciences.* Bloomington: Indiana University Press, 1972.

Fisher, G. *American communication in a global society.* Norwood, N.J.: Ablex, 1979.

Fisher, H., and Merrill, J. (eds.). *International and intercultural communication.* New York: Hastings House, 1976.

Fiske, D., and Maddi, S. (eds.). *Functions of varied experience.* Homewood, Ill.: Dorsey Press, 1961.

Fitchen, R. Observing intercultural communication: A proposal of theory and method. *International Journal of Intercultural Relations,* 1979, 3, 163–174.

Flack, M. Communicable and uncommunicable aspects in personal international relationships. *Journal of Communication,* 1966, 16, 283–290.

Foa, U. Cross-cultural similarity and difference in interpersonal behavior. *Journal of Abnormal and Social Psychology,* 1964, 68, 517–522.

Foa, U. Differentiation in cross-cultural communication. In L. Thayer (ed.), *Communication: Concepts and perspectives.* Washington, D.C.: Spartan Books, 1967.

Foa, U., and Chemers, M. The significance of role behavior differentiation for cross-cultural interaction training. *International Journal of Psychology,* 1967, 2, 45–57.

Foa, U., and Foa, E. *Societal structures of the mind.* Springfield, Ill.: Charles Thomas, 1974.

Fogel, D. Human development and communication competencies. Paper presented at the Speech Communication Association convention, San Antonio, Tex., November, 1979.

Furnham, A., and Bochner, S. Social difficulty in a foreign culture. In S. Bochner (ed.), *Cultures in contact.* Elmsford, N.Y.: Pergamon, 1982.

Gardet, L., et al. *Cultures and time.* Paris: UNESCO, 1976.

Gardner, G. Cross-cultural communication. *Journal of Social Psychology,* 1962, 58, 241–256.

Gertz, C. *The interpretation of culture.* New York: Basic Books, 1973.

Gibbs, J. Norms: The problem of definition and classification. *American Journal of Sociology,* 1965, 70, 586–594.

Giles, H. Accent mobility. *Anthropological Linguistics,* 1973, 15, 87–105.

Giles, H. (ed.). *Language, ethnicity and intergroup relations.* London: Academic Press, 1977.

Giles, H., and St. Clair, R. (eds.). *Language and social psychology.* Baltimore: University Park Press, 1979.

Giles, H., Bourhis, R., and Taylor, D. Toward a theory of language in ethnic group relations. In H. Giles (ed.), *Language, ethnicity and intergroup relations.* London: Academic Press, 1977.

Glenn, E. Semantic difficulties in international communication. *Etc.,* 1954, 11, 163–180.

Glenn, E. Meaning and behavior. *Journal of Communication,* 1966, 16, 248–272.

Glenn, E. *Man and mankind.* Norwood, N.J.: Ablex, 1981.

Glenn, E., Witmeyer, D., and Stevenson, K. Cultural styles and persuasion. *International Journal of Intercultural Relations,* 1977, 1, 52–66.

Glidden, H. The Arab world. *American Journal of Psychiatry,* 1972, 128, 984–988.

Goebel, M., and Cole, S. Mexican-American and white reactions to stimulus persons of same and different race. *Psychological Reports,* 1975, 36, 827–833.

Goff, R. Psychology and intercultural interaction. *Journal of Social Psychology,* 1962, 58, 235–240.

Goffman, E. *Asylums.* New York: Doubleday, 1961.

Goodenough, W. *Cooperation and change.* New York: Russell Sage Foundation, 1963.

Goodenough, W. *Culture, language and society,* 2nd ed. Menlo Park, Calif.: Benjamin Cummings, 1981.

Gorden, R. *Living in Latin America.* Skokie, Ill.: National Textbooks, 1974.

Grant, P., and Holmes, J. The integration of implicit theory schemas and stereotype images. *Social Psychology Quarterly,* 1981, 44, 107–115.

Greenberg, J. *Universals of language.* Cambridge, Mass.: MIT Press, 1966.

Gudykunst, W. Intercultural contact and attitude change. In N. Jain (ed.), *International and intercultural communication annual,* vol. IV. Falls Church, Va.: Speech Communication Association, 1977.

Gudykunst, W. The effects of an intercultural communication workshop on cross-cultural attitudes and interaction. *Communication Education,* 1979, 28, 179–187.

Gudykunst, W. Uncertainty reduction and predictability of behavior in low and high context cultures. *Communication Quarterly,* 1983, 31, 49–55.

Gudykunst, W. (ed.). *Intercultural communication theory.* Beverly Hills, Calif.: Sage, in press (a).

Gudykunst, W. An exploratory comparison of close intracultural and intercultural friendships. *Communication Quarterly,* in press (b).

Gudykunst, W. Similarities and differences in perceptions of initial intracultural and intercultural encounters. *The Southern Speech Communication Journal,* in press (c).

Gudykunst, W. Toward a typology of stranger-host relationships. *International Journal of Intercultural Relations,* in press (d).

Gudykunst, W., and Halsall, S. The application of a theory of contraculture to intercultural communication. In D. Nimmo (ed.), *Communication yearbook 4.* New Brunswick, N.J.: Transaction, 1980.

Gudykunst, W., and Hammer, M. Basic training design: Approaches to intercultural training. In D. Landis and R. Brislin (eds.), *Handbook of intercultural training.* Elmsford, N.Y.: Pergamon, 1983.

Gudykunst, W., and Kim, Y. (eds.). *Intercultural communication research.* Beverly Hills, Calif.: Sage, 1984.

Gudykunst, W., and Nishida, T. Social penetration in close friendships in Japan and the United States. In R. Bostrom (ed.), *Communication yearbook 7.* Beverly Hills, Calif.: Sage, 1983.

Gudykunst, W., Hammer, M., and Wiseman, R. An analysis of an integrated approach to intercultural training. *International Journal of Intercultural Relations,* 1977, 1, 99–110.

Gudykunst, W., Wiseman, R., and Hammer, M. Determinants of a sojourner's attitudinal satisfaction. In B. Ruben (ed.), *Communication year book 1.* New Brunswick, N.J.: Transaction, 1977.

Gulick, S. *The East and the West: A study of their psychic and cultural characteristics.* Rutland, Vt.: Charles E. Tuttle, 1962.

Gumperz, J. *Discourse strategies.* New York: Cambridge University Press, 1982a.

Gumperz, J. (ed.). *Language and social identity.* New York: Cambridge University Press, 1982b.

Hale, C. L. Cognitive complexity-simplicity as a determinant of communication effectiveness. *Communication Monographs,* 1980, 47, 304–311.

Hall, E. T. *The silent language.* New York: Doubleday, 1959.

Hall, E. T. Adumbration as a feature of intercultural communication. *American Anthropologist,* 1964, 154–161. Reprinted in C. D. Mortenson (ed.), *Basic readings in communication theory,* 2nd ed. New York: Harper and Row, 1979.

Hall, E. T. *The hidden dimension.* New York: Doubleday, 1966.

Hall, E. T. *Beyond culture.* New York: Doubleday, 1976.

Hall, E. T. *The dance of life.* New York: Doubleday, 1983.

Hall, E. T., and Whyte, W. F. Intercultural communication. *Human Organization,* 1960, 19, 5–12. Reprinted in C. D. Mortenson (ed.), *Basic readings in communication theory,* 2nd ed. New York: Harper & Row, 1979.

Hamilton, D. (ed.). *Cognitive processes in stereotyping and intergroup behavior.* Hillsdale, N.J.: Lawrence Erlbaum, 1981.

Hamilton, E. *Mythology.* New York: New American Library, 1960.

Hammer, M., Gudykunst, W., and Wiseman, R. Dimensions of intercultural effectiveness. *International Journal of Intercultural Relations,* 1978, 2, 382–393.

Hamnett, M. Ethics and expectations in cross-cultural social science research. In N. Asuncion-Lande (ed.), *Ethical perspectives and critical issues in intercultural communication.* Falls Church, Va.: Speech Communication Association, 1980.

Harms, L. S. *Intercultural communication.* New York: Harper and Row, 1973.

Harms, L. S., and Richstad, J. *Evolving perspectives on the right to communicate.* Honolulu: East-West Center, 1977.

Harris, L. Communication competence. Paper presented at the International Communication Association convention, Philadelphia, Pa., May, 1979.

Harris, M. *Cultural materialism.* New York: Random House, 1979.

Harris, P., and Moran, R. *Managing cultural differences.* Houston, Tex.: Gulf, 1979.

Harrison, R. P. Nonverbal communication. In I. de Sola Pool et al. (eds.), *Handbook of communication.* Chicago: Rand McNally, 1973.

Harvey, O., Hunt, D., and Schroder, H. *Conceptual systems and personality organization.* New York: Wiley, 1961.

Haselden, K. *Morality and the mass media.* Nashville, Tenn.: Broadman Press, 1968.

Herman, S., and Schield, E. The stranger group in a cross-cultural situation. *Sociometry,* 1960, 24, 165–176.

Herskovits, M. J. *Cultural dynamics.* New York: Knopf, 1966.

Herskovits, M. J. *Cultural relativism.* New York: Random House, 1973.

Hess, E., and Petrovich, S. Pupilary behavior in communication. In A. Siegman and S. Feldstein (eds.), *Nonverbal behavior and communication.* Hillsdale, N.J.: Lawrence Erlbaum, 1978.

Hockett, C. F. Chinese vs. English. In P. Gleeson and N. Wakefield (eds.), *Language and culture: A reader.* Columbus, Ohio: Charles E. Merrill, 1968.

Hodges, H. H. *Social stratification.* Cambridge, England: Schenkman, 1964.

Hodges, L., and Byrne, D. Verbal dogmatism as a potentiator of intolerance. *Journal of Personality and Social Psychology,* 1972, 21, 312–317.

Hoebel, E. *The Cheyennes.* New York: Holt, Rinehart, and Winston, 1960.

Hoijer, H. *Language in culture.* Chicago: University of Chicago Press, 1954.

Hoijer, H. The Sapir-Whorf hypothesis. In L. Samovar and R. Porter (eds.), *Intercultural communication: A reader,* 2nd ed. Belmont, Calif.: Wadsworth, 1976.

Holmes, L. *Anthropology.* New York: Ronald Press, 1965.

Hong, K. S. The interest level and exposure to informational contents of mass media. *Shin-Moon-Hak-Bo* (*Journal of Mass Communication*), 1980, 83–93. In Korean.

Honigmann, J. (ed.). *Handbook of social and cultural anthropology.* Chicago: Rand McNally, 1973.

Hoopes, D. S. (ed.). *Readings in intercultural communication,* vols. I–III. Pittsburgh: Intercultural Communication Network, 1972, 1973.

Hoopes, D. S., Pedersen, P., and Renwick, G. (eds.). *Overview of intercultural education training and research,* vols. I–III. Washington, D.C.: Society for Intercultural Education, Training and Research, 1977, 1978.

Hsu, F. *The challenge of the American dream: The Chinese in the United States.* Belmont, Calif.: Wadsworth, 1971.

Hsu, F. *Americans and Chinese,* 3rd ed. Honolulu: University of Hawaii Press, 1981. (First published in 1953.)

Hurh, W. M., and Kim, K. C. Social and occupational assimilation of Korean immigrants in the United States. Paper presented at the Association for Asian Studies convention, Los Angeles, Calif., March, 1979.

Hwang, J., Chase, L., and Kelly, C. An intercultural examination of communication competence. *Communication,* 1980, 9, 70–79.

Hymes, D. Sociolinguistics and the ethnography of speaking. In E. Ardener (ed.), *Social anthropology and language.* New York: Tavistock Publications, 1971.

Infante, D. Cultural influences on interpersonal communication. Paper presented at the Speech Communication Association convention, San Antonio, Tex., November, 1979.

Inglis, M., and Gudykunst, W. Institutional completeness and communication acculturation. *International Journal of Intercultural Relations,* 1982, 6, 251–272.

Ittelson, W. Environment perception and contemporary perceptual theory. In W. Ittelson (ed.), *Environment and cognition.* New York: Seminar Press, 1973.

Jacobson, E., Kumata, H., and Gullahorn, J. Cross-cultural contributions to attitude research. *Public Opinion Quarterly,* 1960, 24, 205–233.

Jaffee, L., and Polanski, N. Verbal inaccessibility in young adolescents showing delinquent trends. *Journal of Health and Social Behavior,* 1962, 3, 105–111.

Jahoda, G. Theoretical and systematic approaches. In H. Triandis and W. Lambert (eds.), *Handbook of cross-cultural psychology,* vol. 1. Boston: Allyn and Bacon, 1980.

Janis, I., and Smith, M. Effects of education and persuasion on national and international images. In H. Kelman (ed.), *International behavior.* New York: Holt, Rinehart, and Winston, 1965.

Jantsch, E. *The self-organizing universe: Scientific and human implications of the emerging paradigm of evolution.* New York: Pergamon, 1980.

Jaspers, J., and Hewstone, M. Cross-cultural interaction, social attribution, and inter-group relations. In S. Bochner (ed.), *Cultures in contact.* Elmsford, N.Y.: Pergamon, 1982.

Jeffries, L., and Hur, K. K. Communication channels within ethnic groups. *International Journal of Intercultural Relations,* 1981, 5, 115–132.

Johnson, C., and Johnson, F. Interaction rules and ethnicity. *Social Forces,* 1975, 54, 452–466.

Johnson, H. G., Ekman, P., and Friesen, W. V. Communicative body movements: American emblems. *Semiotica,* 15, 1975, 335–353.

Johnson, J., and Sarason, I. Life stress, depression and anxiety. *Journal of Psychosomatic Research,* 1978, 22, 205–208.

Johnson, K. Black kinesics. In L. Samovar and R. Porter (eds.), *Intercultural communication: A reader,* 2nd ed. Belmont, Calif.: Wadsworth, 1976.

Jones, E., and Nisbett, R. *The actor and the observer.* Morristown, N.J.: General Learning Press, 1972.

Jones, S. Integrating the etic and emic approaches in the study of intercultural communication. In M. Asante, E. Newmark, and C. Blake (eds.), *Handbook of intercultural communication.* Beverly Hills, Calif.: Sage, 1979.

Jourard, S. A study of self-disclosure. *Scientific American,* 1958, 198, 77–82.

Jourard, S. Self-disclosure patterns in British and American college females. *Journal of Social Psychology,* 1961, 54, 315–320.

Jourard, S. *Self-disclosure.* New York: Wiley, 1971.

Jourard, S. Growing awareness and the awareness of growth. In B. Patton and K. Giffin (eds.), *Interpersonal communication.* New York: Harper and Row, 1974.

Kanouse, D., and Hanson, L. Negativity in evaluations. In E. Jones et al. (eds.), *Attribution.* Morristown, N.J.: General Learning Press, 1972.

Kapoor, S., and Williams, W. Acculturation of foreign students by television. Paper presented at the International Communication Association convention, Philadelphia, Pa., May, 1979.

Katz, D. The functional approach to the study of attitudes. *Public Opinion Quarterly,* 1960, 24, 164–204.

Kelly, G. A. *The psychology of personal constructs.* New York: Norton, 1955.

Kelman, H. (ed.). *International behavior.* New York: Holt, Rinehart, and Winston, 1965.

Kelman, H., and Ezekial, R. *Cross-national encounters.* San Francisco: Jossey-Bass, 1970.

Kelvin, P. *The bases of social power.* New York: Holt, Rinehart, and Winston, 1970.

Kim, J. K. Explaining acculturation in a communication framework. *Communication Monographs,* 1980, 47, 155–179.

Kim, J. K., Lee, B. H., and Jeong, W. J. Use of mass media in acculturation. Paper presented at the Association for Education in Journalism conference, Athens, Ohio, July, 1982.

Kim, Y. Y. Communication patterns of foreign immigrants in the process of acculturation. *Human Communication Research,* 1977a, 4, 66–77.

Kim, Y. Y. Inter-ethnic and intra-ethnic communication. In N. Jain (ed.), *International and intercultural communication annual,* vol. 4. Falls Church, Va.: Speech Communication Association, 1977b.

Kim, Y. Y. Toward a communication approach to the communication process. *International Journal of Intercultural Relations,* 1978a, 197–224.

Kim, Y. Y. Acculturation and patterns of interpersonal communication relationships. Paper presented at the Speech Communication Association convention, Minneapolis, Minn., November, 1978b.

Kim, Y. Y. How do Asian students communicate and why? In *Proceedings of the second annual forum on transcultural adoption.* Chicago: U.S. Office of Education and Illinois Office of Education, 1978c.

Kim, Y. Y. Mass media and acculturation. Paper presented at the Eastern Communication Association convention, Philadelphia, Pa., May, 1979a.

Kim, Y. Y. Toward an interactive theory of communication-acculturation. In

D. Nimmo (ed.), *Communication yearbook 3.* New Brunswick, N.J.: Transaction, 1979b.

Kim, Y. Y. Dynamics of intrapersonal and interpersonal communication: A study of Indochinese refugees in the initial phase of acculturation. Paper presented at the Speech Communication Association convention, San Antonio, Tex., November, 1979c.

Kim, Y. Y. *Psychological, social, and cultural adjustment of Indochinese refugees.* Vol. IV of *Indochinese refugees in the State of Illinois* (5 vols.). Chicago: Travelers Aid Society of Metropolitan Chicago, 1980.

Klass, M., and Hellman, H. *The kinds of mankind.* New York: Lippincott, 1971.

Kleinberg, O. *Tensions affecting international understanding.* New York: Social Science Research Council, Bulletin 62, 1960.

Kleinberg, O. *The human dimension in international relations.* New York: Holt, Rinehart, and Winston, 1964.

Kleinjans, E. Opening remarks at a conference on world communication held at the East-West Center, Honolulu, Hawaii, 1972.

Kluckhohn, F., and Strodtbeck, F. *Variations in value orientations.* New York: Row, Peterson, 1960.

Knapp, M. *Social intercourse.* Boston: Allyn and Bacon, 1978.

Knapp, M., Ellis, D., and Williams, B. Perceptions of communication behavior associated with relationship terms. *Communication Monographs,* 1980, 47, 262–278.

Kochman, T. Cross-cultural communication. *The Florida FL Reporter,* 1971, 3ff.

Kochman, T. (ed.). *Rappin' and stylin' out.* Chicago: University of Chicago Press, 1972.

Kochman, T. *Black and white: Styles in conflict.* Chicago: University of Chicago Press, 1982.

Kohls, L. R. Basic concepts and models of intercultural communication. In M. Prosser (ed.), *USIA intercultural communication course: 1977 proceedings.* Washington, D.C.: United States Information Agency, 1978.

Kohn, M. *Class and conformity: A study in values.* Homewood, Ill.: Dorsey Press, 1969.

Korten, D. *Planned change in a traditional society.* New York: Praeger, 1972.

Korzybski, A. *Science and sanity,* 3rd ed. Lakeville, Conn.: The International Non-Aristotelian Library, 1948 (1933).

Kraft, C. H. Worldview in intercultural communication. In F. Casmir (ed.), *International and intercultural communication.* Washington, D.C.: University Press of America, 1978.

Kuhn, T. *The structure of scientific revolutions,* rev. ed. Chicago: University of Chicago Press, 1970.

Kunihiro, M. U.S.–Japan communications. In H. Rosovsky (ed.), *Discord in the Pacific.* Washington, D.C.: Columbia Books, 1972.

Kunihiro, M. Indigenous barriers to communication. *Japan Interpreter,* 1973, 8, 96–108.

Kurth, S. Friendships and friendly relations. In G. McNall (ed.), *Social relationships.* Chicago: Aldine, 1970.

La Barre, W. The cultural basis of emotions and gestures. *Journal of Personality,* 1947, 16, 49–68.

La Barre, W. Paralinguistics, kinesics, and cultural anthropology. In L. Samovar and R. Porter (eds.), *Intercultural communication: A reader,* 2nd ed. Belmont, Calif.: Wadsworth, 1976.

La France, M., and Mayo, C. Gaze direction in interracial dyadic communication. *Ethnicity,* 1978a, 5, 167–173.

La France, M., and Mayo, C. Cultural aspects of nonverbal communication. *International Journal of Intercultural Relations,* 1978b, 2, 71–89.

Lambert, R., and Bressler, M. *Indian students on an American campus.* Minneapolis: University of Minnesota Press, 1956.

Lambert, W. Psychological approaches to the study of language. *Modern Language Journal,* 1963, 14, 51–62.

Lambert, W. *Language, psychology, and culture.* Stanford, Calif.: Stanford University Press, 1972.

Lambert, W., and Kleinberg, O. *Children's view of foreign peoples.* New York: Appleton-Century-Crofts, 1967.

Lampe, P. Interethnic dating: Reasons for and against. *International Journal of Intercultural Relations,* 1982, 6, 115–126.

Landis, D., and Brislin, R. *Handbook of intercultural training,* vols. I–III. Elmsford, N.Y.: Pergamon, 1983.

Landis, D., McGrew, P., Day, H., Savage, J., and Saral, T. Word meanings in black and white. In H. Triandis (ed.), *Variations in black and white perceptions of the social environment.* Urbana, Ill.: University of Illinois Press, 1976.

Langer, E. Rethinking the role of thought in social interaction. In J. Harvey et al. (eds.), *New directions in attribution research,* vol. 2. Hillsdale, N.J.: Lawrence Erlbaum, 1978.

Lazarsfeld, P., and Merton, R. Friendship as a social process. In M. Berger et al. (eds.), *Freedom and control in modern society.* New York: Octagon Books, 1954.

Lee, D. Lineal and nonlineal codifications of reality. *Psychosomatic Medicine,* 1950, 12, 89–97.

Lee, D. *Freedom and culture.* Englewood Cliffs, N.J.: Prentice-Hall, 1959.

Lee, J. Cultural analysis in overseas operation. *Harvard Business Review,* 1966, 44, 106–114.

Lee, J. Developing managers in overseas operation. *Harvard Business Review,* 1968.

Lefever, E. *Ethics and United States foreign policy.* Cleveland, Ohio: World Publishing Co., 1957.

Lerner, R. A dynamic interactional concept of individual and social relationship development. In R. Burgess and T. Huston (eds.), *Social exchange in developing relationships.* New York: Academic Press, 1979.

Levine, D. *Wax and gold.* Chicago: University of Chicago Press, 1965.

Levine, D. Simmel at a distance. In W. Shack and E. Skinner (eds.), *Strangers in African societies.* Berkeley: University of California Press, 1979.

Levine, R. Socialization, social structure and intersocietal images. In H. Kelman (ed.), *International behavior.* New York: Holt, Rinehart, and Winston, 1965.

Levine, R., and Campbell, D. *Ethnocentrism.* New York: Wiley, 1972.

Lewin, K. *Principles of topological psychology.* New York: McGraw-Hill, 1936.

Lewin, K. Some social-psychological differences between the United States and Germany. In G. Lewin (ed.), *Resolving social conflicts.* New York: Harper, 1948.

Lewin, K. *Field theory in social science.* New York: Harper and Row, 1951.

Liem, N. D. Vietnamese-American intercultural communication. Paper presented at the International Communication Association convention, Acapulco, Mexico, May, 1980.

Lilly, J. *Communication between man and dolphin.* New York: Crown, 1978.

Lindgren, H., and Marrash, J. A comparative study of intercultural insight and empathy. *Journal of Social Psychology,* 1970, 80, 135–141.

Lippman, W. *Public opinion.* New York: Macmillan, 1936.

Lipset, S. The value patterns of democracy. *American Sociological Review,* 1963, 28, 515–531.

Little, K. Cultural variations in social schemata. *Journal of Personality and Social Psychology,* 1968, 10, 1–7.

Littlefield, R. Self-disclosure among Negro, white and Mexican-American adolescents. *Journal of Counseling Psychology,* 1974, 21, 133–136.

Lonner, W. The search for psychological universals. In H. Triandis and W. Lambert (eds.), *Handbook of cross-cultural psychology,* vol. 1. Boston: Allyn and Bacon, 1980.

Loomis, C. Political and occupational cleavages in a Hanoverian village. *Sociometry,* 1938, 1, 375–419.

Lukens, J. Ethnocentric speech. *Ethnic Groups,* 1978, 2, 35–53.

Lum, J. Marginality and multiculturalism. In L. Samovar and R. Porter (eds.), *Intercultural communication: A reader,* 3rd ed. Belmont, Calif.: Wadsworth, 1982.

Lundstedt, S. An introduction to some evolving problems in cross-cultural research. *Journal of Social Issues,* 1963, 14, 1–9.

Lutzker, D. Internationalism as a predictor of cooperative behavior. *Journal of Conflict Resolution,* 1960, 4, 426–430.

Lysgaard, S. Adjustment in a foreign society. *International Social Science Bulletin,* 1955, 7, 45–51.

MacCannell, D. *The tourist.* New York: Schocken, 1976.

Manheim, K. *Ideology and utopia.* New York: Harcourt, Brace and World, 1936.

Mann, L. Cross-cultural studies of small groups. In H. Triandis and R. Brislin (eds.), *Handbook of cross-cultural psychology,* vol. 5. Boston: Allyn and Bacon, 1980.

Mansell, M. Transcultural experience and expressive response. *Communication Education,* 1981, 30, 93–108.

Maslow, A. H. *Motivation and personality,* 2nd ed. New York: Harper and Row, 1970. (First published in 1954.)

Maslow, A. H. *The farther reaches of human nature.* New York: Viking, 1971.

Masuda, M. Ethnic identity in three generations of Japanese Americans. *Journal of Social Psychology,* 1970, 81, 199–207.

Mazur, A. Interpersonal spacing on public benches in contact vs. noncontact cultures. *Journal of Social Psychology,* 1977, 101, 53–58.

McGranahan, D., and Wayne, I. German and American traits reflected in popular drama. *Human Relations,* 1954, 1, 429–455.

McGuire, W. The nature of attitudes and attitude change. In G. Lindzey and E. Aronson (eds.), *Handbook of social psychology,* 2nd ed., vol. 3. Reading, Mass.: Addison-Wesley, 1969.

McLemore, S. Simmel's 'stranger': A critique of the concept. *Pacific Sociological Review,* 1970, 13, 86–94.

McLuhan, M. *The Gutenberg galaxy.* New York: New American Library, 1962.

Mead, M. Culture change and character structure. In M. Stein et al. (eds.), *Identity and anxiety.* Glencoe, Ill.: Free Press, 1963.

Meggers, B. J. Environmental limitations on the development of culture. *American Anthropologist,* 1954, 56, 801–824.

Melikan, L. Self-disclosure among university students in the Middle East. *Journal of Social Psychology,* 1962, 57, 257–263.

Merton, R. K. *Social theory and social structure.* New York: Free Press, 1957.

Milgram, S. The experience of living in cities. *Science,* 1970, 167, 1461–1468.

Miller, D., Hintz, R., and Couch, J. Elements and structure of openings. *Sociological Quarterly,* 1975, 16, 479–499.

Miller, G., and Steinberg, M. *Between people.* Chicago: Science Research Associates, 1975.

Miller, G., and Sunnafrank, M. All is for one but one is not for all: A conceptual perspective of interpersonal communication. In F. Dance (ed.), *Human communication theory.* New York: Harper and Row, 1982.

Mintz, N. Effects of esthetic surroundings II. *Journal of Personality,* 1956, 41, 459–466.

Mir-Djalali, E. The failure of language to communicate. *International Journal of Intercultural Relations,* 1980, 4, 307–328.

Mischel, W. Toward a cognitive social learning reconceptualization of personality. *Psychological Review,* 1973, 80, 252–283.

Montagu, A. *Man's most dangerous myth.* New York: Harper and Row, 1952.

Montagu, A. *Statement on race.* New York: Oxford University Press, 1972.

Montagu, A., and Matson, F. *The human connection.* New York: McGraw-Hill, 1979.

Montero, D. *Vietnamese Americans.* Boulder, Colo.: Westview Press, 1979.

Morris, D., et al. *Gestures.* New York: Stein and Day, 1979.

Morris, R. T. *The two-way mirror.* Minneapolis: University of Minnesota Press, 1960.

Morsbach, H. Aspects of nonverbal communication in Japan. In L. Samovar and R. Porter (eds.), *Intercultural communication: A reader,* 2nd ed. Belmont, Calif.: Wadsworth, 1976.

Mosel, J. Status and role analysis. Lecture to Japan and East Asia Area Studies Course, Foreign Service Institute, Washington, D.C., May 17, 1973.

Nakane, C. The social system reflected in interpersonal communication. In J. Condon and M. Saito (eds.), *Intercultural encounters with Japan.* Tokyo: Simul Press, 1974.

Neisser, U. *Cognition and reality.* San Francisco: W. H. Freeman, 1976.

Nisbett, R., Caputo, C., Legant, P., and Marecek, J. Behavior as seen by the actor and as seen by the observer. *Journal of Personality and Social Psychology,* 1973, 27, 154–165.

Nishida, T. Comparing Japanese-American person-to-person communication. Ph.D. dissertation, University of Minnesota, 1979.

Nishida, T., and Gudykunst, W. *Readings in intercultural communication.* Tokyo: Geirinshobo Publishing Co., 1981.

Nist, J. The language of the socially disadvantaged. In L. Samovar and R. Porter (eds.), *Intercultural communication: A reader,* 2nd ed. Belmont, Calif.: Wadsworth, 1976.

Noesjirwan, J. A rule-based analysis of cultural differences in social behavior. *International Journal of Psychology,* 1978, 13, 305–316.

Oberg, K. Culture shock and the problem of adjustment to new cultural environments. Washington, D.C.: Department of State, Foreign Service Institute, 1958.

Okabe, R. Cultural assumptions of East and West: Japan and the United States. In W. Gudykunst (ed.), *Intercultural communication theory: Current perspectives.* Beverly Hills, Calif.: Sage, 1983.

O'Keefe, D., and Sypher, H. Cognitive complexity measures and the relationship of cognitive complexity to communication. *Human Communication Research,* 1981, 8, 72–92.

Oliver, R. *Culture and communication.* Springfield, Ill.: Charles C Thomas, 1962.

Oliver, R. *Communication and culture in ancient India and China.* Syracuse, N.Y.: Syracuse University Press, 1971.

Olsen, M. *The process of social organization,* 2nd ed. New York: Holt, Rinehart, and Winston, 1978.

Ornstein, R. *The psychology of consciousness.* New York: Pelican Books, 1972.

Osgood, C. Semantic differential technique in the comparative study of cultures. *American Anthropologist,* 1964, 66, 171–200.

Osgood, C. Cross-cultural comparability in attitude measurement via multilingual semantic differentials. In I. Steiner and M. Fishbein (eds.), *Current studies in social psychology.* New York: Holt, Rinehart, and Winston, 1965.

Osgood, C., and Richards, M. From YANG and YIN to OR and BUT. *Language,* 1973, 49, 380–412.

Osgood, C., May, H., and Miron, S. *Cross-cultural universals of affective meaning.* Urbana: University of Illinois Press, 1972.

Ouchi, W. *Theory Z.* Reading, Mass.: Addison-Wesley, 1981.

Padilla, A. Introduction. In A. Padilla (ed.), *Acculturation.* Boulder, Colo.: Westview Press, 1980.

Palisi, B. Ethnic patterns of friendship. *Phylon,* 1966, 217–225.

Palmore, E. Ethnophaulisms and ethnocentrism. *American Journal of Sociology,* 1962, 67, 442–445.

Park, R. Reflections on communication and culture. *American Journal of Sociology,* 1939, 44, 191–205.

Parrillo, V. N. *Strangers to these shores.* Boston: Houghton Mifflin, 1980.

Parsons, T. *The social system.* Glencoe, Ill.: Free Press, 1951.

Parsons, T. Some comments on the state of the general theory of action. *American Sociological Review,* 1953, 18, 618–631.

Parsons, T., and Shils, E. *Toward a general theory of action.* Cambridge, Mass.: Harvard University Press, 1951.

Pascale, R., and Athos, A. *The art of Japanese management.* New York: Simon and Schuster, 1981.

Patai, R. *The Arab mind.* New York: Scribner's, 1976.

Patterson, O. *Ethnic chauvinism.* New York: Stein and Day, 1977.

Pearce, W. B., and Branham, R. The ineffable: An examination of the limits of expressibility and the means of communication. In B. Ruben (ed.), *Communication yearbook 2.* New Brunswick, N.J.: Transaction, 1978.

Pearce, W. B., and Harris, L. Optimizing the acculturation process. Paper presented at the Society for Intercultural Education, Training and Research convention, Mount Pocono, Pa., March, 1980.

Pearce, W. B., and Stamm, K. Communication behavior and coorientation relations. In P. Clark (ed.), *New models for communication research.* Beverly Hills, Calif.: Sage, 1973.

Pearce, W. B., and Wiseman, R. Rules theories. In W. Gudykunst (ed.), *Intercultural communication theory.* Beverly Hills, Calif.: Sage, 1983.

Pedersen, P., Lonner, W., and Draguns, J. *Counseling across cultures.* Honolulu: University of Hawaii Press, 1975.

Pedone, R. J. *The retention of minority language in the United States.* Washington, D.C.: National Center for Education Statistics, 1980.

Peng, F. Communicative distance. *Language Sciences,* 1974, 31, 32–38.

Pettigrew, T. Personality and sociocultural factors in intergroup attitudes. *Journal of Conflict Resolution,* 1958, 2, 29–42.

Pettigrew, T. Three issues in ethnicity. In J. Yinger and S. Cutler (eds.), *Major social issues.* New York: Free Press, 1978.

Pike, K. L. Etic and emic standpoints for the description of behavior. In A. Smith (ed.), *Communication and culture.* New York: Holt, Rinehart, and Winston, 1966.

Piker, S. Friendship to the death in rural Thai society. *Human Organization,* 1968, 200-204.

Plog, S. The disclosure of self in the United States and Germany. *Journal of Social Psychology,* 1965, 65, 193-203.

Pool, I. de Sola. Effects of cross-national contact on national and international images. In H. Kelman (ed.), *International behavior.* New York: Holt, Rinehart, and Winston, 1965.

Power, W. T. Feedback: Beyond behaviorism. *Science,* 1973, 179, 351–356.

Presidential Commission on Foreign Language and International Studies. *Strength through wisdom.* Washington, D.C.: U.S. Government Printing Office, 1979.

Prosser, M. *Intercommunications among nations and people.* New York: Harper and Row, 1973.

Prosser, M. *The cultural dialogue.* Boston: Houghton Mifflin, 1978.

Pusch, M. *Multicultural education.* Chicago: Intercultural Press, 1979.

Quisumbing, M. Life events, social support and personality: Their impact upon Filipino psychological adjustment. Ph.D. dissertation, University of Chicago, 1982.

Rahula, W. *What the Buddha taught.* New York: Grove Press, 1959.

Ramsey, C. E., and Smith, R. J. Japanese and American perceptions of occupations. *American Sociological Review,* 1960, 65, 475–479.

Ramsey, S. J. Nonverbal communication: An intercultural perspective. In M. Asante, E. Newmark, and C. Blake (eds.), *Handbook of intercultural communication.* Beverly Hills, Calif.: Sage, 1979.

Rapoport, A. *House form and culture.* Englewood Cliffs, N.J.: Prentice-Hall, 1969.

Reina, R. Two patterns of friendship in a Guatemalan community. *American Anthropologist,* 1959, 44–61.

Remy, R. C., Nathan, J. A., Becker, J. M., and Torney, J. V. *International learning and international education in a global age.* Washington, D.C.: National Council for Social Science, 1975.

Renwick, G. W. *Australians and North Americans.* Chicago: Intercultural Press, 1980.

Rhoode, N. *Intergroup accommodation in plural societies.* New York: St. Martin's, 1979.

Rich, A. L. *Interracial communication.* New York: Harper and Row, 1973.

Rich, A. L., and Ogawa, D. M. Intercultural and interracial communication. In L. Samovar and R. Porter (eds.), *Intercultural communication: A reader,* 2nd ed. Belmont, Calif.: Wadsworth, 1976.

Ricks, D., Fu, Y., and Arpan, J. *International business blunders.* Columbus, Ohio: Grid, 1974.

Rigney, J., Bieri, J., and Tripodi, T. Social concept attainment and cognitive complexity. *Psychological Reports,* 1964, 15, 503–509.

Robinson, J. W., and Preston, J. D. Equal status contact and modification of racial prejudice: A reexamination of the contact hypothesis. *Social Forces,* 1976, 54, 911–924.

Rogers, E. M., and Bhowik, D. K. Homophily-heterophily. *Public Opinion Research,* 1971, 34, 523–531.

Rogers, E. M., and Kincaid, D. L. *Communication networks.* New York: Free Press, 1981.

Rogers, E. M., and Shoemaker, F. *Communication of innovations,* 2nd ed. New York: Free Press, 1971.

Rogler, L. H., et al. Intergenerational change in ethnic identity in Puerto Rican family. *International Migration Review,* 1980, 14, 193–214.

Rokeach, M. (ed.). *The open and closed mind.* New York: Basic Books, 1960.

Rokeach, M. *Beliefs, attitudes and values.* San Francisco: Jossey-Bass, 1972.

Rokeach, M., Smith, P., and Evans, R. Two kinds of prejudice or one? In M. Rokeach (ed.), *The open and closed mind.* New York: Basic Books, 1960.

Rosenblatt, P. C. Origins and effects of group ethnocentrism and nationalism. *Journal of Conflict Resolution,* 1964, 8, 131–146.

Rosenblatt, P. C. Cross-cultural perspective on attraction. In T. Huston (ed.), *Foundations of interpersonal attraction.* New York: Academic Press, 1974.

Rosenfeld, H. Conversational control functions of nonverbal behavior. In A. Siegman and S. Feldstein (eds.), *Nonverbal behavior in communication.* Hillsdale, N.J.: Lawrence Erlbaum, 1978.

Ross, L. D. The intuitive psychologist and his shortcomings: Distortions in the attribution process. In L. Berkowitz (ed.), *Advances in experimental psychology,* vol. 10. New York: Academic Press, 1977.

Ross, R. L. (ed.). *Interethnic communication*. Athens, Ga.: University of Georgia Press, 1978.

Ruben, B. D. Intrapersonal, interpersonal and mass communication process in individual and multi-person systems. In B. Ruben and J. Kim (eds.), *General systems theory and human communication*. Rochelle Park, N.J.: Hayden, 1975.

Ruben, B. D. Assessing communication competency for intercultural adaptation. *Group and Organizational Studies*, 1976, 1, 334–354.

Ruben, B. D. Guidelines for cross-cultural communication effectiveness. *Group and Organizational Studies*, 1977a, 2, 470–479.

Ruben, B. D. Human communication and cross-cultural effectiveness. In N. Jain (ed.), *International and intercultural communication annual*. Falls Church, Va.: Speech Communication Association, 1977b.

Ruben, B. D., and Kealey, D. J. Behavioral assessment of communication competency and the prediction of cross-cultural adaptation. *International Journal of Intercultural Relations*, 1979, 3, 15–48.

Ruechelle, R. C. Communication and the Peace Corps. *Journal of Communication*, 1962, 12, 135–141.

Ryan, E. Why do low-prestige language varieties persist? In H. Giles and R. St. Clair (eds.), *Language and social psychology*. Baltimore: University Park Press, 1979.

Ryan, E., and Giles, H. (eds.). *Attitudes toward language variation*. London: Edward Arnold, Ltd., 1982.

Ryu, J. S. New-socialization function of mass media working among foreign students. Paper presented at the Western States Speech Communication Association convention, San Francisco, November, 1976.

Saarinen, E. *The search for form*. New York: Reinhold, 1948.

Safire, W. Should we export our morality? *New York Times*, August 14, 1975.

Sapir, E. *Culture, language and personality*. Berkeley: University of California Press, 1970.

Saral, T. Intercultural communication theory and research. In B. Ruben (ed.), *Communication yearbook 1*. New Brunswick, N.J.: Transaction, 1977.

Saral, T. The consciousness theory of intercultural communication. In M. Asante, E. Newmark, and C. Blake (eds.), *Handbook of intercultural communication*. Beverly Hills, Calif.: Sage, 1979.

Sarbaugh, L. *Intercultural communication*. Rochelle Park, N.J.: Hayden, 1979.

Sarbin, T., and Allen, V. Role theory. In G. Lindzey and E. Aronson (eds.), *Handbook of social psychology*, 2nd ed. Reading, Mass.: Addison-Wesley, 1968.

Schaefer, R. *Racial and ethnic groups*. Boston: Little, Brown, 1979.

Schatzman, L., and Strauss, A. Social class and modes of communication. In A. G. Smith (ed.), *Communication and culture*. New York: Holt, Rinehart, and Winston, 1966.

Schaupp, D. L. *A cross-cultural study of a multinational company*. New York: Praeger, 1978.

Scheflen, A. E. *Human territories*. Englewood Cliffs, N.J.: Prentice-Hall, 1976.

Scherer, K., and Giles, H. (eds.). *Social markers in speech*. Cambridge: Cambridge University Press, 1979.

Schiffrin, D. Opening encounters. *American Sociological Review,* 1977, 42, 679–690.

Schild, E. The foreign student as stranger, learning the norm of the host culture. *Journal of Social Issues,* 1962, 18, 41–54.

Schneider, M., and Jorden, W. Perception of the communicative performance of Americans and Chinese in intercultural dyads. *International Journal of Intercultural Relations,* 1981, 5, 175–192.

Schroder, H., Driver, M., and Streufert, S. *Human information processing: Individuals and groups functioning in complex social situations.* New York: Holt, Rinehart, and Winston, 1967.

Schuetz, A. The stranger. *American Journal of Sociology,* 1944, 49, 499–507. Reprinted in M. Stein and A. Vidich (eds.), *Identity and anxiety.* Glencoe, Ill.: Free Press, 1963.

Schuetz, A. The homecomer. *American Journal of Sociology,* 1945, 50, 369–376.

Schwartz, T. (ed.). *Socialization as cultural communication.* Berkeley: University of California Press, 1976.

Scott, F. *The American experience of Swedish students.* Minneapolis: University of Minnesota Press, 1956.

Scott, W. Psychological and social correlates of international images. In H. Kelman (ed.), *International behavior.* New York: Holt, Rinehart, and Winston, 1965.

Sechrest, L., Fay, T., and Zaidi, S. Problems of translation in cross-cultural communication. *Journal of Cross-Cultural Psychology,* 1972, 3, 41–56.

Seelye, H. N., and Wasilewski, J. *Social competency development in multicultural children, aged 6–13.* Final report of exploratory research on Hispanic-background children (NIE contract no. 400-80-0003). National Institute of Education, March 1981.

Segall, M. H. *Cross-cultural psychology: Human behavior in global perspective.* Monterey, Calif.: Brooks/Cole, 1979.

Selltiz, C., and Cook, S. Factors influencing attitudes of foreign students toward the host country. *Journal of Social Issues,* 1962, 18, 7–23.

Selltiz, C., Christ, J., Havel, J., and Cook, S. *Attitudes and social relations of foreign students in the United States.* Minneapolis: University of Minnesota Press, 1963.

Sewell, W., and Davidsen, O. *Scandinavian students on an American campus.* Minneapolis: University of Minnesota Press, 1961.

Shack, W. Open systems and closed boundaries. In W. Shack and E. Skinner (eds.), *Strangers in African society.* Berkeley: University of California Press, 1979.

Sherif, M., and Sherif, C. *Groups in harmony and tension.* New York: Harper, 1953.

Shibutani, T., and Kwan, M. *Ethnic stratification.* New York: Macmillan, 1965.

Shuter, R. Proxemics and tactility in Latin America. *Journal of Communication,* 1976, 26, 46–52.

Shuter, R. A field study of nonverbal communication in Germany, Italy, and the United States. *Communication Monographs,* 1977a, 44, 298–305.

Shuter, R. Cross-cultural small group research. *International Journal of Intercultural Relations,* 1977b, 1, 90–104.

Shuter, R. Eye contact in interracial and intraracial interactions. In N. Jain (ed.), *International and intercultural communication annual,* vol. IV. Falls Church, Va.: Speech Communication Association, 1977c.

Shuter, R. The dap in the military. *Journal of Communication,* 1979, 29, 136–142.

Shuter, R. Initial interaction of American blacks and whites in interracial and intraracial dyads. *Journal of Social Psychology,* 1982, 117, 45–52.

Sigman, S. On communication rules from a social perspective. *Human Communication Research,* 1980, 7, 37–51.

Simard, L. M. Cross-cultural interaction: Potential invisible barriers. *Journal of Social Psychology,* 1981, 113, 171–192.

Simard, L. M., and Taylor, D. M. The potential for bicultural communication in a dyadic situation. *Canadian Journal of Behavioral Science,* 1973, 5, 211–225.

Simard, L. M., Taylor, D. M., and Giles, H. Attributional processes and interpersonal accommodation. *Language and Speech,* 1976, 19, 374–387.

Simmel, G. The stranger. In K. Wolff (trans. and ed.), *The sociology of Georg Simmel.* New York: Free Press, 1950.

Simons, H., Berkowitz, N., and Moyer, R. Similarity, credibility, and attitude change: A review and a theory. *Psychological Bulletin,* 1970, 73, 1–16.

Sitaram, K., and Cogdell, R. *Foundations of intercultural communication.* Columbus, Ohio: Charles E. Merrill, 1976.

Slocum, J., and Topichak, P. Do cultural differences affect job satisfaction? *Journal of Applied Psychology,* 1971, 55, 177–178.

Smalley, W. Culture shock, language shock and the shock of self-discovery. *Practical Anthropology,* 1963, 10, 49–56.

Smith, A. G. *Communication and culture.* New York: Holt, Rinehart, and Winston, 1965.

Smith, A. L. *How to talk with people of other races, ethnic groups, and cultures.* Los Angeles: Trans Ethnic Education Communication Foundation, 1972.

Smith, A. L. *Transracial communication.* Englewood Cliffs, N.J.: Prentice-Hall, 1973.

Smith, H. *The Russians.* New York: Ballantine Books, 1976.

Smith, H. P. Do intercultural experiences affect attitudes? *Journal of Abnormal Psychology,* 1955, 51, 469-477.

Smith, V. L. *Hosts and guests: The anthropology of tourism.* Philadelphia: University of Pennsylvania Press, 1977.

Smutkupt, S., and Barna, L. Impact of nonverbal communication in an intercultural setting: Thailand. In F. Casmir (ed.), *International and intercultural communication annual,* vol. III. Falls Church, Va.: Speech Communication Association, 1976.

Smuts, J. C. *Holism and evolution.* New York: Viking, 1967. (First published in 1926.)

Spaulding, S., and Flack, M. *The world's students in the United States.* New York: Praeger, 1976.

Spielbergen, C. D., and Guerrers, R. D. (eds.). *Cross-cultural anxiety.* New York: Wiley, 1976.

Spradley, J. P. (ed.). *Culture and cognition.* San Francisco: Chandler, 1972.

Srivastava, S. Patterns of ritual friendship in tribal India. *International Journal of Comparative Sociology,* 1960, 239-247.

Stagner, R. *Psychological aspects of international conflicts.* Belmont, Calif.: Brooks/Cole, 1967.

Starr, P. D. Continuity and change in social distance. *Social Forces,* 1978, 56, 1221-1227.

Stenning, B. W., and Everett, J. E. Direct and stereotype cultural differences. *Journal of Cross-Cultural Psychology,* 1979, 10, 203-220.

Stewart, E. C. The simulation of cultural differences. *Journal of Communication,* 1966, 15, 291-304.

Stewart, E. C. *American cultural patterns: A cross-cultural perspective.* Chicago: Intercultural Network, 1972.

Stewart, E. C. Outline of intercultural communication. In F. Casmir (ed.), *International and intercultural communication.* Washington, D.C.: University Press of America, 1978.

Stewart, J. *Bridges not walls.* Reading, Mass.: Addison-Wesley, 1977.

Stoner, J., Aram, J., and Rubin, I. Factors associated with effective performance in overseas work assignments. *Personnel Psychology,* 1972, 25, 303-318.

Strassberg, D., and Anchor, K. Rating intimacy of self-disclosure. *Psychological Reports,* 1975, 37, 562.

Suleiman, M. W. The Arabs and the West: Communication gap. In M. Prosser (ed.), *Intercommunication among nations and peoples.* New York: Harper and Row, 1973.

Sumner, W. G. *Folkways.* Boston: Ginn, 1940.

Sunnafrank, M. J., and Miller, G. R. The role of initial conversation in determining attraction to similar and dissimilar strangers. *Human Communication Research,* 1981, 8, 16–25.

Suttles, G. Friendship as a social institution. In G. McNall (ed.), *Social relationships.* Chicago: Aldine, 1970.

Suttles, G. *The social construction of communities.* Chicago: University of Chicago Press, 1972.

Suzuki, D. T. *The essence of Buddhism.* Kyoto, Japan: Hozokan, 1968.

Szalay, L. B. Intercultural communication—A process model. *International Journal of Intercultural Relations,* 1981, 5, 133–146.

Szalay, L. B., and Deese, J. *Subjective meaning and culture.* Hillsdale, N.J.: Lawrence Erlbaum, 1978.

Szapocznik, J., et al. *Acculturation: Theory, measurement and clinical implications.* (NIDA grant no. NIDA-sh-81-DA-01-696-02). Rockville, Md.: National Institute on Drug Abuse, 1975.

Tafoya, D. Ethics and intercultural communication research. In N. Asuncion-Lande (ed.), *Ethical perspectives and critical issues in intercultural communication.* Falls Church, Va.: Speech Communication Association, 1980.

Tafoya, D. Perceptions of the roots of conflict: A theory and typology. In W. Gudykunst (ed.), *Intercultural communication theory.* Beverly Hills, Calif.: Sage, 1983.

Taft, R. Coping with unfamiliar cultures. In N. Warren (ed.), *Studies in cross-cultural psychology,* vol. 1. New York: Academic Press, 1977.

Tagore, R. *Toward universal man.* New York: Asia Publishing House, 1961.

Tajfel, H. Second thoughts about cross-cultural research and international relations. *International Journal of Psychology,* 1958, 3, 213–219.

Tajfel, H. Social and cultural factors in perception. In G. Lindzey and A. Aronson (eds.), *The handbook of social psychology,* 2nd ed. Reading, Mass.: Addison-Wesley, 1969a.

Tajfel, H. Cognitive aspects of prejudice. *Journal of Social Issues,* 1969b, 25, 79–97.

Tajfel, H. Experiments in a vacuum. In J. Israel and H. Tajfel (eds.), *The context of social psychology.* London: Academic Press, 1972.

Tajfel, H. Social identity and intergroup behaviour. *Social Science Information,* 1974, 13, 65–93.

Tajfel, H. *Differentiation between social groups.* London: Academic Press, 1978.

Tajfel, H. *Human groups and social categories.* Cambridge, England: Cambridge University Press, 1982a.

Tajfel, H. (ed.). *Social identity and intergroup relations.* London: Cambridge University Press, 1982b.

Tajfel, H., and Dawson, J. *Disappointed guests.* London: Oxford University Press, 1965.

Tajfel, H., Jahoda, G., Nemeth, C., Campbell, J., and Johnson, N. The development of children's preference for their own country: A cross-cultural study. *International Journal of Psychology,* 1970, 4, 245-253.

Taylor, D. M., and Gardner, R. C. Bicultural communication: A study of communicational efficiency and person perception. *Canadian Journal of Behavioral Science,* 1970, 2, 67-81.

Taylor, D. M., and Simard, L. M. Social interaction in a bilingual setting. *Canadian Psychological Review,* 1975, 16, 240-254.

Taylor, S. E., and Fiske, S. T. Point of view and perceptions of causality. *Journal of Personality and Social Psychology,* 1975, 32, 439-445.

Taylor, S. E., and Koivumaki, J. H. The perception of self and others. *Journal of Personality and Social Psychology,* 1976, 33, 403-408.

Terpstra, V. *The cultural environment of international business.* Cincinnati, Ohio: South-Western Publishing Co., 1978.

Tessler, M. A., O'Ban, W. M., and Spain, D. H. *Tradition and identity in changing Africa.* New York: Harper and Row, 1973.

Textor, R. B. (ed.). *Cultural frontiers of the Peace Corps.* Cambridge, Mass.: MIT Press, 1966.

Thiagarajan, K. M., and Deep, S. D. A study of supervisor-subordinate influence and satisfaction in four cultures. *Journal of Social Psychology,* 1972, 82, 173-180.

Ting-Toomey, S. Talk as a cultural resource in the Chinese-American speech community. *Communication,* 1980, 9, 193-203.

Ting-Toomey, S. Ethnic identity and close friendship in Chinese-American college students. *International Journal of Intercultural Relations,* 1981, 5, 383-406.

Ting-Toomey, S. Toward a theory of conflict and culture. Paper presented at the Speech Communication Association convention, Louisville, Ky., November, 1982.

Tiryakian, E. A. Perspectives on the stranger. In S. TeSelle (ed.), *The rediscovery of ethnicity.* New York: Harper and Row, 1973.

de Tocqueville, A. *Democracy in America.* New York: Knopf, 1945.

Toffler, A. *The third wave.* New York: Bantam Books, 1980.

Trager, G. L., and Hall, E. T. Culture and communication. *Explorations,* 1954, 3, 137-149.

Triandis, H. C. Cultural influences upon cognitive processes. In L. Berkowitz (ed.), *Advances in experimental social psychology,* vol. 1. New York: Academic Press, 1964.

Triandis, H. C. Interpersonal relations in international organizations. *Journal of Organizational Behavior and Human Performance,* 1967, 7, 316-328.

Triandis, H. C. Culture training, cognitive complexity and interpersonal attitudes. In R. Brislin, S. Bochner, and W. Lonner (eds.), *Cross-cultural perspectives on learning.* New York: Wiley, 1975.

Triandis, H. C. (ed.). *Variations in black and white perceptions of the social environment.* Urbana: University of Illinois Press, 1979.

Triandis, H. C., and Vassiliou, V. Interpersonal influence and employee selection in two cultures. *Journal of Applied Psychology,* 1972, 56, 140–145.

Triandis, H. C., Vassiliou, V., and Nassiakou, M. Three cross-cultural studies of subjective culture. *Journal of Personality and Social Psychology,* 1968, 8 (Monograph Supplement No. 4), 1–42.

Triandis, H. C., et al. *The analysis of subjective culture.* New York: Wiley, 1972.

Triandis, H. C., et al. (eds.). *Handbook of cross-cultural psychology,* vols. 1–6. Boston: Allyn and Bacon, 1980.

Tseng, W. Adjustment in intercultural marriage. In W. Tseng, J. McDermott, and T. Maretzki (eds.), *Adjustment in intercultural marriage.* Honolulu: University of Hawaii Press, 1977.

Turnbull, C. *The forest people.* New York: Simon and Schuster, 1961.

Turner, J., and Giles, H. (eds.). *Intergroup behavior.* Chicago: University of Chicago Press, 1981.

Tversky, A., and Kahnerman, D. Judgment under uncertainty. *Science,* 1974, 185, 1124–1131.

Tyrwhitt, J. The moving eye. In E. Carpenter and M. McLuhan (eds.), *Explorations in communication.* Boston: Beacon, 1960.

Useem, J., and Useem, R. *The Western educated man in India.* New York: Dryden Press, 1955.

Useem, J., Useem, R., and Donoghue, J. Men in the middle of the third culture. *Human Organization,* 1963, 22, 169–179.

Van den Berghe, P. L. The benign quota. *The American Sociologist,* 1971, 6, 40–43.

Vander Zanden, J. W. *Sociology: A systematic approach.* New York: Ronald Press, 1965.

Vassiliou, V., Triandis, H., Vassiliou, G., and McGuire, H. Interpersonal contact and stereotyping. In H. Triandis, *The analysis of subjective culture.* New York: Wiley, 1972.

Verbrugge, L. M. The structure of adult friendship choices. *Social Forces,* 1977, 56, 576–597.

Von Wright, G. *Explanation and understanding.* Ithaca, N.Y.: Cornell University Press, 1971.

Waley, A. (trans.). *The analects of Confucius.* New York: Vintage Books, 1938.

Wallach, M. A. The influence of classification requirements on gradients of response. *Psychological Monographs,* 1959, 73, no. 478.

Walsh, J. E. *Intercultural education in the community of man.* Honolulu: University of Hawaii Press, 1973.

Walsh, J. E. *Humanistic culture learning.* Honolulu: University of Hawaii Press, 1979.

Watson, J., and Lippitt, R. *Learning across cultures.* Ann Arbor: University of Michigan, 1955.

Watson, J., and Lippitt, R. Cross-cultural experience as a source of attitude change. *Journal of Conflict Resolution,* 1958, 2, 61–66.

Watson, O. M. *Proxemic behavior: A cross-cultural study.* The Hague: Mouton, 1970.

Watzlawick, P. *How real is real?* New York: Random House, 1976.

Watzlawick, P., Beavin, J., and Jackson, D. *The pragmatics of human communication.* New York: Norton, 1967.

Wedge, B. *Visitors to the United States and how they see us.* Princeton, N.J.: Van Nostrand, 1965.

Wei, A. Y. Cultural variations in perception. Paper presented at 6th Annual Third World Conference, Chicago, March, 1980.

Weinstall, T. D. (ed.). *Culture and management.* New York: Penguin Books, 1977.

Weinstock, A. Some factors that retard or accelerate the rate of acculturation. *Human Relations,* 1964, 17, 321–340.

Wen, K. Theories of migration and mental health. *Social Science and Medicine,* 1976, 10, 297–306.

Wendt, J. Description, interpretation and evaluation. Department of Speech Communication, University of Minnesota, undated mimeo.

Westin, A. *Privacy and freedom.* New York: Atheneum, 1970.

Whorf, B. *Collected papers on metalinguistics.* Washington, D.C.: Department of State Foreign Service Institute, 1952.

Whorf, B. L. *Language, thought, and reality.* New York: Wiley, 1956.

Whorf, B. L. An American Indian model of the universe. In P. Gleeson and N. Wakefield (eds.), *Language and culture.* Columbus, Ohio: Charles E. Merrill, 1968.

Whyte, W. F., and Holmberg, A. R. Human problems of U.S. enterprise in Latin America. *Human Organization,* 1956, 15, 1–4.

Wigland, R. T., and Barnett, G. A. Multidimensional scaling of cultural processes. In F. Casmir (ed.), *International and intercultural communication annual,* vol. III. Falls Church, Va.: Speech Communication Association, 1976.

Williams, R. M. *The reduction of intergroup tensions.* New York: Social Science Research Council, 1947.

Williams, R. M. *Strangers next door: Ethnic relations in American communities.* Englewood Cliffs, N.J.: Prentice-Hall, 1974.

Wilmont, W. *Dyadic communication,* 2nd ed. Reading, Mass.: Addison-Wesley. 1980.

Wirth, L. The problem of minority groups. In R. Linton (ed.), *The science of man in the world crisis.* New York: Columbia University Press, 1945.

Wish, M. Comparisons among multidimensional structures of nations based on different measures of subjective similarity. In L. von Bertalanffy and A. Rapoport (eds.), *General systems.* Ann Arbor, Mich.: Society for General Systems Research, 1970.

Wish, M., Deutsch, M., and Kaplan, S. Perceived dimensions of interpersonal relations. *Journal of Personality and Social Psychology,* 1976, 33, 409-421.

Witkin, H. A., Dyk, R. B., Faterson, H. F., Goodenough, D. R., and Karp, S. A. *Psychological differentiation.* New York: Wiley, 1962.

Witkin, H. A., Lewis, H. B., Hertzman, M., Machover, K., Missner, P., and Wapner, S. *Personality through perception.* New York: Harper and Row, 1954.

Wolfgang, A., and Weiss, D. A locus of control and social distance: Comparison of Canadian and West Indian-born students. *International Journal of Intercultural Relations,* 1980, 4, 295-305.

Wolken, G., Moriwaki, S., and Williams, K. Race and social class as factors in the orientation toward psychotherapy. *Journal of Counseling Psychology,* 1973, 20, 312-316.

Wong-Rieger, D. Testing a model of emotional and coping responses to problems in adaptation. Paper presented at the Society for Intercultural Education, Training and Research conference, Long Beach, Calif., March, 1982.

Wood, M. M. *The stranger: A study in social relationships.* New York: Columbia University Press, 1934.

Wright, P. H. Toward a theory of friendship based upon a conception of self. *Human Communication Research,* 1978, 4, 196-207.

Yinger, M. J. Contraculture and subculture. *American Sociological Review,* 1960, 25, 625-635.

Yoshikawa, M. Some Japanese and American cultural characteristics. In M. Prosser, *The cultural dialogue.* Boston: Houghton Mifflin, 1978.

Yousef, F. S. The integration of local nationals into managerial hierarchy of American overseas subsidiaries. *Academy of Management Journal,* 1973, 16, 25-35.

Yousef, F. S. Cross-cultural communication. *Human Organization,* 1974, 33, 383-387.

Yum, J. O. Communication diversity and information acquisition among Korean immigrants in Hawaii. *Human Communication Research,* 1982, 8, 154-169.

Zajonic, R. Aggressive attitudes of the "stranger" as a function of conformity pressures. *Human Relations,* 1952, 5, 205-216.

Zavalloni, M. Values. In H. Triandis and R. Brislin (eds.), *Handbook of cross-cultural psychology,* vol. 5. Boston: Allyn and Bacon, 1980.

Zax, M., and Takahashi, S. Cultural influences on response style. *Journal of Social Psychology,* 1967, 71, 3-10.

Zurcher, L. Particularism and organizational position: A cross-cultural analysis. *Journal of Applied Psychology,* 1968, 52, 139-144.

Zweigenhaft, R. L. American Jews: In or out of the upper class? *Insurgent Sociologist,* 1979-1980, 9, 24-37.

Index